Pro Windows Subsystem for Linux (WSL)

Powerful Tools and Practices for Cross-Platform Development and Collaboration

Hayden Barnes

Apress®

Pro Windows Subsystem for Linux (WSL): Powerful Tools and Practices for Cross-Platform Development and Collaboration

Hayden Barnes
Columbus, GA, USA

ISBN-13 (pbk): 978-1-4842-6872-8   ISBN-13 (electronic): 978-1-4842-6873-5
https://doi.org/10.1007/978-1-4842-6873-5

Managing Director, Apress Media LLC: Welmoed Spahr
Acquisitions Editor: Joan Murray
Development Editor: Laura Berendson
Coordinating Editor: Jill Balzano

Cover image designed by Freepik (www.freepik.com)

Distributed to the book trade worldwide by Springer Science+Business Media LLC, 1 New York Plaza, Suite 4600, New York, NY 10004. Phone 1-800-SPRINGER, fax (201) 348-4505, e-mail orders-ny@springer-sbm.com, or visit www.springeronline.com. Apress Media, LLC is a California LLC and the sole member (owner) is Springer Science + Business Media Finance Inc (SSBM Finance Inc). SSBM Finance Inc is a **Delaware** corporation.

For information on translations, please e-mail booktranslations@springernature.com; for reprint, paperback, or audio rights, please e-mail bookpermissions@springernature.com.

Apress titles may be purchased in bulk for academic, corporate, or promotional use. eBook versions and licenses are also available for most titles. For more information, reference our Print and eBook Bulk Sales web page at http://www.apress.com/bulk-sales.

Any source code or other supplementary material referenced by the author in this book is available to readers on GitHub via the book's product page, located at www.apress.com/9781484268728. For more detailed information, please visit http://www.apress.com/source-code.

Printed on acid-free paper

This book is dedicated to the
Windows Subsystem for Linux community.

Table of Contents

About the Author

 **Hayden Barnes** is the Senior Engineering Manager for Windows Containers at SUSE and a recognized Microsoft MVP. Hayden was previously Engineering Manager for Ubuntu on Windows Subsystem for Linux (WSL) at Canonical. Hayden regularly presents on the topic of WSL at conferences such as Microsoft Build and is the founder of WSLConf, the first community conference dedicated to WSL. He has consulted for enterprises, academic institutions, and government agencies to help them deploy WSL. Before joining Canonical, Hayden founded Whitewater Foundry, the first company to create a custom Linux distribution built specifically for WSL. He is passionate about WSL because it opens up a myriad of opportunities for cross-platform development, open source development, and collaboration between Linux and other communities.

About the Technical Reviewer

Nuno Do Carmo is an IT professional with 20 years of experience in various Windows domains, such as Windows OS support, Active Directory management, and application support.

He was also a Unix, HP/UX and Solaris 10, and Linux system administrator for HP for more than five years.

It is this mix of experiences that motivated him to start using WSL since its inception in 2016, and he was very happy to find other (crazy) persons who had the same interest in this incredible technology.

One of those persons was a certain Hayden Barnes.

Today, Nuno is a Microsoft MVP, Windows Insider MVP, CNCF Ambassador, and Docker Captain, and he is specially interested or invested in bringing the Cloud Native technologies to WSL to allow a broader user base to use these amazing projects.

On the personal side, Nuno lives in tiny Switzerland, the French side, with his wife, stepdaughter, stepson, and four cats.

He can be reached at

LinkedIn: www.linkedin.com/in/ndocarmo/

Twitter: https://twitter.com/nunixtech

Website: https://wsl.dev

Acknowledgments

I would like to acknowledge the following persons, without whom this book would not be possible:

Taylor Brown

Kayla Cinnamon

Sarah Cooley

Nuno Do Carmo

Yosef Durr

Sven Groot

Scott Hanselman

Ben Hillis

Dustin Howett

Igor Ljubuncic

Daniel Llewellyn

Craig Loewen

Kim Mullis

Tara Raj

Carlos Ramirez

Sohini Roy

Clint Rutkas

Mark Shuttleworth

John Starks

Rich Turner

Martin Wimpress

Patrick Wu

And everyone at Microsoft who contributed to the development of WSL and the community around WSL.

Introduction

Pro Windows Subsystem for Linux

This book will equip you with a wide breadth of WSL knowledge to tackle a range of challenges on WSL, from IT administration to development work, including:

- Connecting to popular Integrated Development Environments

- Building a custom Linux kernel for WSL 2

- Building a derivative Linux distro with your own packages

- Automating emails in Outlook from a bash script in WSL

It will also cover advanced settings, customization, and optimizations for both WSL and WSL 2, from the command line to the Registry. This will include each configuration option in wsl.conf and .wslconfig and recommendations for best performance.

First, we will cover the early development of WSL.

History of Windows Subsystem for Linux

What we now call WSL 1 began as an effort inside Microsoft, code-named Project Astoria, to support Android applications on the ill-fated Windows Phone. Project Astoria, known publicly as Windows Bridge for Android, was announced at the Microsoft Build conference for developers in 2015 (Figure I-1).

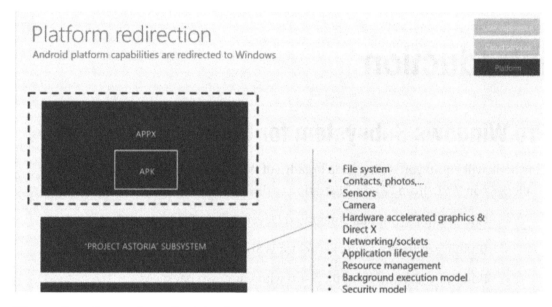

Figure I-1. *Screenshot of original presentation on Project Astoria, 2015. Source:* `https://channel9.msdn.com/Events/Build/2015/2-702`

Project Astoria built on virtualization concepts from a Microsoft Research project known as Project Drawbridge. Project Drawbridge was a prototype of a new form of virtualization for application sandboxing based on pico processes. Project Drawbridge included a version of Windows built to run inside pico processes. In Project Astoria, the pico process environment was modified to run Linux-based Android applications.

A single build of Windows 10 Phone was leaked from Microsoft containing Project Astoria. This build allowed rudimentary Android applications to be sideloaded and run on Windows Phone devices. Project Astoria was never officially released and was terminated by Microsoft along with Windows Phone in 2017. The underlying technology in Project Astoria survived though. After all, Android is based on Linux.

Bash on Ubuntu on Windows

In 2016, the technology underneath Project Astoria was recycled as Bash on Ubuntu on Windows. Instead of running Android applications, the technology was used to run a Bash terminal for developers on Windows (Figure I-2). The core of the technology was a binary translation layer that ran Linux binaries on an NT kernel inside pico processes, discussed in Chapter 1, "WSL Architecture."

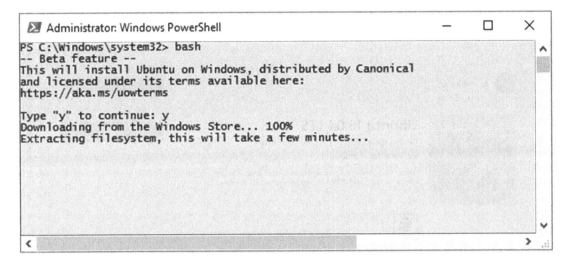

Figure I-2. *Screenshot of Bash on Ubuntu on Windows*

Microsoft partnered with Canonical, the publishers of Ubuntu, to bring this first version of WSL to Windows. Bash on Ubuntu on Windows shipped in Windows 10 Anniversary Update, also known as Windows 10 1607. The partnership between Microsoft and Canonical was a milestone in Microsoft's increasing adoption of Linux and open source software.

Windows Subsystem for Linux

In 2017, Bash on Ubuntu on Windows became Windows Subsystem for Linux with Windows 10 1709. Linux distributions could now be installed on WSL from the Microsoft Store (Figure I-3), and the number of available distributions expanded. A complete list of available WSL distributions is in Chapter 2, "Enabling WSL." This version of WSL based on the binary translation layer is what we now call WSL 1 following the announcement of WSL 2 in 2019.

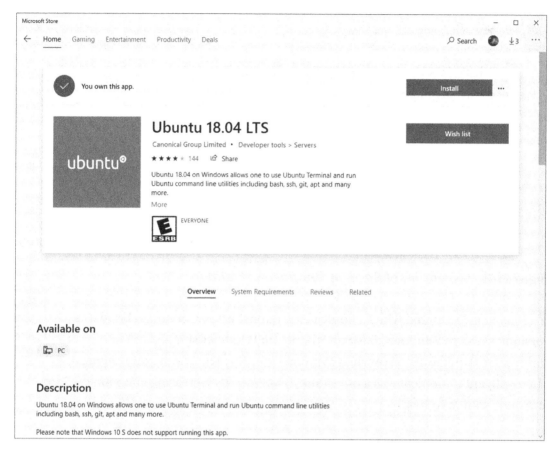

Figure I-3. *Ubuntu 18.04 LTS on the Microsoft Store*

Why "Windows Subsystem for Linux"?

Some people wonder why Windows Subsystem for Linux is so awkwardly named. From a historical perspective, Windows Subsystem for Linux matches the naming structure of Windows Services for UNIX, the previous POSIX compatibility layer for Windows NT. According to Rich Turner, Senior Program Manager at Microsoft, it was trademark concerns that prevented Microsoft from starting the product name with Linux. At the time, WSL did not contain the Linux kernel like it would with WSL 2. We ended up with Windows Subsystem for Linux, which you can think about as a subsystem of Windows to run Linux.

Windows Subsystem for Linux 2

WSL 2 was announced at Microsoft Build 2019 and reached general availability in Windows 10 2004. The core of WSL 2 was not a binary translation layer like WSL 1 but a full Linux kernel and environment running in a lightweight Hyper-V container. Unlike traditional Hyper-V, which is limited to Windows 10 Enterprise, Professional, Education, and Server, WSL 2 is available for all Windows 10 editions, including Windows 10 Home. WSL 2 offered significant improvements in application compatibility and performance over WSL 1. WSL 2 enabled several highly requested features to be brought to WSL, including GPU acceleration, official GUI support, and nested virtualization for KVM guests.

CHAPTER 1

WSL Architecture

To get the most out of Windows Subsystem for Linux, it is useful to understand its underlying architecture and history. If you plan to hack on WSL or just deploy it in your enterprise, it is necessary to know. This chapter will cover the architecture of WSL 1 and WSL 2, how we got here, and then dive into some of the bleeding edge features on the WSL platform.

WSL 1 vs. WSL 2

WSL 1 creates a Linux environment on Windows through the use of a Linux binary translation layer. WSL 2 does so with a lightweight virtualization platform based on Hyper-V. Both are unique and fascinating approaches to achieving Linux and Windows interoperability.

Kernel Drivers

When WSL is enabled on Windows 10, two NT core kernel drivers are loaded by Windows 10 (Figure 1-1). These drivers are Lxss.sys, a stub driver loaded early in the boot process, and LxCore.sys, the full WSL driver, which is loaded later in the boot process.

© Hayden Barnes 2021
H. Barnes, *Pro Windows Subsystem for Linux (WSL)*, https://doi.org/10.1007/978-1-4842-6873-5_1

Pico Processes

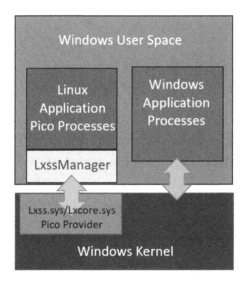

Figure 1-1. *Diagram of WSL 1 architecture*

Linux applications in WSL are executed in *pico processes*, lightweight virtual spaces created in Windows user space. LxCore.sys acts as a *pico provider* simulating a Linux environment in the virtual space inside WSL pico processes. LxCore.sys also performs the syscall translation in WSL 1, which is discussed in more detail below.

Linux applications running in a pico process are completely unaware they are running on Windows. Pico process technology can theoretically be used to simulate *any* operating system environment. Similar pico process technology is used by Microsoft to allow Windows 10 IoT to run legacy Windows CE applications and was used, in reverse, to port Microsoft SQL Server to Linux.

LxssManager

LxssManager is a Windows Service (Figure 1-2) that serves as a broker to LxCore.sys. An NT call to execute a Linux binary is routed by LxssManager to LxCore.sys. LxssManager also monitors the WSL user state and ensures smooth installation and uninstallation of WSL distributions (Figure 1-2).

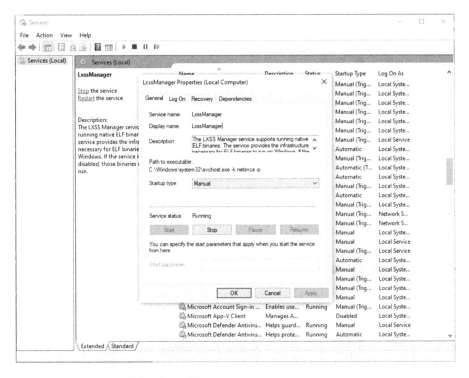

Figure 1-2. *Properties of the LxssManager service*

Syscall Translation in WSL 1

LxCore.sys must translate Linux kernel system calls from Linux applications into NT system calls. System calls are the low-level requests made by compiled binaries to an operating system kernel to perform tasks, such as apportion memory, open files, and read from devices.

To read the system calls created by a simple application, install `strace` on Ubuntu on WSL:

```
$ sudo apt install strace -y
```

Then run a simple application with strace, outputting the system call trace output to a file called output.txt:

```
$ strace -o output.txt echo 'hello world'
```

You can then read the strace output with cat:

```
$ cat output.txt
```

And you can see the Linux system calls made from simply running echo 'hello world' (Figure 1-3):

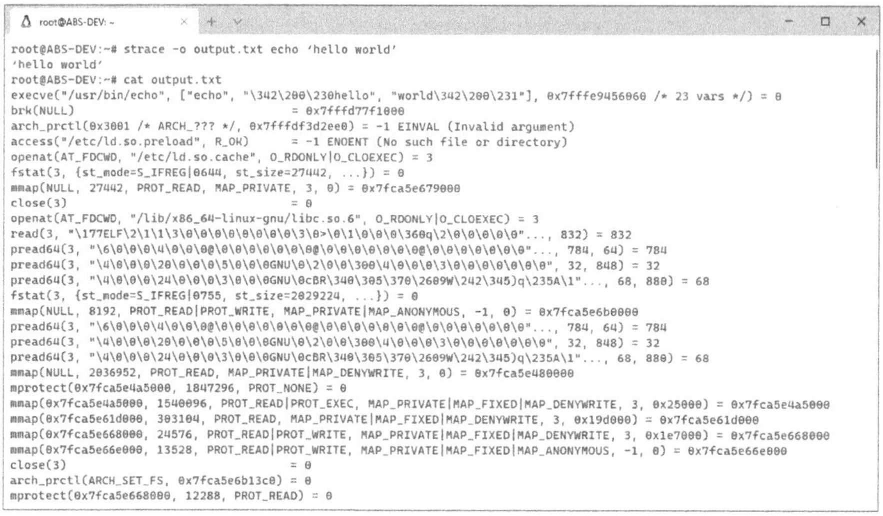

Figure 1-3. *System calls made by the command echo 'hello world'*

These system calls involve executing the binary, opening files, assigning memory, and writing the output to the console.

The Linux and Windows NT kernels were both created in the early 1990s. Linux was created by Linus Torvalds in 1991, inspired by MINIX, a research operating system, which was itself inspired by UNIX from Bell Labs. The Windows NT kernel was designed in 1993 by a team at Microsoft under David N. Cutler whose background at Digital Equipment Corporation on the VMS operating system heavily influenced the design of NT. Like Linux, NT was originally designed to be POSIX standards compatible. Like Linux, NT also had distinct modes of execution, a kernel privileged mode and a user unprivileged mode. Despite their very distinct implementations, the NT and Linux kernels were influenced by the same operating system theories and trends in the early to mid-1990s.

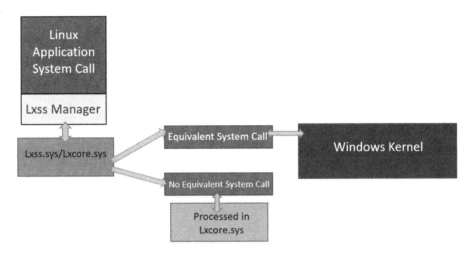

Figure 1-4. *Diagram of system call handling in WSL 1*

Despite their distinct implementations, thanks to their common influences in some cases there are direct translations of Linux to NT kernel system calls. When a Linux binary is executed in a pico process and a 1-1 Linux to NT system call exists, these can be passed directly by LxCore.sys to the NT kernel (Figure 1-4).

When a 1-1 Linux to NT system call does not exist, but a similar NT system call exists for a Linux system call, LxCore will translate the Linux system call into an NT system call by reordering or refactoring the call from a Linux to an NT call.

In other cases, where there is no equivalent for a Linux system call. Here, LxCore must handle the system call itself. This is handled in a clean room implementation of the Linux kernel API and contains no Linux kernel code.

Not all possible Linux system calls are implemented in WSL 1, and some of the more obscure system calls will never be. WSL 1 achieves close to 90% binary compatibility with Linux with this translation layer. Early in WSL 1 development, the Linux Test Project (https://linux-test-project.github.io/) was used to validate Linux compatibility.

WSL 2

WSL 2 is a vastly different architectural approach from WSL 1. By leveraging a Linux kernel and a lightweight Hyper-V container, WSL 2 addresses many of the issues users encountered with WSL 1, such as syscall incompatibility.

Hyper-V

WSL 2 addresses the challenge of implementing complete system call translation support for every possible Linux system call by implementing a true Linux kernel in a lightweight virtualization platform built on Hyper-V (Figure 1-5).

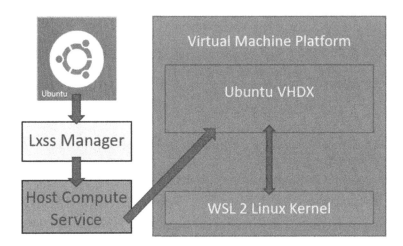

Figure 1-5. *Diagram of WSL 2 architecture*

Hyper-V is the native virtualization technology built into the Windows NT kernel, equivalent to the native virtualization implementations such as KVM on Linux or Hypervisor.Framework on macOS.

Hyper-V is a Type 1 hypervisor, which means it runs at the NT kernel level. Third-party hypervisors, like VirtualBox and VMware, are Type 2 hypervisors which load kernel-level drivers but are mostly implemented user space.

This is why Hyper-V and third-party hypervisors clash. You cannot run VirtualBox and WSL 2 on the same Windows installation.

Virtual Machine Platform

WSL 2 uses the Windows Host Compute Service, an API built on Hyper-V and exposed by enabling the Virtual Machine Platform in Windows 10.

WSL 2 defines a lightweight Linux environment through a series of API calls to the Host Compute Service, including attaching virtual file systems and virtual network adapters.

In contrast with WSL 1, where calls to open files or to open a networking port on WSL 1 are handled directly by the NT kernel, calls to open files or a networking port on WSL 2 are handled by the Linux kernel which then interacts with virtual Hyper-V devices.

Calls to open files on WSL 2 are directed to the Linux kernel which interacts with a virtual file system emulated by Hyper-V. The virtual file system is a hard disk image mounted as a virtual block device upon which the file system is stored. This provides greater performance and lower overhead than emulating a physical IDE, SATA, or NVMe device.

Calls to open a networking port on WSL 2 are directed to the Linux kernel which interacts with a virtual network adapter emulated by Hyper-V.

You can view the virtual file systems and network adapters in WSL 2 by running

```
$ lshw
```

The device drivers for these virtual Hyper-V file systems and devices have been included in the upstream Linux kernel since 2009. Here is an example of a virtual network adapter:

```
*-network:0
     description: Ethernet interface
     physical id: 1
     logical name: eth0
     serial: 00:10:4d:eb:01:ab
     size: 10Gbit/s
     capabilities: ethernet physical
     configuration: autonegotiation=off broadcast=yes driver=hv_netvsc
     duplex=full firmware=N/A ip=172.24.18.219 link=yes multicast=yes
     speed=10Gbit/s
```

WSL 2 Kernel

The Linux kernel in WSL 2 is a slightly modified Linux kernel optimized to run in the Hyper-V-based WSL 2 environment. The source is made available under GPL 2.0 at `https://github.com/microsoft/WSL2-Linux-Kernel`. Updates to the Linux kernel in WSL 2 are provided by Windows Update (Figure 1-6).

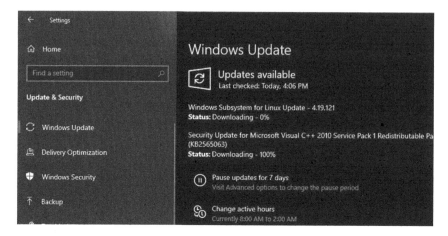

Figure 1-6. *Screenshot of Windows Update in Windows 10 Settings*

Some users will need to manually install the WSL 2 kernel (Figure 1-7) from an installer when upgrading from previous version of Windows 10 by downloading it from `https://aka.ms/wsl2kernel`. A version of the WSL 2 kernel for ARM64 devices is also available.

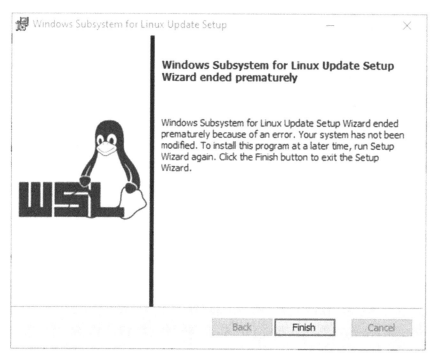

Figure 1-7. *Screenshot of Windows Subsystem for Linux 2 kernel installer*

Building your own kernel for WSL is detailed in Chapter 8 "Going Further with WSL2".

WSL 1 vs. WSL 2

Availability

WSL 1 is currently available on more versions of Windows 10, including Windows Server 2019. WSL 1 is your only choice on Windows 10 versions 1709 to 1809.

WSL 2 is available on the Windows 10 May 2019 update, known as version 1903, with recent updates applied, specifically build 18362.1049 and higher. If you are running this version of Windows 10 or higher, I strongly recommend you try WSL 2.

WSL 2 was originally launched on Windows 10 May 2020 Update, version 2004, but was then backported to Windows 10 May 2019, version 1903, later in 2020.

Why You Would Choose WSL 1

WSL 1 has lower system overhead than WSL 1. It may make a better choice on a lower-resource machine, such as a Surface Go, on which power usage takes precedence over performance.

WSL 1 also has simplified networking compared to WSL 2. WSL 1 simply adopts the networking configuration of your host Windows machines, whereas WSL 2 must implement an entire NAT network inside the virtual environment which can complicate some workflows.

Note   NAT stands for Network Address Translation. Each WSL 2 distro has its own individual IP address that is only accessible from the Windows device on which it is running. Windows translates outgoing connections to look like they are coming from the Windows device.

WSL 1 has compatibility with many Linux applications. If you are limited to WSL 1, you should not be dismayed. It is still a viable option for some users. Note though it is not expected to get new features.

Why You Would Choose WSL 2

You should choose WSL 2 if your application requires it, such as Docker or microk8s. WSL 2 is also more performant than WSL 1, by a significant factor. If you want to maximize WSL performance, then WSL 2 is a breakthrough for your workflow.

WSL 2 has a more complicated networking setup than WSL 1. WSL 2 implements an entire NAT network inside the virtual environment. Extra steps are required to connect to WSL 2 services from other devices, something to keep in mind while planning your WSL deployment or migration from WSL 1 to WSL 2.

WSL 2 also allows you to compile and run your own Linux kernel if you need kernel features not provided by the default Microsoft WSL 2 kernel.

The Future of WSL

2020 brought announcements of more architectural changes to WSL 2. Chief among them is support for GPU computing tasks, which are accelerated by DirectX, Direct3D, and DirectML. Support for OpenGL, OpenCL, and Vulkan is expected later. These new GPU compute features required updates to the WSL 2 kernel and how GPU devices are handled by WSL 2. These represent the next major architectural advances since the introduction of WSL 2.

GPU Compute

Windows 10 builds with GPU compute support were released to the Insider Dev Channel in June 2020 and are expected to be a feature in a release of Windows 10 in 2021.

The new GPU compute functionality is based on a para-virtualized GPU in the WSL 2 environment. GPU acceleration will allow a whole new category of GPU-driven compute, artificial intelligence, machine learning, and statistical analysis workloads on WSL.

A GPU-accelerated workflow setup is detailed in Chapter 10, "Using WSL for Enterprise Development."

/dev/dxgkrnl

The para-virtualized GPU is powered by a new Linux kernel device. A new Linux kernel driver, /dev/dxgkrnl, provides a series of device calls that are similar to what DirectX provides in the NT kernel via the Windows Display Driver Model (WDDM). This allows APIs and drivers written to work on WDDM to run within WSL.

/dev/dxgkrnl connects outside the WSL environment through the Hyper-V VM Bus (Figure 1-8) using the WDDM Paravirtualization Protocol. /dev/dgkrnl then communicates over the VM Bus directly with dxgkrnl, the DirectX component in the NT kernel, which passes requests to the GPU kernel mode driver and ultimately the GPU.

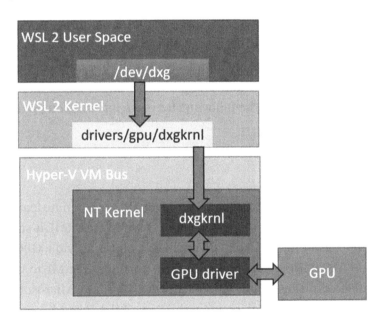

Figure 1-8. *Diagram of DirectX implementation in WSL 2*

The NT kernel treats GPU processes on WSL and Windows equally and will dynamically allocate available GPU resources between them. /dev/dxgkrnl is a pass-through driver, similar in some ways to accelerated graphics drivers on other virtualization platforms, like VirtualBox.

Only GPU compute and off-screen rendering is currently provided by /dev/dxgkrnl; there is no display capability. Read the following for more on official GUI support coming to WSL 2.

/dev/dxgkrnl does not contain DirectX, but it is open source and can be viewed at `https://github.com/microsoft/WSL2-Linux-Kernel/tree/linux-msft-wsl-4.19.y/drivers/gpu/dxgkrnl`. Microsoft has initiated the process for the driver to be sent "upstream" to the mainline Linux kernel.

GPU compute currently requires at least Windows 10 build 20150 and WSL-aware drivers for Windows from your GPU chipset manufacturer. Beta drivers for Nvidia GPU chipsets are available through the Nvidia Developer Program. Eventually, these drivers will be released via Windows Update.

Direct3D 12

Direct3D is part of DirectX. Direct3D is a real-time API for rendering three-dimensional graphics in applications and games. The extension of WDDM to Linux allowed Microsoft to port the Direct3D 12 API to Linux. A complete Direct3D library is compiled for Linux from the source code of the Windows Direct3D library. Currently, Direct3D can only be used for off-screen rendering; see the following for more information on official GUI support coming to WSL 2.

DirectML

DirectML is a part of DirectX. DirectML is a low-level API for machine learning that should be familiar with developers experienced in DirectX. DirectML is supported on all DirectX-compatible hardware. Unlike CUDA, which requires a Nvidia GPU, DirectML works on Intel and AMD GPUs. In conjunction with porting DirectML to WSL, Microsoft also released a preview of TensorFlow with a DirectML backend. Microsoft is working with the TensorFlow community to upstream the DirectML backend.

OpenGL and OpenCL

Most graphics rendering on Linux uses the open source OpenGL and OpenCL APIs. Microsoft has been working with Collabora to provide mapping layers for OpenGL and OpenCL on top of DirectX through the open source Mesa library (Figure 1-9). This will allow OpenGL and OpenCL applications to be seamlessly DirectX accelerated when executed on WSL. This work is not complete and will be coming in an update to the Mesa library in the future. Once distributions like Ubuntu update to the new Mesa libraries, three-dimensional acceleration for OpenGL and OpenCL will be automatic. Microsoft has said they are still exploring how best to support Vulkan on WSL.

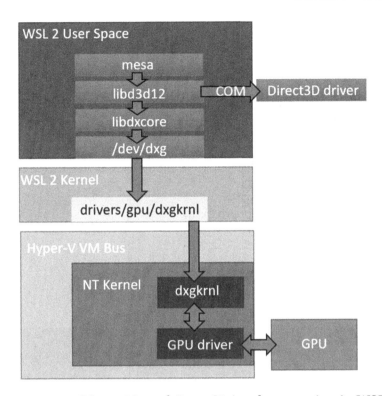

Figure 1-9. *Diagram of OpenGL and OpenCL implementation in WSL 2*

Nvidia CUDA

CUDA is a cross-platform parallel processing API created by Nvidia. Microsoft worked with Nvidia to build a version of CUDA for Linux that targeted the WDDM layer through the /dev/dxgkrnl device driver (Figure 1-10). This provides CUDA acceleration to applications such as TensorFlow in WSL and to Docker containers run with the Nvidia runtime.

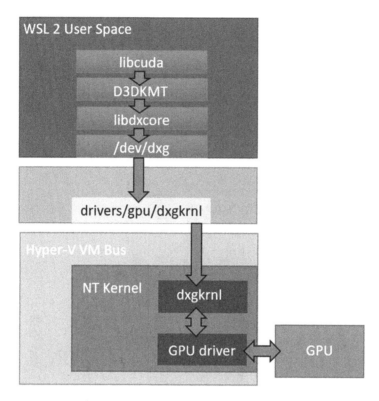

Figure 1-10. *Diagram of CUDA implementation in WSL 2*

Libraries

The libraries needed to access advanced GPU features in WSL are overlaid onto the WSL file system at /usr/lib/wsl/lib for glibc-based distributions. No Linux-specific drivers are required. Distributions such as Alpine which use musl libc instead of glibc are not currently supported.

The Direct3D library (libd3d12), DirectML (libdirectml), CUDA (libcuda), and a related driver ported to Linux, DxCore (libdxcore), are not open source.

GUI Support

At Build 2020, Microsoft also announced that official GUI support would be coming to WSL 2. As detailed in Chapter 7 "Customizing WSL," it is possible to run a GUI application on WSL 1 and 2 today using a Windows-based X server such as VcXsrv or X410. More details about official GUI support for WSL 2 are coming in 2021.

We do know the forthcoming GUI support will use a Wayland compositor based on Weston and also include PulseAudio support. Microsoft's compositor will forward raw visual elements over RDP to the RDP client built into Windows (Figure 1-11). The graphical rendering itself occurs on Windows. The visual elements of the Linux GUI, including application windows, are drawn by Windows using your computer's GPU. Windows will also listen for keyboard and mouse input to transmit back to Linux.

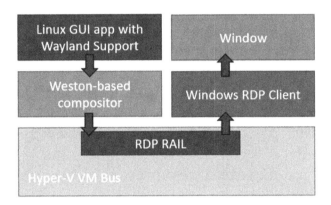

Figure 1-11. *Diagram of Wayland application support in WSL 2*

Microsoft's Weston-based compositor will have support for Xwayland, a compatibility layer for Linux GUI applications built against Xorg libraries (Figure 1-12). Xwayland contains an Xserver that uses Wayland input devices and forwards output to Wayland surfaces.

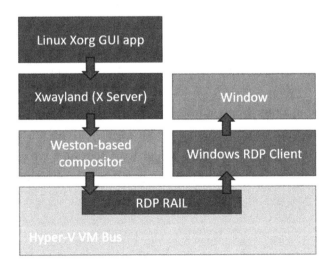

Figure 1-12. *Diagram of Xorg application support in WSL 2*

15

As of writing, Microsoft uses the Remote Desktop Protocol (RDP) Remote Application Integrated Locally (RAIL) channel to send graphical data from Linux to Windows. Microsoft has proposed an extension to the RDP called Virtual Application Integrated Locally (VAIL), which is currently only in use between Windows clients (Figure 1-13).

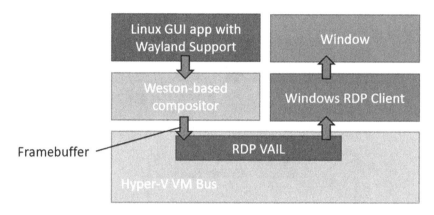

Figure 1-13. *Diagram of RDP over VAIL*

If VAIL is upstreamed into the RDP standard, then, instead of using the RAIL channel to send graphical data, the video framebuffer could be copied directly from Linux to Windows. This will dramatically improve GUI performance and is similar to Intel GVT-g technology. It could also have other applications for remote and virtual desktop interoperability between Windows and Linux. Microsoft has said their Wayland compositor, contributions to FreeRDP, and RDP extension will be open source.

Microsoft has also announced that audio support will accompany GUI support in WSL 2, provided by a minimal PulseAudio layer running in a special sidecar container, which the UNIX domain socket needed for communication mounted into your WSL 2 distro.

The push toward using a real, open source Linux kernel with open protocols being pushed upstream represents a dramatic shift for Microsoft. With an understanding of the architecture of how WSL 1, WSL 2, and its pieces work together, we can begin to understand how to exploit these pieces for fun and profit in the following chapters.

## CHAPTER 2

Enabling WSL

WSL does not come enabled by default in Windows; it must be enabled via the GUI or command line. WSL can be enabled on all editions or "SKUs" of Windows, including Windows 10 Home, Professional, Enterprise, and Server. There are multiple ways to enable WSL on Windows 10. How you enable WSL depends on your comfort level. New users may wish to use the GUI option, experienced users may wish to use PowerShell, and system administrators managing fleets of Windows machines may use DISM.

In Programs and Features

In Windows 10, click the Start button, type "features," and select "Turn Windows features on or off." In the "Windows Features" menu (Figure 2-1), scroll down, and check "Windows Subsystem for Linux" to enable WSL 1. To enable WSL 2, also select "Virtual Machine Platform."

© Hayden Barnes 2021
H. Barnes, *Pro Windows Subsystem for Linux (WSL)*, https://doi.org/10.1007/978-1-4842-6873-5_2

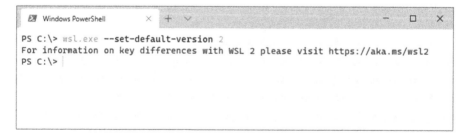

Figure 2-1. *Graphical menu to turn Windows features on or off*

Click "OK," allow the features to be enabled, and then restart.

One disadvantage to the GUI method is that WSL 1 will remain your default even if you enable WSL 2 on Windows 10 1909 and later. To set WSL 2 as your default (Figure 2-2), open PowerShell as Administrator, and run

```
wsl.exe --set-default-version 2
```

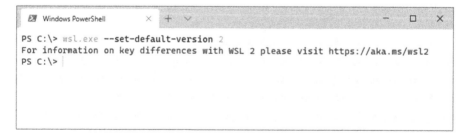

Figure 2-2. *Setting WSL 2 as the default WSL version*

Using PowerShell

To enable WSL using PowerShell (Figure 2-3), open PowerShell as Administrator, and run

```
Enable-WindowsOptionalFeature -Online -FeatureName Microsoft-Windows-
Subsystem-Linux -NoRestart
```

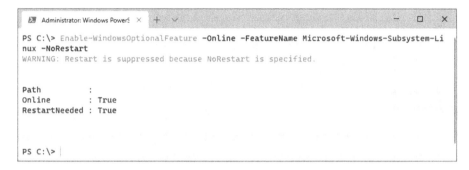

Figure 2-3. *Enabling the WSL 1 feature in Windows 10 using PowerShell*

To then enable WSL 2 on Windows 10 1909 or later (Figure 2-4), run

```
Enable-WindowsOptionalFeature -Online -FeatureName VirtualMachinePlatform
-NoRestart
```

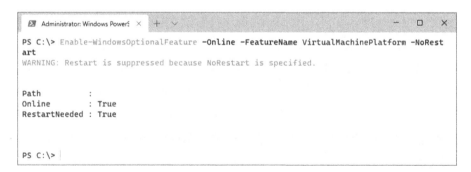

Figure 2-4. *Enabling the WSL 2 feature in Windows 10 using PowerShell*

Allow the features to be enabled, and then restart:

```
Restart-Computer
```

If you enabled WSL 2, you can sct WSL 2 as your default (Figure 2-5). Open PowerShell as Administrator, and run (Figure 2-5)

```
wsl.exe --set-default-version 2
```

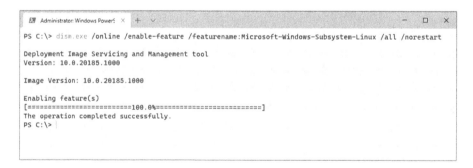

```
PS C:\> wsl.exe --set-default-version 2
For information on key differences with WSL 2 please visit https://aka.ms/wsl2
PS C:\>
```

Figure 2-5. *Setting WSL 2 as the default WSL version*

Using DISM

Some administrators may be more familiar with the Deployment Image Servicing and Management (DISM) tool. To enable WSL 1 using DISM (Figure 2-6), open PowerShell as Administrator, and run

```
dism.exe /online /enable-feature /featurename:Microsoft-Windows-Subsystem-
Linux /all /norestart
```

```
PS C:\> dism.exe /online /enable-feature /featurename:Microsoft-Windows-Subsystem-Linux /all /norestart

Deployment Image Servicing and Management tool
Version: 10.0.20185.1000

Image Version: 10.0.20185.1000

Enabling feature(s)
[==========================100.0%==========================]
The operation completed successfully.
PS C:\>
```

Figure 2-6. *Enabling the WSL 1 feature in Windows 10 using DISM*

Then, to enable WSL 2 using DISM (Figure 2-7), run

```
dism.exe /online /enable-feature /featurename:VirtualMachinePlatform /all /
norestart
```

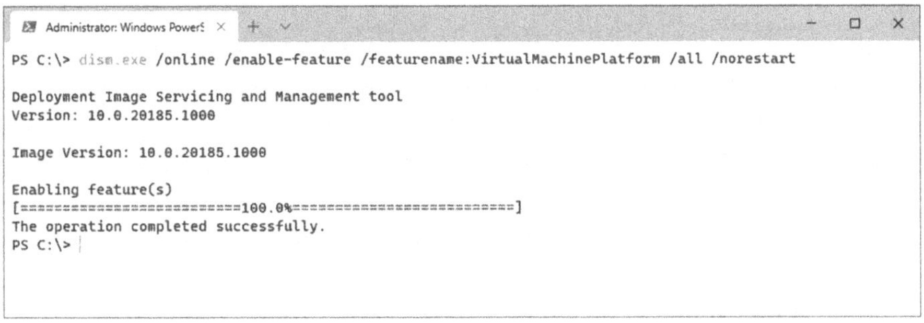

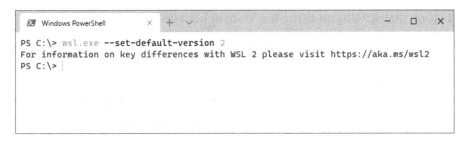

Figure 2-7. *Enabling the WSL 2 feature in Windows 10 using DISM*

Allow the features to be enabled, and then restart:

```
Restart-Computer
```

If you enabled WSL 2, you can set WSL 2 as your default (Figure 2-8). Open PowerShell as Administrator, and run

```
wsl.exe --set-default-version 2
```

Figure 2-8. *Setting WSL 2 as the default WSL version*

Using wsl.exe --install

At Build 2020, Microsoft announced that a new feature would be coming to Windows to enable WSL on all eligible versions of Windows 10. To enable WSL using this method (Figure 2-9), open PowerShell as Administrator, and run

```
wsl.exe --install
```

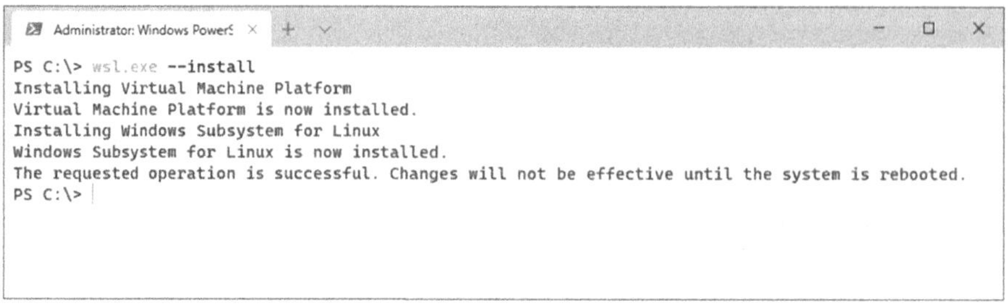

```
Administrator: Windows PowerS   ×   +  ∨                              –   □   ×
PS C:\> wsl.exe --install
Installing Virtual Machine Platform
Virtual Machine Platform is now installed.
Installing Windows Subsystem for Linux
Windows Subsystem for Linux is now installed.
The requested operation is successful. Changes will not be effective until the system is rebooted.
PS C:\>
```

Figure 2-9. *Enabling the WSL n Windows 10 using wsl.exe –install*

This feature will eventually be backported to existing Windows 10 service channels still in support. It will enable WSL 2 by default, update the WSL 2 kernel, and install GUI support on eligible versions of Windows 10.

Installing a Distribution with wsl.exe –install

A further feature of the `wsl.exe` utility, made available in Windows builds numbered 20211 and above, is the capability to install Linux distributions directly from the Windows Store, that is, without using the Store application to search for them.

To see a list of available distributions, run

```
wsl.exe --list --online
```

This will print a two-column table listing all the available distributions in the Windows Store (Figure 2-10). The table shows each distribution's name, as you will use to install with wsl.exe, and a "friendly name" as a description allowing you to clearly see what each distro is.

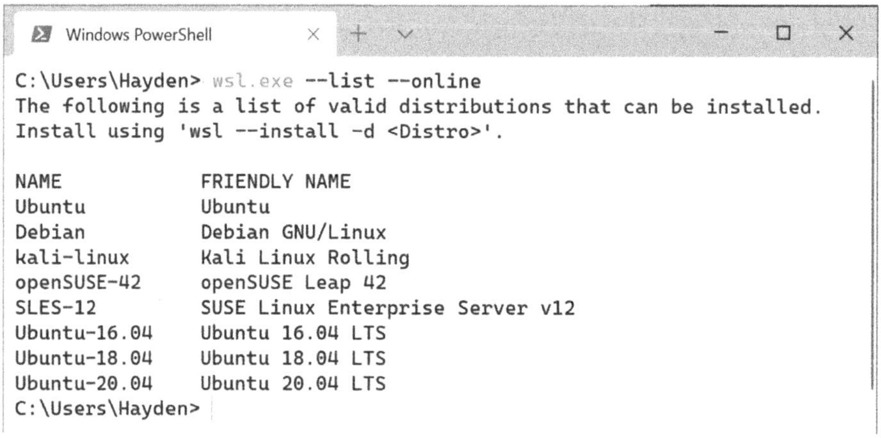

```
Windows PowerShell          ×   +  ∨                      –   □   ×
C:\Users\Hayden> wsl.exe --list --online
The following is a list of valid distributions that can be installed.
Install using 'wsl --install -d <Distro>'.

NAME              FRIENDLY NAME
Ubuntu            Ubuntu
Debian            Debian GNU/Linux
kali-linux        Kali Linux Rolling
openSUSE-42       openSUSE Leap 42
SLES-12           SUSE Linux Enterprise Server v12
Ubuntu-16.04      Ubuntu 16.04 LTS
Ubuntu-18.04      Ubuntu 18.04 LTS
Ubuntu-20.04      Ubuntu 20.04 LTS
C:\Users\Hayden>
```

Figure 2-10. *The output of wsl.exe --list --online showing all installable distros*

To install a distro from the list, such as "Ubuntu-16.04," run (Figure 2-11)

```
wsl.exe --install -d Ubuntu-16.04
```

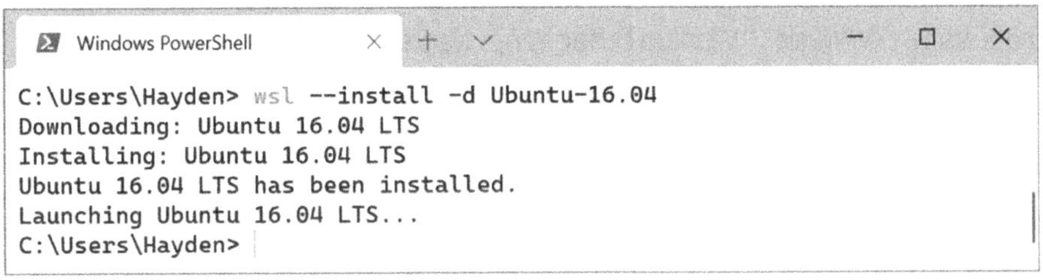

Figure 2-11. *Using wsl.exe to install Ubuntu 16.04 in WSL*

A new terminal window should now pop up with the distro's usual setup flow. For Ubuntu-16.04, this involves setting a username and password for your Linux user.

Using DISM to Enable WSL in Images

WSL can be enabled in a Windows image for imaging purposes using DISM. Create a Windows image, enable WSL, sideload your WSL distro from the .appx, and then follow the steps to generalize your image and create an installable derivative image:

https://docs.microsoft.com/en-us/windows-hardware/manufacture/desktop/work-with-windows-images

In Hyper-V Guests

WSL is supported in Windows 10 guests on Hyper-V. Hyper-V can be useful for trying new features in WSL in Windows 10 Dev Channel and Beta Channel builds prior to deployment into production.

Hyper-V requires Windows 10 Pro, Enterprise, or Education editions and an Intel processor with VT-x virtualization extensions. The Intel virtualization extensions must first be enabled in your system BIOS/EFI. As of this writing, Microsoft has announced preliminary support for nested virtualization on AMD processors, with support for nested KVM to follow.

Once enabled in your BIOS/EFI, the virtualization extensions must be exposed to your Hyper-V guest. To expose virtualization extensions to your Hyper-V guest, open PowerShell as Administrator on your host device, and run (Figure 2-12)

```
Set-VMProcessor -VMName "Virtual Machine Name"
-ExposeVirtualizationExtensions $true
```

where "Virtual Machine Name" is the name of your Hyper-V guest. If you encounter issues starting your Hyper-V guest or Hyper-V-related features in your guest are disabled, double-check virtualization extensions are enabled in your BIOS/EFI and you have exposed virtualization extensions for the correct Hyper-V guest.

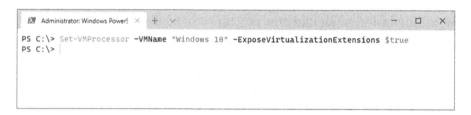

Figure 2-12. *Exposing virtualization extensions to a Hyper-V guest virtual machine*

Installing a Linux Distribution on WSL

Choice of Distribution

Once WSL is enabled, you must install a Linux distribution, commonly abbreviated as "distro." As of publication, the following distributions are available for WSL on the Microsoft Store:

- Ubuntu
- Ubuntu 20.04 LTS
- Ubuntu 18.04 LTS
- Debian
- Pengwin
- Pengwin Enterprise
- Fedora Remix for WSL

- SUSE Linux Enterprise Server 15 SP1

- SUSE Linux Enterprise Server 12 SP5

- openSUSE Leap 15.2

- Alpine WSL

You may already be familiar with some of the preceding distributions. Factors to consider when selecting a distribution include

Familiarity with distro-specific tools – For example, Ubuntu, Debian, and Pengwin use the apt package manager, which use .deb package files. Fedora uses dnf as a package manager, and openSUSE and SUSE use zypper, which uses .rpm package files.

Distribution support by the Linux applications you would like to use – You should check to make sure the Linux applications you would like to use are available in the repositories of the distro you choose. If not, many upstream projects will offer Ubuntu-compatible .deb files or even their own apt repository.

Availability of support for WSL use in production environments – Paid support is available from Canonical for Ubuntu and from Whitewater Foundry for Pengwin.

WSL-specific features in distributions – Ubuntu, Pengwin, and Fedora Remix for WSL include wslutilities, an open source set of utilities for WSL.

Consideration: WSL Version When Installing

When you enable WSL 1 and WSL 2, you have the option of installing distros under either 1 or 2.

If you install a distro from the Store or manually using an .appx package file as detailed in the following, it will install to your default WSL version choice.

To set your default WSL version choice, open PowerShell, and run

```
wsl.exe --set-default-version <version>
```

To set WSL 2 as your default, run the following (Figure 2-13):

```
wsl.exe --set-default-version 2
```

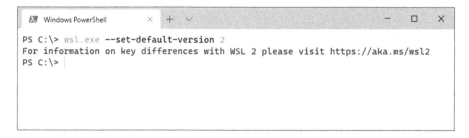

Figure 2-13. *Setting WSL 2 as the default WSL version*

Converting distros between WSL 1 and 2 is covered in Chapter 3, "Managing WSL Distros."

Install from the Microsoft Store

The recommended method of installing WSL distros is from the Microsoft Store. No account is necessary to download free distributions like Ubuntu. To install a distribution, search the Store for its entry. Once located (Figure 2-14), click "Get" followed by "Install." Wait for the download to complete, and then click "Launch."

Figure 2-14. *Ubuntu for WSL on the Microsoft Store*

You can also run the distro from the Start Menu or its executable alias from PowerShell, for example, "ubuntu.exe" for Ubuntu. This book will primarily use Ubuntu in examples.

On the first run, the distro will be unpacked, and you will set up a default non-root user (Figure 2-15). This user is separate from your Windows username and password.

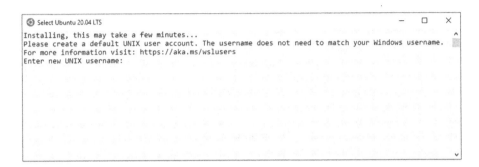

Figure 2-15. *Create a default new user on Ubuntu on WSL*

On most WSL distros, this non-root user will be added to the sudo or wheel Linux user group, so you can issue privileged commands with sudo followed by an administrative command. A more detailed discussion of sudo is included in Chapter 4, "Linux Distro Maintenance."

Sideload an .appx File in Developer Mode

There are more options to install WSL distros if you do not have access to the Microsoft Store. Linux distros on the Microsoft Store are packaged using the .appx application packaging format. It is possible to sideload .appx packages on devices that do not have the Microsoft Store enabled. To allow sideloading of applications, Windows 10 must be set to developer mode. This can be done in Settings ➤ Update & Security ➤ For developers and by toggling the switch for "Install apps from any source, including loose files" to On (Figure 2-16).

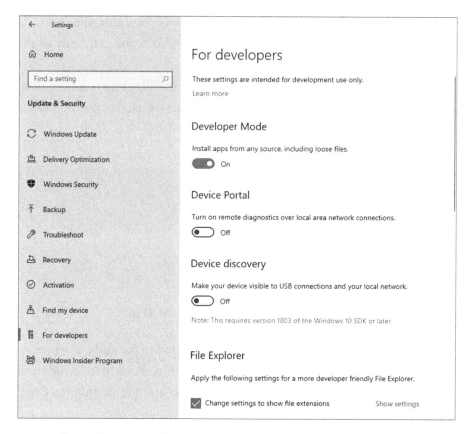

Figure 2-16. *"For developers" panel in Windows 10 Settings to enable .appx sideloading, also known as "developer mode"*

You will be prompted with a message warning you about the risk of installing and running apps from outside the Microsoft Store (Figure 2-17).

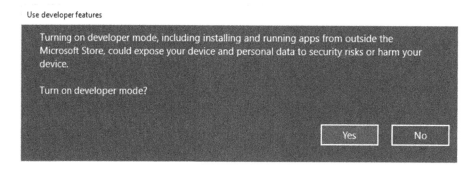

Figure 2-17. *Warning message displayed when enabling developer mode*

There is a risk in sideloading .appx. You should treat .appx like you would an .exe and verify its source before installation. WSL .appx are not contained like other Store applications and have full access to most of your Windows system. You can enable developer mode if you take reasonable precautions. Verified .appx of most Linux distros available for WSL can be downloaded directly from Microsoft at `https://docs.microsoft.com/en-us/windows/wsl/install-manual`.

You can also find .appx of Linux distros from projects on GitHub. Check the reputation of the project before installing a WSL .appx you find online. A harmful .appx could cause serious damage to your system.

To install an .appx, double-click the .appx in File Explorer, and click "Install" (Figure 2-18).

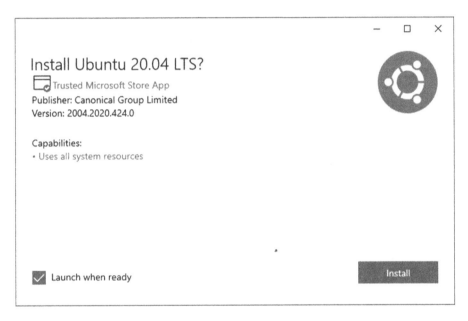

Figure 2-18. *Install menu when sideloading a WSL distro from .appx*

Import a Tarball Using wsl.exe --import

WSL distros can also be installed directly from a root file system tar file. A root file system, called a rootfs, is a snapshot of a working Linux distribution installation, archived in a tar file, and compressed as a gzip file. They will have a file extension of .tar.gz.

Rootfs can be downloaded directly from some Linux distributions. There are also third-party rootfs builds on GitHub. Ubuntu provides nightly builds of rootfs for its Long Term Support versions (18.04, 20.04, etc.) that are on the Microsoft Store. Ubuntu also provides nightly builds of rootfs for its interim versions, which are released every six months and have bleeding-edge versions of packages. Ubuntu publishes rootfs tarballs for WSL on their cloud image server at `https://cloud-images.ubuntu.com/` organized by release code name (Figure 2-19).

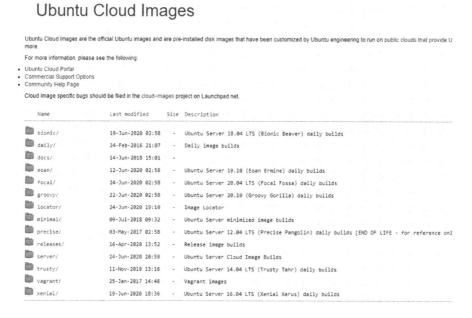

Figure 2-19. *Directory listing of Ubuntu images by release code name*

Find the code name of the Ubuntu release you would like to download. To match a code name to an Ubuntu version number, such as 20.04, check `https://releases.ubuntu.com/` (Figure 2-20).

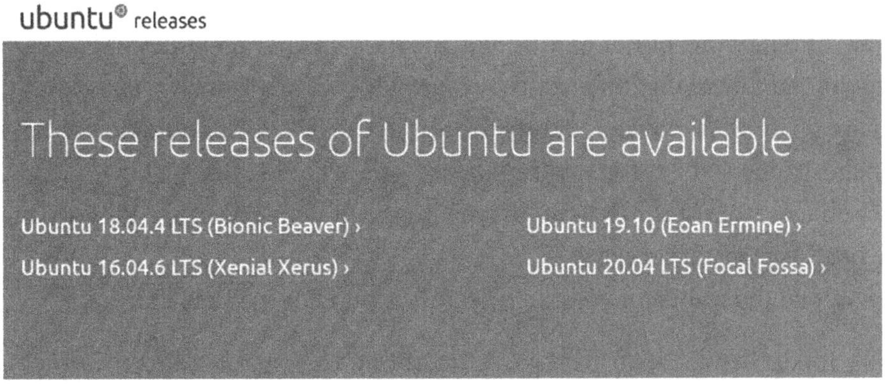

ubuntu® releases

These releases of Ubuntu are available

Ubuntu 18.04.4 LTS (Bionic Beaver) ›   Ubuntu 19.10 (Eoan Ermine) ›

Ubuntu 16.04.6 LTS (Xenial Xerus) ›   Ubuntu 20.04 LTS (Focal Fossa) ›

Figure 2-20. *Listing of currently supported Ubuntu releases*

A detailed explanation of the Ubuntu release cycle can be found at `https://ubuntu.com/about/release-cycle`.

In this example, we will download Ubuntu Groovy Gorilla, the code name of the Ubuntu 20.10 interim release. We will begin at `https://cloud-images.ubuntu.com/` (Figure 2-17). Click "groovy" and then "current," and you will find yourself at a page listing builds for a wide range of platforms (Figure 2-21).

Ubuntu 20.10 (Groovy Gorilla) Daily Build [20200621]

The Ubuntu Cloud image can be run on your personal Ubuntu Cloud, or on public clouds that provide Ubuntu Certified Images.

To find a listing of our public images on supported Clouds, please use the Cloud Image Locator:

- Released Image locator
- Daily Image Locator

Cloud image specific bugs should be filed in the cloud-images project on Launchpad.net.
A full list of available files can be found below.

Name	Last modified	Size	Description
Parent Directory		-	
MD5SUMS	21-Jun-2020 17:56	2.3K	
MD5SUMS.gpg	21-Jun-2020 17:56	836	
SHA1SUMS	21-Jun-2020 17:58	2.5K	
SHA1SUMS.gpg	21-Jun-2020 17:58	836	
SHA256SUMS	21-Jun-2020 17:59	3.3K	
SHA256SUMS.gpg	21-Jun-2020 17:59	836	
groovy-server-cloudimg-amd64-azure.vhd.manifest	21-Jun-2020 11:58	16K	Package manifest file
groovy-server-cloudimg-amd64-azure.vhd.zip	21-Jun-2020 17:04	524M	Windows Azure/Hyper-V image
groovy-server-cloudimg-amd64-disk-kvm.img	21-Jun-2020 11:58	501M	Ubuntu Server 20.10 (Groovy Gorilla) daily builds

Figure 2-21. *Listing of builds of Ubuntu for a range of platforms*

Builds for WSL end with -<platform>-wsl.rootfs.tar.gz. Locate the correct build for your system architecture, either amd64 or arm64. Users on Intel and AMD processors should download the amd64 image: `groovy-server-cloudimg-amd64-wsl.rootfs.tar.gz`. If you are on an ARM device, such as the Surface Pro X, you should download the arm64 image: `groovy-server-cloudimg-arm64-wsl.rootfs.tar.gz.`

Rootfs images from Ubuntu have "server" in the filename because they are built from the same base as Ubuntu server.

To download the rootfs for your architecture, open PowerShell, and run

```
wsl.exe --import <name for distro> <location to unpack rootfs> <location of
rootfs> [optionally: --version <version of WSL to install in>]
```

For example, as seen in Figure 2-22:

```
wsl.exe --import UbuntuGroovy-2 C:\WSL\Ubuntu-Groovy-2 $HOME\Downloads\
groovy-server-cloudimg-amd64-wsl.rootfs.tar.gz --version 2
```

Figure 2-22. *Importing an Ubuntu groovy build from rootfs and then listing all installed WSL distros*

It is possible to install the same rootfs under different distro names to have multiple distros for different purposes. In Figure 2-22, you can see there are multiple versions of Ubuntu Groovy installed, under Ubuntu-Groovy, Ubuntu-Groovy-2, and a special-purpose one I created for GPU work called Ubuntu-Groovy-GPU. Duplicating installed distros is covered in Chapter 3, "Managing WSL Distros."

When you install a rootfs using wsl.exe --import, there is no icon created in the Start Menu; you must launch the distro from PowerShell using

```
wsl.exe -d <name for distro>
```

However, if you are using the new Windows Terminal, it will automatically populate with your imported distributions (Figure 2-23).

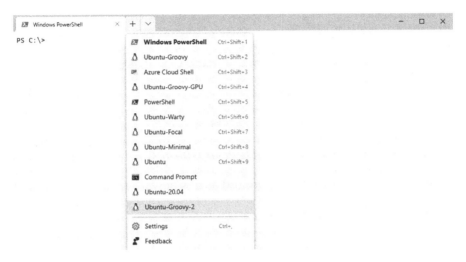

Figure 2-23. *Installed WSL distros listed in the new Windows Terminal*

The new Windows Terminal is available to download from the Microsoft Store (`www.microsoft.com/store/productId/9N0DX20HK701`) and GitHub (`https://github.com/microsoft/terminal`).

Windows Terminal is a significant upgrade from the legacy console application in Windows 10. It is highly recommended for use with WSL and PowerShell.

When you install a rootfs using wsl.exe –import, there is no default unprivileged user created. Instead, you launch the distribution as root.

You can create a new default user on Ubuntu (Figure 2-24) with

```
$ adduser <username>
```

For example:

```
$ adduser hayden
```

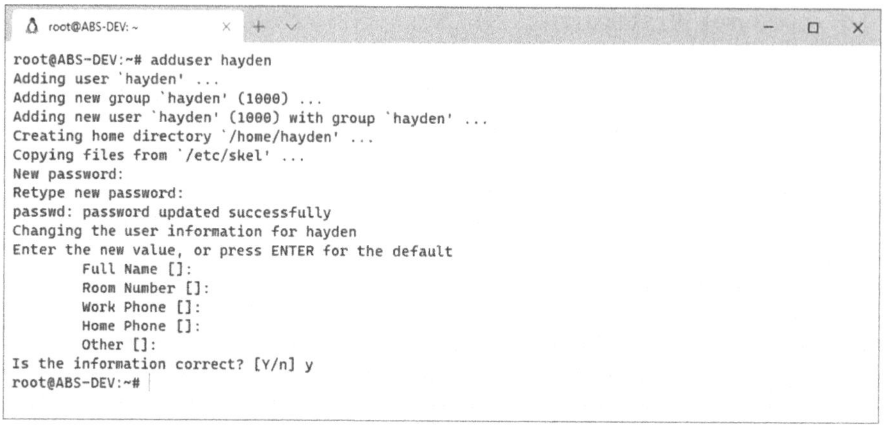

Figure 2-24. *Manually creating a new user in Ubuntu*

If you would like to use the sudo command as this new user, you should add the new user to the sudo group:

```
$ usermod -aG sudo <username>
```

For example:

```
$ usermod -aG sudo hayden
```

To switch to this new user from root (Figure 2-25), use

```
$ su hayden
```

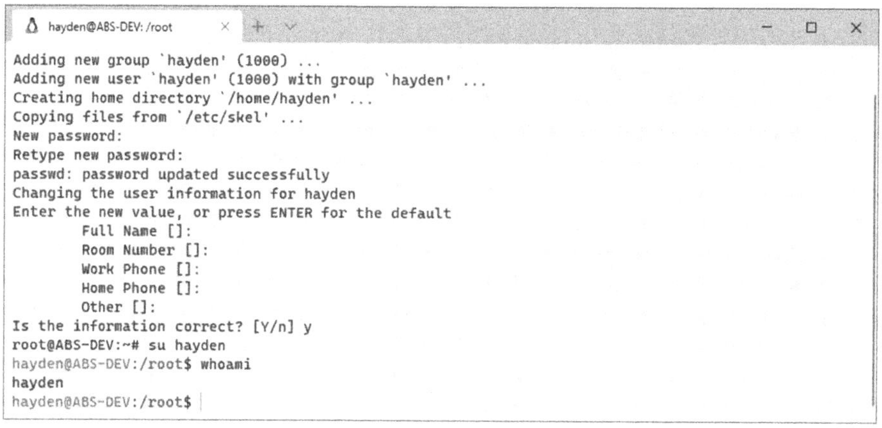

Figure 2-25. *Using the su command to switch to a new user, followed by whoami to verify*

To start a distribution as a user you have created, from PowerShell (Figure 2-26), run

```
wsl.exe -d <distro name> -u <username>
```

For example:

```
wsl.exe -d Ubuntu-Groovy -u hayden
```

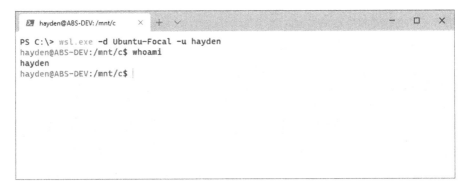

Figure 2-26. *Starting a WSL distro as a specific user from PowerShell*

WSL Installation Mechanics

Installation Location

WSL distributions are installed as rootfs images, whether they come bundled from the Store, in appx, or the raw rootfs. When installed from the Microsoft Store or sideloaded via .appx, the rootfs is bundled with extra plumbing to register the distro via the WSL API, create Start Menu icons, provide an executable alias ("ubuntu.exe"), and create a default user with sudo privileges. This extra plumbing varies slightly based on distro. The official template from Microsoft is available from `https://github.com/microsoft/WSL-DistroLauncher`.

Distros installed from the Store or sideloaded via .appx will be installed alongside other Windows UWP packages in `C:\Users\<username>\AppData\Local\Packages\`.

On WSL 1, the rootfs is unpacked on the first run into a file system at `C:\Users\<username>\AppData\Local\Packages\<Store package name>\LocalState` (Figure 2-27).

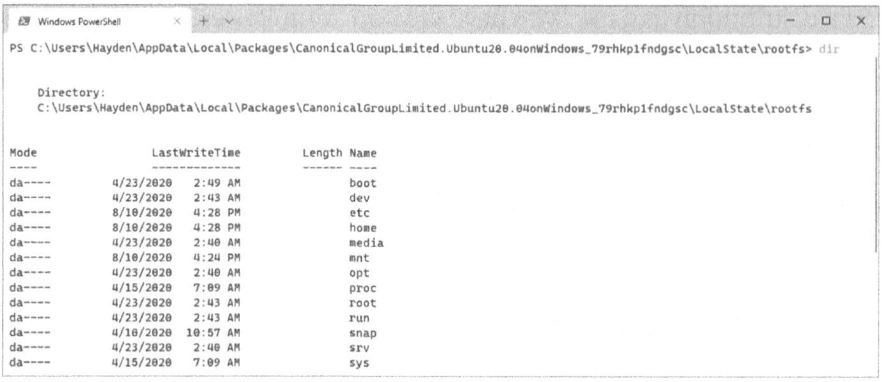

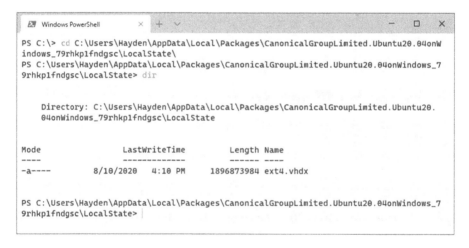

Figure 2-27. *Directory listing of WSL 1 unpacked file system*

On WSL 2, the rootfs is unpacked into a Hyper-V .vhdx file at `C:\Users\<username>\`
`AppData\Local\Packages\<Store package name>\LocalState\ext4.vhdx` (Figure 2-28).

Figure 2-28. *Directory listing of WSL 2 file system location in a VHDX file*

Warning   You should not attempt to access your WSL file system via this method;
doing so could cause irreparable damage to the data. You should only access your
WSL file system via \\wsl$\<distro name> or in the Quick Access menu in File
Explorer on Windows 10 version 2010 and later.

When you install a rootfs using wsl.exe --import, none of the extra plumbing beyond
registering the distro with WSL is included, and creation of a default user other than root
must be completed manually, if desired.

When you import a rootfs using wsl.exe --import, the rootfs will be unpacked at the location specified in your command:

```
wsl.exe --import <name for distro> <location to unpack rootfs> <location of
rootfs> [optionally: --version <version of WSL to install in>]
```

For WSL 1, it will unpack the Linux file system, which as discussed earlier is important you do not edit directly. For WSL 2, it will unpack into a VHDX, a virtual hard disk image file (Figure 2-29).

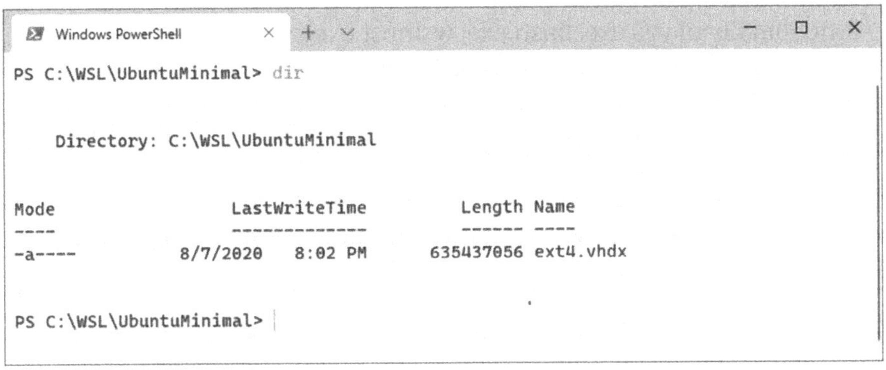

Figure 2-29. *Directory listing of WSL 2 file system custom location in a VHDX file*

WSL Tooling

WSL 2 uses several components located at %SystemRoot%\system32\lxss\ to perform its basic functions (Figure 2-30).

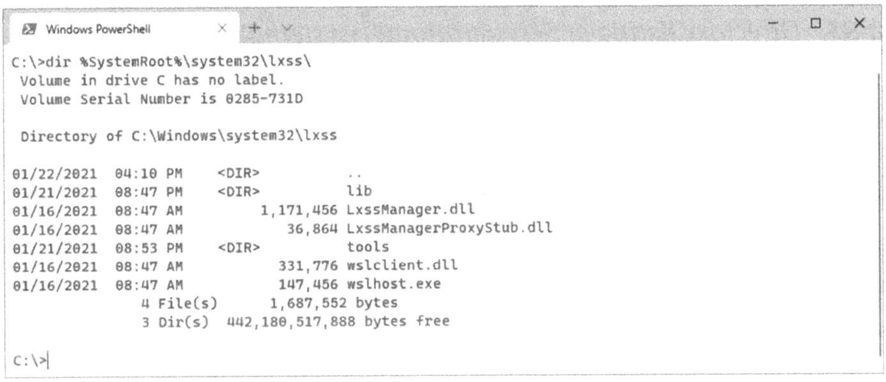

Figure 2-30. *Directory listing of %SystemRoot%\system32\lxss*

%SystemRoot%\system32\lxss\ contains

- LxssManager.dll – Services for managing the WSL environment

- LxssManagerProxyStub.dll – An initial stub for loading LxssManager. dll later in the boot process

- tools/ – A folder containing several other tools (see in the following)

- lib/ – A folder containing several libraries (see in the following)

- wslclient.dll – A new library in builds 19555+ used to consolidate the functionality of wsl.exe, bash.exe, wslhost.exe, wslconfig.exe, and LxssManager.dll into a single library

- wslhost.exe – A tool used to maintain Windows interoperability for background tasks on WSL 1

In the tools/ folder, there are several key components of WSL 2 (Figure 2-31).

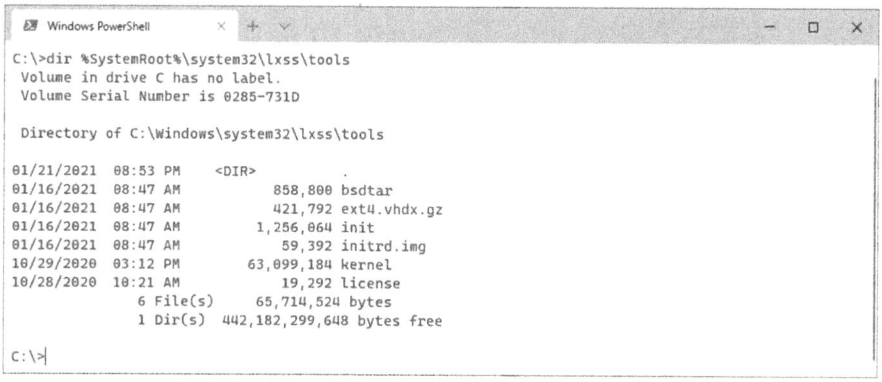

Figure 2-31.   *Directory listing of %SystemRoot%\system32\lxss\tools*

The subdirectory \tools\ (Figure 2-31) is home to

- bsdtar – The utility for converting WSL installations to and from tar.gz balls

- ext4.vhdx.gz – A preformatted blank ext4 file system

- init – The WSL 2 init process, which operates as PID 1 on WSL 2 containers

- initrd.img – The initial RAM disk loaded by the WSL 2 kernel as part of the "boot" process

- kernel – The WSL 2 Linux kernel

- license – A copy of the GNU General Public License 2 covering the Linux kernel

In the lib/ folder, there are several libraries used by WSL 2 for GPU on builds 20150+ (Figure 2-30).

```
Windows PowerShell        ×    +   ∨                            –   □   ×

C:\>dir %SystemRoot%\system32\lxss\lib\
 Volume in drive C has no label.
 Volume Serial Number is 0285-731D

 Directory of C:\Windows\system32\lxss\lib

01/21/2021  08:47 PM    <DIR>          .
12/15/2020  07:32 PM           133,088 libcuda.so
12/15/2020  07:32 PM           133,088 libcuda.so.1
12/15/2020  07:32 PM           133,088 libcuda.so.1.1
01/16/2021  04:59 AM           785,480 libd3d12.so
01/16/2021  04:59 AM         5,346,360 libd3d12core.so
01/16/2021  04:59 AM        25,263,592 libdirectml.so
01/16/2021  04:59 AM           827,904 libdxcore.so
12/15/2020  07:32 PM           192,160 libnvidia-ml.so.1
12/15/2020  07:32 PM        48,606,768 libnvwgf2umx.so
               9 File(s)     81,421,528 bytes
               1 Dir(s)  442,215,612,416 bytes free

C:\>|
```

Figure 2-32. *Directory listing of %SystemRoot%\system32\lxss\lib*

The subdirectory \lib\ (Figure 2-32) is home to the following:

- libcuda.so, libnvidia-ml.so.1, libnvwgf2umx.so, and related libraries provide support for Nvidia CUDA, machine learning, and other GPU compute functionalities.

- libdxcore.so, libd3d12.so, libd3d12core.so, libdirectml.so, and related libraries provide support for DirectX-powered Direct3D GPU acceleration and DirectML machine learning.

This subdirectory is linked into place inside WSL distros at /usr/lib/wsl/lib/ (Figure 2-33).

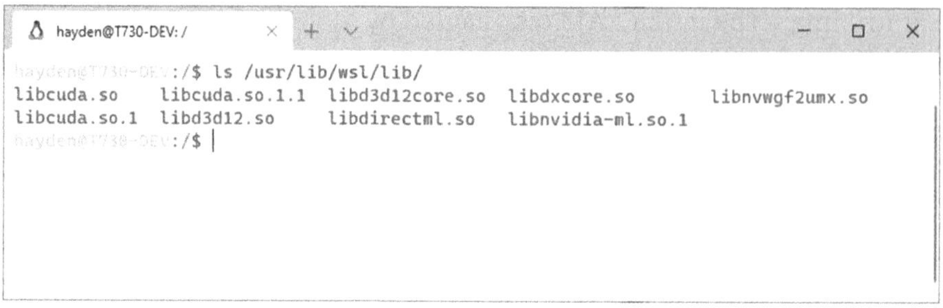

```
△ hayden@T730-DEV: /        ×    + ∨                                      —    □    ×

hayden@T730-DEV:/$ ls /usr/lib/wsl/lib/
libcuda.so      libcuda.so.1.1  libd3d12core.so  libdxcore.so        libnvwgf2umx.so
libcuda.so.1    libd3d12.so     libdirectml.so   libnvidia-ml.so.1
hayden@T730-DEV:/$ |
```

Figure 2-33. *Directory listing of /usr/lib/wsl/lib mirrored from %SystemRoot%\ system32\lxss\lib on Windows*

WSL API in Windows 10

For a closer examination of what occurs when a WSL distro is installed, the WSL-DistroLauncher template provided by Microsoft can provide some insight. DistroLauncher is comprised of a classic Win32 C++ application, launcher.exe, bundled with Store Assets and a rootfs tarball into a UWP package. This code calls the WSL API in Windows 10 to check the distro install status, install, and register the distro.

The main code in launcher.exe is located at DistroLauncher/DistroLauncher.cpp. It checks if WSL is enabled, and if not, display a message:

```
if (!g_wslApi.WslIsOptionalComponentInstalled()) {
      Helpers::PrintMessage(MSG_MISSING_OPTIONAL_COMPONENT);
```

It then checks if the WSL distribution is installed and, if not, installs it:

```
if (!g_wslApi.WslIsDistributionRegistered()) {
```

```
// If the "--root" option is specified, do not create a user account.
    bool useRoot = ((installOnly) && (arguments.size() > 1) &&
    (arguments[1] == ARG_INSTALL_ROOT));
    hr = InstallDistribution(!useRoot);
      if (FAILED(hr)) {
          if (hr == HRESULT_FROM_WIN32(ERROR_ALREADY_EXISTS)) {
          Helpers::PrintMessage(MSG_INSTALL_ALREADY_EXISTS);
          }
      } else {
```

```
        Helpers::PrintMessage(MSG_INSTALL_SUCCESS);
    }
    exitCode = SUCCEEDED(hr) ? 0 : 1;
}
```

Creating a new user and adding them to sudo is handled in DistroLauncher/ DistributionInfo.cpp and calls directly inside the WSL distro:

```
bool DistributionInfo::CreateUser(std::wstring_view userName)
{
    // Create the user account.
    DWORD exitCode;
    std::wstring commandLine = L"/usr/sbin/adduser --quiet --gecos '' ";
    commandLine += userName;
    HRESULT hr = g_wslApi.WslLaunchInteractive(commandLine.c_str(), true,
    &exitCode);
    if ((FAILED(hr)) || (exitCode != 0)) {
        return false;
    }
    // Add the user account to any relevant groups.
    commandLine = L"/usr/sbin/usermod -aG adm,cdrom,sudo,dip,plugdev ";
    commandLine += userName;
    hr = g_wslApi.WslLaunchInteractive(commandLine.c_str(), true, &exitCode);
    if ((FAILED(hr)) || (exitCode != 0)) {
        // Delete the user if the group add command failed.
        commandLine = L"/usr/sbin/deluser ";
        commandLine += userName;
        g_wslApi.WslLaunchInteractive(commandLine.c_str(), true, &exitCode);
        return false;
    }
    return true;
}
```

The WSL API calls available in the Windows 10 WSL API from wslapi.dll are detailed in DistroLauncher/WslApiLoader.cpp:

```
WslIsOptionalComponentInstalled()
WslIsDistributionRegistered()
WslRegisterDistribution()
WslConfigureDistribution()
WslLaunchInteractive()
WslLaunch()
```

These API calls are not otherwise documented. However, third-party projects, such as Docker Desktop and Raft WSL, do use them. Community projects use them to create custom launchers built on top of WSL.

CHAPTER 3

Managing WSL Distros

WSL includes a set of command line Linux distribution management tools. This chapter will examine these tools with discussions, examples, and screenshots of each.

Listing All Distros

The names, state, and WSL version number of all installed WSL distros can be listed (Figure 3-1) by opening PowerShell and running

```
wsl.exe --list --verbose --all
```

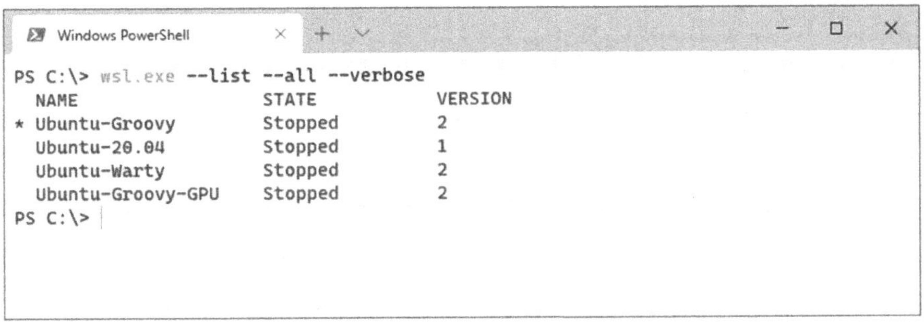

Figure 3-1. *Listing all WSL distros installed with their current state and WSL version*

Under "NAME," you will see there are four distributions installed. This name is a unique identifier in WSL for each distro installed. It is set by the publisher in WSL distros that are installed from the Microsoft Store or sideloaded from an .appx package. The name can be manually set when WSL distros are installed using wsl.exe --import (see section "Import/Restore Distro"). Most WSL commands refer to the distro by this name.

An asterisk (*) appears next to your default WSL distro. For more on the default distro setting, see section "Setting a Default Distro."

© Hayden Barnes 2021
H. Barnes, *Pro Windows Subsystem for Linux (WSL)*, https://doi.org/10.1007/978-1-4842-6873-5_3

Under "STATE," you see that, here, none of them are running. WSL distros will open when you open a WSL shell, run WSL from an existing shell, or browse WSL files using \\wsl$\<distroname>, for example, \\wsl$\Ubuntu-20.04\, and in newer Windows 10 builds using \\wsl\<distroname>, for example, \\wsl\Ubuntu.

Under "VERSION," you see that Ubuntu-Groovy, Ubuntu-Warty, and Ubuntu-Groovy-GPU are installed as WSL 2 distros, while Ubuntu-20.04 is installed as a WSL 1 distro. It is possible to have WSL 1 and 2 distributions side by side. It is easy to convert existing WSL distros between WSL 1 and 2 (see section "Converting Distros Between WSL Versions").

Listing Running Distros

To see the names of the WSL distros that are running (Figure 3-2), use

```
wsl.exe --list –running
```

Example:

```
wsl.exe --list --running ·
```

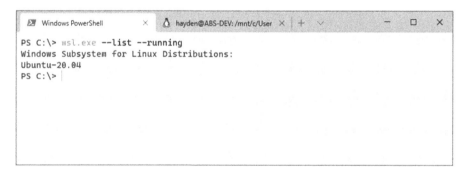

Figure 3-2. *Listing the WSL distros that are running*

Running a Default Distro

WSL sets one of your distros as the default distro. This distro is launched when you run `wsl.exe` from PowerShell without the -d parameter. To change the default distro, see the "Setting a Default Distro" section.

Start the default WSL distro from PowerShell (Figure 3-3) using

```
wsl.exe
```

```
hayden@ABS-DEV:/mnt/c        ×    +  ∨                                    –   □   ×

PS C:\> wsl.exe
To run a command as administrator (user "root"), use "sudo <command>".
See "man sudo_root" for details.

hayden@ABS-DEV:/mnt/c$ |
```

Figure 3-3. *Starting the default WSL distro*

Setting a Default Distro

As discussed in the preceding, the default distro is the distro launched when you run wsl.
exe without the -d parameter. Some third-party tools also use wsl.exe to interface with
WSL. You may need to change the default distro to work with your preferred distro in
these tools.

Set the default WSL distro (Figure 3-4) using

```
wsl.exe --set-default <name of distribution>
```

where <name of distribution> is the name of the WSL distro registered in WSL you would
like to set as default. To see all the distros you have installed, see section "Listing All
Distros."

Example:

```
wsl.exe --set-default Ubuntu-20.04
```

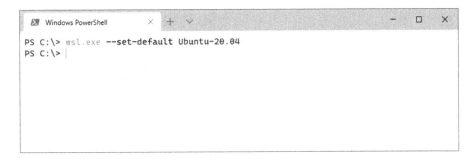

Figure 3-4. *Setting Ubuntu-20.04 as the default distro in WSL*

Running a Specific Distro

Start a specific WSL distro (Figure 3-5), such as one other than your default, from PowerShell using

```
wsl.exe --distribution <name of distribution>
```

where <name of distribution> is the name of the WSL distro registered in WSL. You need the exact name of the WSL distro; see the "Listing All Distros" section if you need to look it up.

Example:

```
wsl.exe --distribution Ubuntu-20.04
```

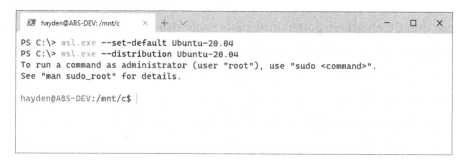

Figure 3-5. *Starting Ubuntu-20.04*

WSL distros installed from the Microsoft Store or a sideloaded .appx package can also be launched by their Start Menu icon (Figure 3-6).

Figure 3-6. *Icon for Ubuntu on Windows Start Menu next to some of the author's favorite development applications*

WSL distros installed from the Microsoft Store or a sideloaded .appx package also include an application alias and can be run from PowerShell (Figure 3-7). These are not created when manually importing WSL distros using `wsl.exe --import`.

Example:

`ubuntu2004.exe` will run Ubuntu 20.04 LTS from the Microsoft Store.

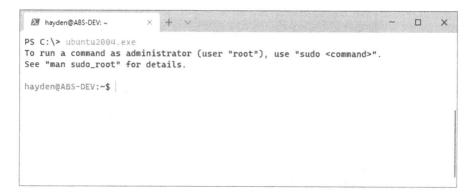

Figure 3-7. *Starting Ubuntu 20.04 installed from the Microsoft Store using the application alias*

Running as a Specific User

To start a specific WSL distro from PowerShell as a specific user (Figure 3-8), use

```
wsl.exe --distribution <name of distribution> --user <name of user>
```

where <name of distribution> is the name of the WSL distro registered in WSL you would like to run and <name of user> is the username of an existing user you would like to start the WSL distro as.

Example:

```
wsl.exe --distribution Ubuntu-20.04 --user root
```

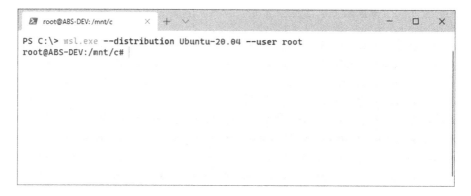

Figure 3-8. *Starting Ubuntu-20.04 as a specific user, in this case, the root user*

Note that the user must exist in the WSL distro; otherwise, you will receive an error (Figure 3-9).

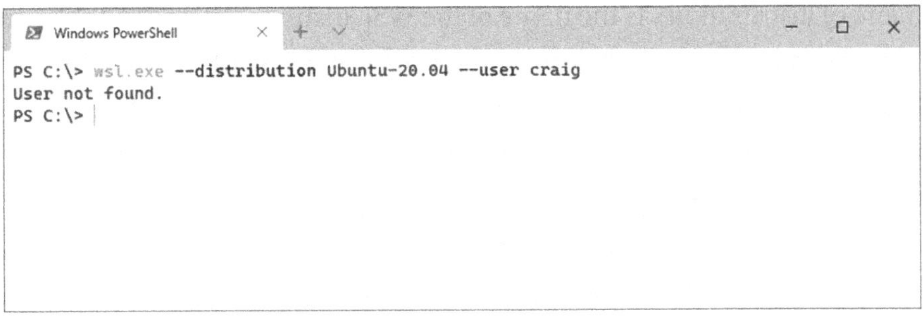

```
Windows PowerShell           ×    +  ∨                    —  □  ×
PS C:\> wsl.exe --distribution Ubuntu-20.04 --user craig
User not found.
PS C:\>
```

Figure 3-9. *Error when starting Ubuntu-20.04 as a specific user when that user does not exist*

Executing Single Commands

To run commands on your default WSL distribution (Figure 3-10), use

`wsl.exe --exec <command to run>`

where <command to run> is the command you would like to execute as the default user on your default WSL distro.

Example:

`wsl.exe --exec echo 'hello world'`

```
Windows PowerShell           ×    +  ∨                    —  □  ×
PS C:\> wsl.exe --exec echo 'hello world'
hello world
PS C:\>
```

Figure 3-10. *Running a single command on the default WSL distro using wsl.exe*

To run commands on a specific WSL distribution, add --distribution and the name of the distribution (Figure 3-11):

`wsl.exe --distribution <name of distribution> --exec <command to run>`

where <name of distribution> is the name of the WSL distro registered in WSL you would like to run and <command to run> is the command you would like to execute on the default shell.

Example:

```
wsl.exe --distribution Ubuntu-20.04 --exec cat /etc/os-release
```

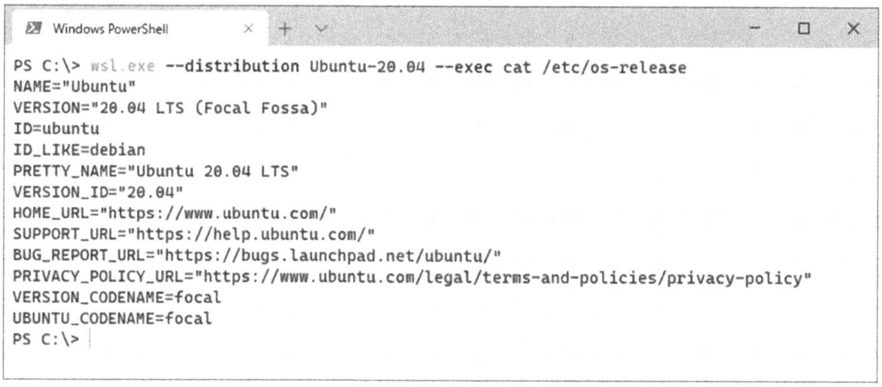

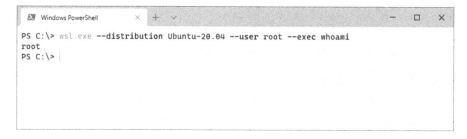

Figure 3-11. *Running a single command on a specific WSL distro using wsl.exe*

You can optionally add --user and run the command as a specific user (Figure 3-12):

```
wsl.exe --distribution <name of distribution> --user <name of user> --exec
<command to run>
```

Example:

```
wsl.exe --distribution Ubuntu-20.04 --user root --exec whoami
```

Figure 3-12. *Running a single command on a specific WSL distro as a specific user using wsl.exe*

Shutdown

Some tasks will require you to restart the WSL 2 virtual machine environment.

You must restart the WSL 2 environment after changing settings in your .wslconfig such as setting a custom WSL kernel or changing your memory usage limits.

It is also possible, more so on Insider builds, that the WSL 2 environment could become unstable, particularly if you are hacking on the subsystem like many of you will.

To shut down the WSL 2 environment (Figure 3-13), run the following:

```
wsl.exe --shutdown
```

This will initiate a shutdown, notifying running Linux processes of the shutdown via SIGTERM, and then terminate the WSL instance. Starting any distro now will restart the WSL 2 environment.

Example:

```
wsl.exe --shutdown
```

Figure 3-13. *Shutting down the WSL 2 environment*

In the tab Ubuntu-20.04 was opened in, you will see (Figure 3-14) that it exited.

Figure 3-14. *The state of Ubuntu 20.04 after issuing the shutdown command*

Terminate

Very rarely a WSL distro or Linux process in a WSL distro will become unresponsive, and it becomes necessary to forcibly terminate it. Terminating a WSL distro immediately halts all running processes and should be avoided if a process could be writing critical data.

To terminate a WSL distro (Figure 3-15), run the following:

```
wsl.exe –terminate <name of distribution>
```

where <name of distribution> is the name of the WSL distro registered in WSL you would like to terminate.

Example:

```
wsl.exe --terminate Ubuntu-20.04
```

Figure 3-15. *Terminating a WSL distro*

In the tab Ubuntu-20.04 was opened in, you will see (Figure 3-16) that it exited.

Figure 3-16. *The state of Ubuntu 20.04 after issuing the terminate command*

Converting Distros Between WSL Versions

Converting WSL distros between WSL 1 and 2 is relatively simple; however, large installations can take time, so patience is required.

On a recent Intel Core i7 with moderate specs, converting a 500 MB environment between WSL 1 and 2 takes about a minute. Large WSL distro installations, of 10 GB or more, could take up to an hour depending on your hardware. If it appears stuck, give "Enter" a try and see what happens.

To learn more about how WSL 1 and 2 files are managed, see section "WSL Installation Mechanics" in Chapter 2, "Enabling WSL."

To convert a distro between 1 and 2 (Figure 3-17), run

```
wsl.exe --set-version <name of distribution> <version number>
```

Note there is no status or progress indicator.

Examples:

```
wsl.exe --set-version Ubuntu-20.04 1
wsl.exe --set-version Ubuntu-20.04 2
```

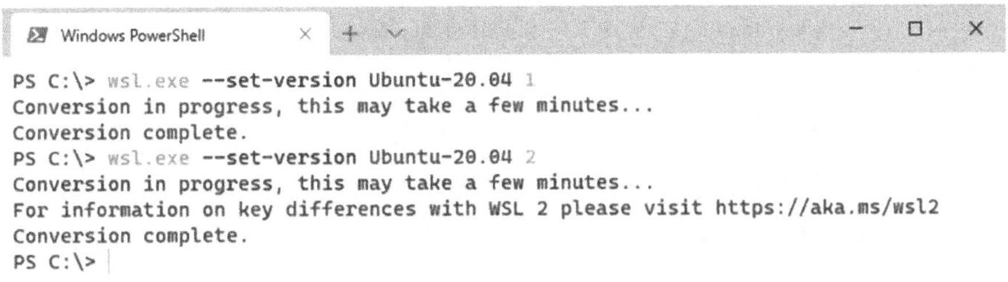

Figure 3-17. *Converting a WSL distro between WSL 1 and 2*

Export/Backup Distro

We should all make regular backups of our systems. This is particularly true if you have configured your WSL distro with all your preferred packages and settings. You may also want to share your WSL distro with a colleague working on the same project.

The same warning about the length of time this process can take from the "Converting Distros Between WSL Versions" section applies here too. This is a file I/O-intensive process that can take a long time to complete.

To back up or export a WSL distribution (Figure 3-18), run the following:

```
wsl.exe --export <name of distribution> <filename of exported image>
```

where <name of distribution> is the name of the WSL distro registered in WSL you would like to export and where <filename of exported image> is the filename of the WSL distro image to export to. Note there is no status or progress indicator.

Example:

```
wsl.exe --export Ubuntu-20.04 C:\WSL\ubuntu-focal-backup.tar.gz
```

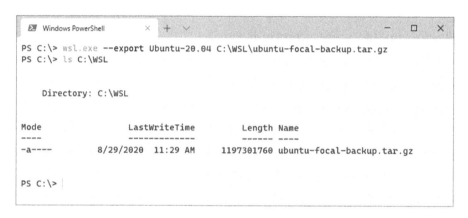

Figure 3-18. *Backing up or exporting a WSL distro*

Import/Restore Distro

In addition to installing WSL distros from the Microsoft Store and sideloaded .appx packages, you can also import Linux rootfs images directly into WSL. These can include

- Linux rootfs images downloaded directly from Web, such as from Ubuntu at https://cloud-images.ubuntu.com/

- WSL images exported for backup purposes

- WSL images exported to have multiple WSL distributions from the same image

Importing an image is accomplished as follows:

```
wsl.exe --import <name of imported distro> <location to store unpacked file
system> <filename of exported image> --version <1 or 2>
```

where <name of imported distro> is the unique name to register your WSL distro as in WSL. This is the name you will use to interact with the distribution and what will appear in wsl.exe –list and in the Windows Terminal drop-down.

<location to store unpacked file system> is a directory for storing WSL-related files. This is handled automatically in WSL distros from the Microsoft Store and a sideloaded .appx, but when importing manually, you must specify a directory. Your Windows user must have read/write permissions for this folder. Using drives other than C:\ is possible, but using network-mounted storage is not recommended.

<filename of exported image> is the filename of your Linux rootfs to import.

WSL will import the rootfs as WSL 1 or 2 based on your default setting. Reminder: To set WSL 2 as your default, use `wsl.exe --set-default-version 2`.

--version <1 or 2> is an optional setting to override the default WSL setting and import the rootfs specifically as WSL 1 or 2 (Figure 3-19).

Example:

```
wsl.exe --import Ubuntu-Groovy C:\WSL\Ubuntu-Groovy\ C:\Users\Hayden\
Downloads\groovy-server-cloudimg-amd64-wsl.rootfs.tar.gz --version 2
```

This example imports the export of our Ubuntu 20.04 WSL 1 image as a WSL 2. This way we can test the same Ubuntu 20.04 image we have customized for ourselves in WSL 1 or WSL 2.

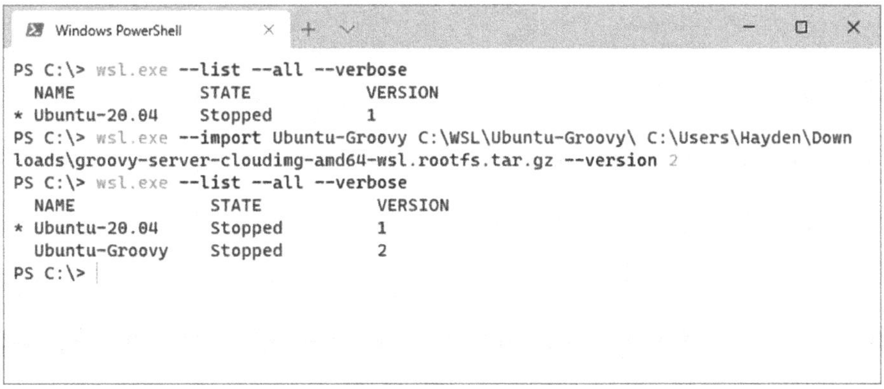

Figure 3-19. *Restoring or importing a WSL distro*

Duplicate Distros

In certain cases, you may want to duplicate an existing WSL distro that is installed. This is useful when you want to clone an existing development stack that you have configured to your exact specifications, perhaps to test a change to the configuration without disrupting your existing workflow. To do this, we export an image of the distro we want to make a duplicate of and then import it under a new WSL distro name.

First, export

```
wsl.exe --export <name of distribution> <filename of exported image>
```

Example:

```
wsl.exe --export Ubuntu-20.04 C:\WSL\ubuntu-focal-backup.tar.gz
```

Then, we import the rootfs file under a new distro name (Figure 3-20):

```
wsl.exe --import <name of imported distro> <location to store unpacked file system> <filename of exported image> --version <1 or 2>
```

Example:

```
wsl.exe --import Ubuntu-20.04-2 C:\WSL\Ubuntu-20.04-2\ C:\WSL\ubuntu-focal-backup.tar.gz --version 2
```

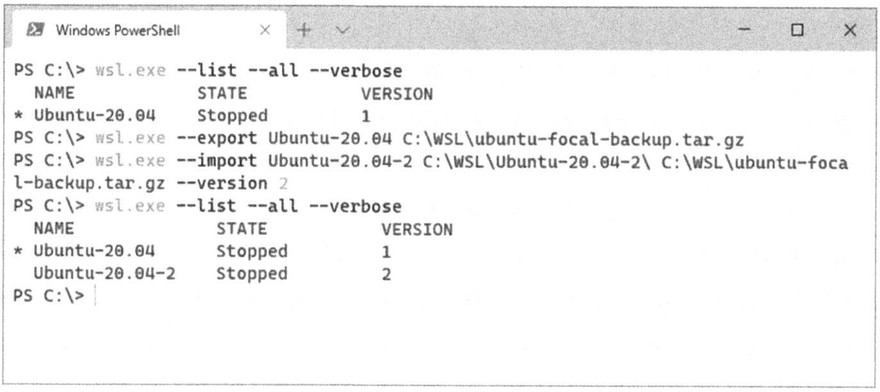

Figure 3-20. *Duplicating a WSL distro by combining the export and import functions*

Resetting Distros

If you have installed your WSL distro from the Microsoft Store or a sideloaded .appx, you have a few additional GUI options to manage your distro, including the option to "Reset" to a fresh installation, by virtue of being bundled as UWP app.

Open WSL Distro "App" Settings

Click the Windows Start button, and locate your WSL distro in the Windows Start Menu, either in the alphabetical list or on a pinned tile. Right-click your distro, hover over "More," and, in the expanded menu, click "App Settings" (Figure 3-21).

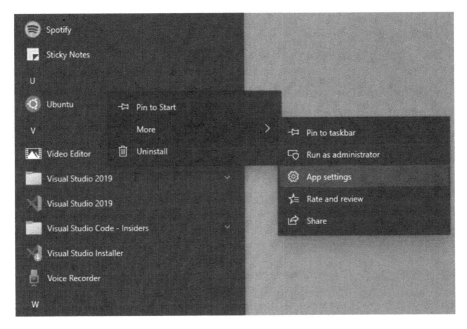

Figure 3-21. *Opening App Settings of a WSL distro installed from the Microsoft Store*

Alternatively, you can also access application settings by clicking the Windows Start button and clicking the Settings gear icon (Figure 3-22).

Figure 3-22. *Opening Settings from the Windows Start button*

Click Apps in Windows Settings (Figure 3-23).

Figure 3-23. *The Apps category in Windows Settings*

And then scroll down or search for your distro installed from the Microsoft Store in "Apps & features" (Figure 3-24):

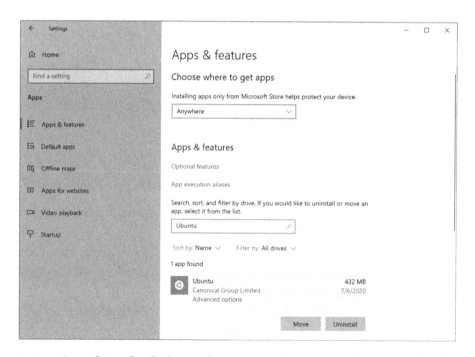

Figure 3-24. *Searching for "Ubuntu" in Apps & features in Windows Settings*

From "Apps & features," you can easily relocate your WSL distro to another drive (possible but not recommended) and uninstall. Before you attempt to move your WSL distro to another drive, make sure you take a complete backup (see section "Export/ Backup Distro").

Advanced Options in WSL Distro "App" Settings

To access additional options for your WSL distro, click "Advanced options," which will take you to the following pane (Figure 3-25).

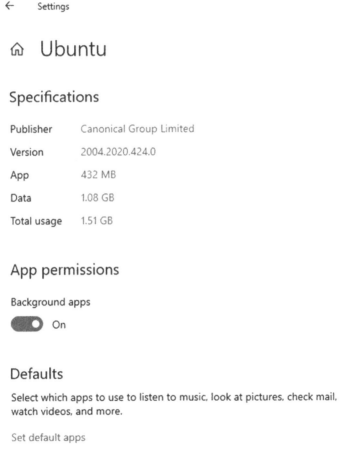

Figure 3-25. *Advanced options for Ubuntu installed from the Microsoft Store*

Publisher and Version

This pane gives some basic information, such as WSL distro publisher and version.

App Storage Space

The app storage space is the size of the original image published by the distro maker that is unpacked on installation. A copy of this original image is kept on the system and is updated behind the scenes when a new update is made available. However, this does not update your existing distribution installation. Existing installations are updated via the distro's respective package manager, such as apt for Ubuntu. This updated image will be unpacked when you reset as follows.

Data Storage Space

The data storage space is the size of your existing distribution installation, which includes the unpacked image plus any additional programs and files you may have installed.

Considerations: Resetting WSL Distro

If you wish to reset your existing WSL distro installation to the most recent original image published by your distro publisher on the Microsoft Store, scroll down on the "Advanced options" pane (Figure 3-26), and click "Reset." There is no confirmation. This will immediately and irreparably erase all files on your WSL distro at /. It will leave you with a fresh WSL distro install. Make sure you have backed up all important files by copying them to a secure location on Windows via /mnt/c or by making a backup image using wsl.exe --export as described earlier.

Figure 3-26. *Further down the "Advanced options" pane for Ubuntu installed from the Microsoft Store, where the "Reset" option is visible*

Uninstall Distros from the Microsoft Store

If you have installed your WSL distro from the Microsoft Store (or a sideloaded .appx), you have some additional options for uninstalling.

From the Windows Start Menu

Click the Windows Start button, and locate your WSL distro, either in the alphabetical list or on a pinned tile (Figure 3-27). Right-click your distro, and click "Uninstall."

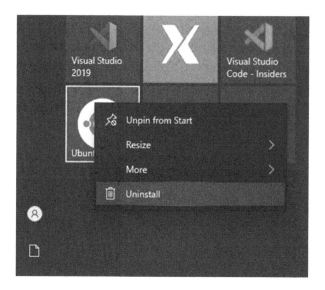

Figure 3-27. *Uninstalling a WSL distro from the Windows Start Menu*

From Advanced Options in WSL Distro "App" Settings

Access the "Advanced options" pane as described earlier (Figure 3-28), but instead of clicking "Reset," click "Uninstall."

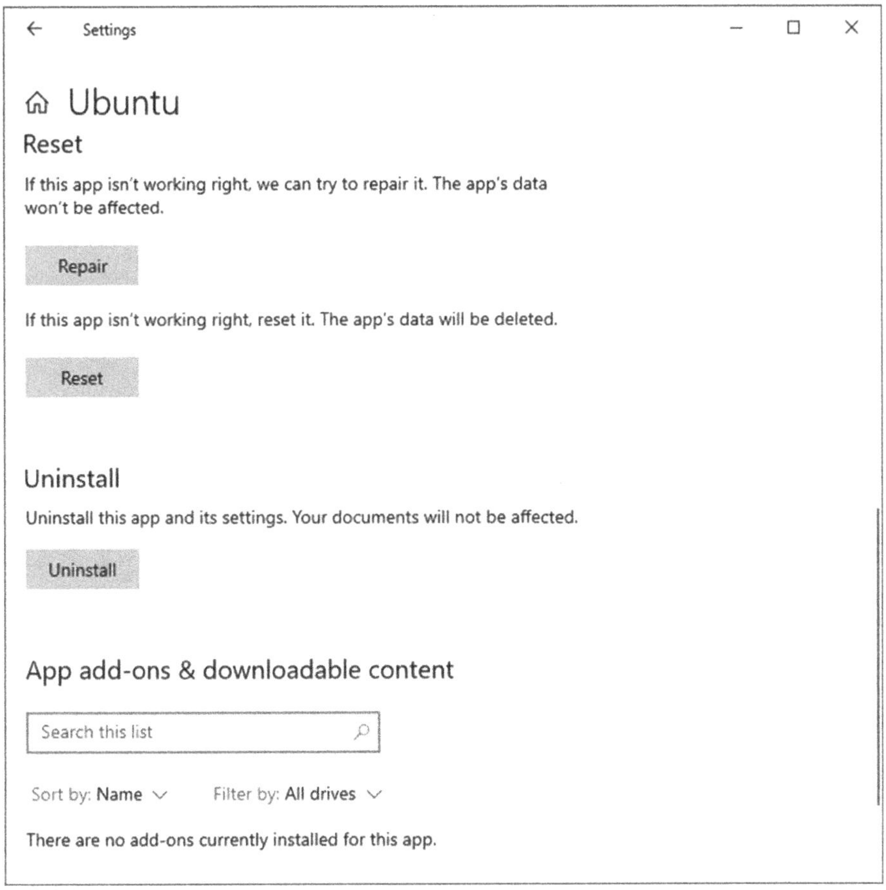

Figure 3-28. *The "Advanced options" pane for Ubuntu installed from the Microsoft Store, where the "Uninstall" option is visible*

Using PowerShell

You may also remove a WSL distro installed from the Microsoft Store or a sideloaded .appx using PowerShell.

First, locate the package's full name (Figure 3-29) using:

```
Get-AppxPackage -Name "*<distroname>*" | Select PackageFamilyName
```

Example:

```
Get-AppxPackage -Name "*ubuntu*" | Select PackageFullName
```

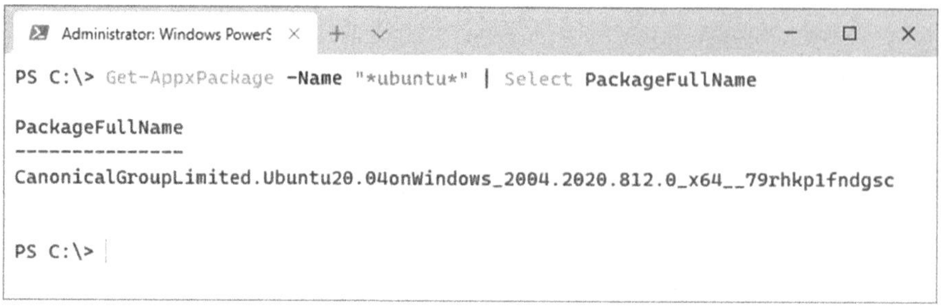

Figure 3-29. *Output of installed appx packages containing "ubuntu" in PowerShell*

Then copy and paste the PackageFullName as follows (Figure 3-30):

```
Remove-AppxPackage -Package <PackageFullName>
```

Example:

```
Remove-AppxPackage -Package "CanonicalGroupLimited.
UbuntuonWindows_2004.2020.424.0_x64__79rhkp1fndgsc"
```

Figure 3-30. *Uninstalling the Ubuntu WSL appx package in PowerShell*

Uninstall Distros Installed Using wsl.exe --import

If you manually import a WSL distro using `wsl.exe --import` and wish to remove it, you must unregister the distro. Unregister the distro as follows (Figure 3-31):

```
wsl.exe -unregister <name of distribution>
```

Example:

```
wsl.exe --unregister Ubuntu
```

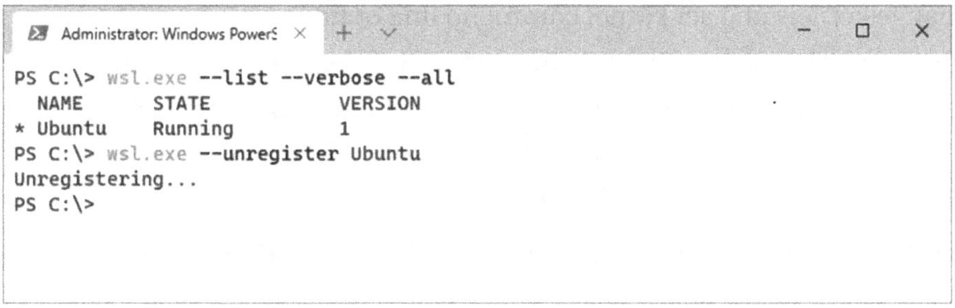

Figure 3-31. *Manually unregistering a WSL distro installed via --import*

After unregistering the WSL distro, you may then wish to delete the folder where the WSL distro was originally unpacked. In PowerShell, this can be performed with (Figure 3-32):

```
rmdir <path to WSL distro folder>
```

Example:

```
rmdir C:\WSL\ubuntu-hirsute
```

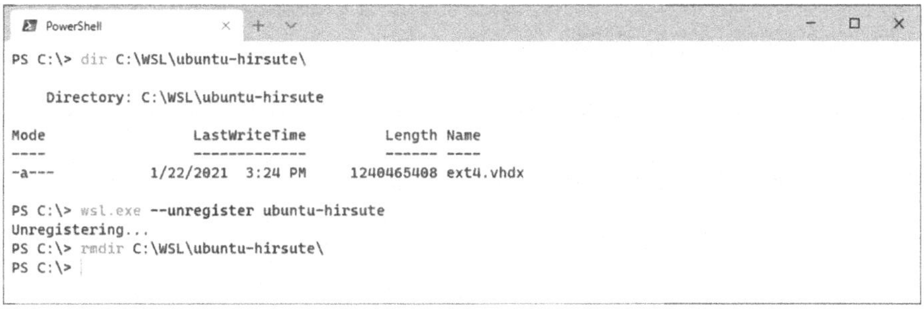

Figure 3-32. *Removing the folder where the WSL distro was originally unpacked*

WSL 2 Kernel Management

With the arrival of WSL 2, a Linux kernel is powering the WSL environment, to provide complete application binary interface compatibility.

The WSL 2 kernel is distributed separately from the kernel inside a WSL image. Changing the kernel inside the distribution will not change the "kernel" that WSL distros are launched with.

To change kernels and set kernel command line options, you must configure .wslconfig, in your Windows user directory, which can be referred to by the Windows environmental variable %USERPROFILE%. See "Configure WSL 2 Settings" for more configuration settings in .wslconfig and "Customizing WSL" for how to build your own WSL 2 kernel.

The standard WSL 2 kernel is updated via the Windows Update infrastructure. To ensure Windows updates of the WSL 2 kernel, enable "Receive updates for other Microsoft products when you update Windows" in the "Advanced options" page of Windows Update (Figure 3-33).

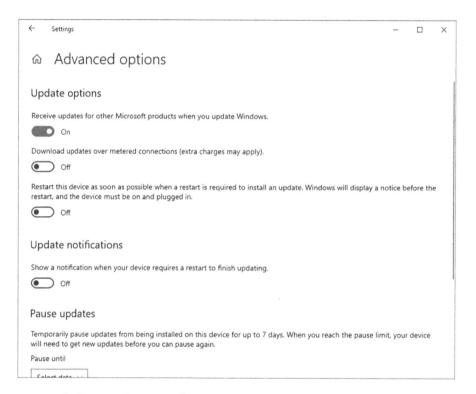

Figure 3-33. *"Advanced options" in "Windows Update" in Windows Settings*

Checking for Available Updates

Check for available kernel updates with the following. If no kernel updates are available, the current kernel version will be displayed (Figure 3-34).

```
wsl.exe --update
```

```
PS C:\> wsl.exe --update
Checking for updates...
Downloading updates...
Installing updates...
This change will take effect on the next full restart of WSL. To force a restart, please run 'wsl --shutdown'.
Kernel version: 4.19.128
PS C:\>
```

Figure 3-34. *Updating the WSL kernel using wsl.exe --update*

Note that if you have installed a custom kernel, then updating the kernel with this method will not affect the kernel you have specified in .wslconfig.

If you get the message "The requested operation requires elevation," then you need to run PowerShell as Administrator. To start an elevated prompt from an existing PowerShell (Figure 3-35), run

```
Start-Process WT -Verb runAs
```

```
PS C:\> Start-Process WT -Verb runAs
PS C:\>
    PS C:\>
```

Figure 3-35. *Launching an elevated Administrator PowerShell prompt to update the WSL 2 kernel*

And then run wsl.exe --update again in the elevated PowerShell prompt window.

Checking Kernel Update Status

Check the last update date, automatic update status, and current version of the WSL 2 kernel (Figure 3-36) with the following:

```
wsl.exe --update --status
```

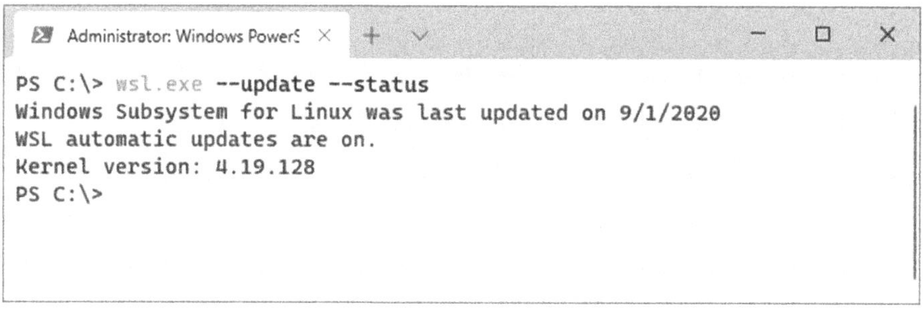

Figure 3-36. *Checking the last update date, automatic update status, and current version of the WSL 2 kernel*

Rolling Back Kernel Updates

If a kernel upgrade were to cause a problem, there should be a built-in mechanism to roll back to the most recent working kernel.

To roll back, you need to run PowerShell as Administrator. To start an elevated prompt from an existing PowerShell, run

```
Start-Process WT -Verb runAs
```

Then to roll back the WSL 2 kernel update (Figure 3-37), run

```
wsl.exe --update --rollback
```

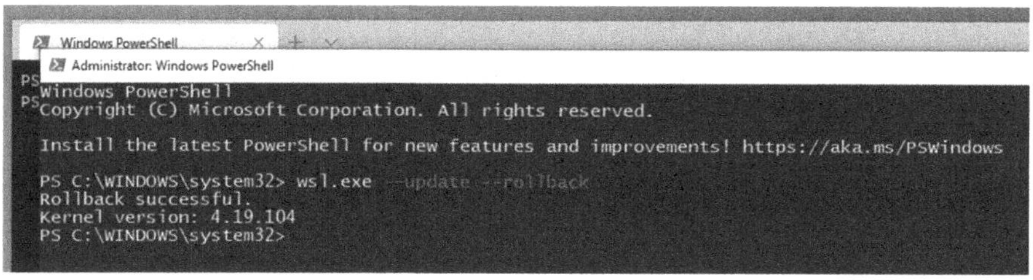

Figure 3-37. *Rolling back the most recent WSL 2 kernel update to the previous kernel*

Mounting External Volumes

A new feature in Windows builds starting from number 20211 is the ability to use wsl.exe to mount disks and disk images to your WSL distros. This lets you access a disk's actual file system data in addition to the files it stores. You cannot mount a disk or a partition that is on your primary Windows drive that contains your C: partition.

Unmounting from Windows

If your desired disk is currently accessible from within Windows via a drive letter, you must first unmount it. Right-click the Windows Start Menu icon, and choose "Disk Management" (Figure 3-38).

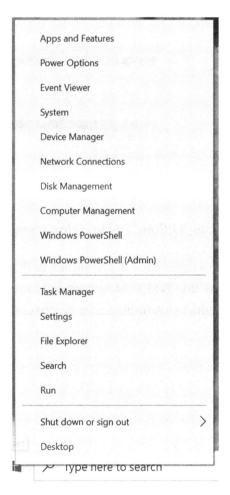

Figure 3-38. *Opening Disk Management via the Start Menu*

You now need to locate the disk you wish to make available to WSL. Any mounted partitions are labeled with their Windows drive letters to help you locate the drive. Once you have located it in the bottom half of the Disk Management window, right-click the disk, and choose "Offline" (Figure 3-39).

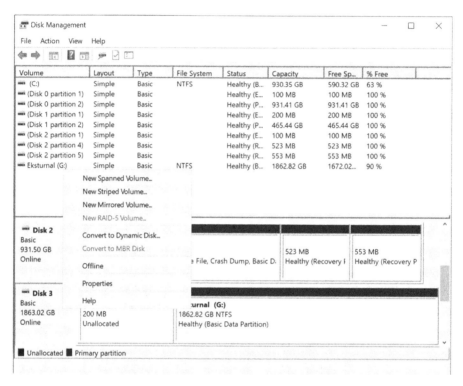

Figure 3-39. *Setting a disk to "Offline" in Disk Management*

While you are here, make a note of the disk number. In this case, it is disk 3. We need this number to mount the disk into WSL 2. Mounting disks into WSL requires running as Administrator, so open a terminal as Administrator before continuing.

We can mount the drive to WSL and check that it is visible with (Figure 3-40)

```
wsl.exe --mount \\.\PHYSICALDRIVE<disk number> --bare
wsl.exe --exec lsblk
```

where <disk number> is the drive number from Disk Management.

Example:

```
wsl.exe --mount \\.\PHYSICALDRIVE3 --bare
wsl.exe --exec lsblk
```

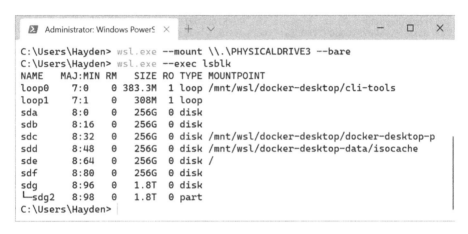

Figure 3-40. *Mounting a block device into WSL 2 and showing it is present as sdg, with a single partition numbered 2, via lsblk*

We can double-check that we have the correct \\.\PHYSICALDRIVE path by running

```
wmic diskdrive list brief
```

Because we specified the –bare flag, the disk was inserted into WSL but not mounted, instead exposing every partition for further use as we want. We can also mount individual partitions and cause their file systems to be loaded in one step, so that we do not need to determine the /dev node that is associated with the disk. Remembering the limitation that we cannot mount partitions on the same disk as our C: partition, we mount a partition with (Figure 3-41)

```
wsl.exe --mount \\.\PHYSICALDRIVE<disk number> --partition <partition
number> [optionally: --type <filesystem type>] [optionally: --options
<filesystem mount options>]
```

where <disk number> is the disk number from Disk Management; <partition number> is the partition number from Disk Management; <filesystem type> is the type of file system stored within the partition as Linux refers to it, the default being ext4; and <filesystem mount options> is the parameters used in Linux to mount the file system as would be used with Linux's mount command's -o flag.

Example:

```
wsl.exe --mount \\.\PHYSICALDRIVE0 --partition 2
```

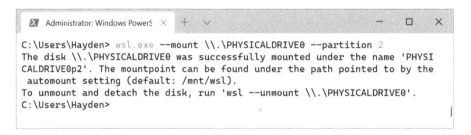

Figure 3-41. *Successfully mounting an ext4 partition in WSL*

CHAPTER 4

Linux Distro Maintenance

This chapter will discuss maintaining your Linux distro installed on WSL, beginning with how the distro is updated, how to apply upgrades, and how to find and install specific packages. The chapter will conclude with a guide on generating your own special-purpose Ubuntu WSL image.

Once your Linux distro of choice is installed on WSL, you must maintain it. On WSL 2, the Linux kernel and the underlying WSL platform in Windows 10 will be maintained by Microsoft through Windows Update. However, updates to the respective Microsoft Store app for your WSL distro do not automatically upgrade your WSL distro once it is installed. The Microsoft Store and Windows Update do not reach inside your WSL distro to update packages there. Everything inside your Linux distro is up to you and is managed with distro-specific tools.

There is also no automatic upgrade mechanism in Linux distros on WSL at this time; updates must be performed manually from the command line or scheduled to occur automatically using a custom Windows Service, Windows Task Scheduler, or the new [boot] option in Windows builds 21286+. See "Rolling your own init" in Chapter 7 "Customizing WSL" on ways to accomplish this.

It is important to understand how to update your WSL distro, which will depend on your specific distro, because package management varies from distro to distro and upgrades provide important feature and security updates.

Packages

All Linux distributions come with a package manager and packages available in an online repository or archive. Packages are how software and software updates are delivered on Linux. The same applies to Linux distros on WSL. Learning how to use the package manager for your Linux distro of choice will unlock thousands of free and open source applications for you to explore. In fact, you may find the package manager to be a major factor in which Linux distro you choose as your daily driver.

© Hayden Barnes 2021
H. Barnes, *Pro Windows Subsystem for Linux (WSL)*, https://doi.org/10.1007/978-1-4842-6873-5_4

On Ubuntu, Debian, Pengwin, and Kali distros, WSL package management is done with the apt package manager. This is the most common package manager you will find on WSL distros. The instructions in this chapter are therefore focused on apt.

Other distros, like Fedora Remix, Alpine, and OpenSUSE, use their own package managers, and you should refer to those respective distros' documentation for usage of their package managers. Covering the usage of every distro package manager could be its own book.

The general principles here, regarding checking for updates, getting upgrades, and the importance of doing so, are generally applicable to most Linux package managers, even if the syntax and package names in other distro package managers may differ.

Distro	Package Files	Package Manager
Ubuntu, Debian, Pengwin, Kali	.deb	apt
Fedora	.rpm	dnf
OpenSUSE and SUSE Enterprise Linux	.rpm	zypper
Red Hat Enterprise Linux, Oracle Linux, and Pengwin Enterprise	.rpm	yum
Alpine	.apk	apk

Dependencies

Often a package will rely on another package to provide some of its functionality, such as a software library (which tends to start with "lib"). These are called dependencies. When you install a package, you will see it installs other packages that are its dependencies. Sometimes, dependencies can change, which is why when upgrading, you will occasionally see new packages need to be installed and old packages will be reported as no longer required.

Completing Administrative Tasks with sudo

Most package operations, including installing and upgrading packages, are considered administrator-level tasks and therefore require elevated privileges on Linux. If you installed WSL from the Store and created a new WSL user account and password, you have been added to the "sudo" or "wheel" user group in most distros, capable of running elevated commands with the sudo command. You can execute commands with elevated privilege by prefacing them with the sudo command followed by the command you want to run with elevated privileges. You will then be prompted to enter your user password before running the command with elevated privileges (Figure 4-1).

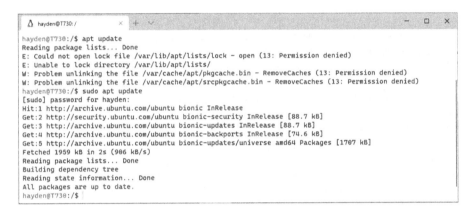

Figure 4-1. Running apt without sudo, failing with permission denied, and then again successfully with sudo

---

Tip If you manually imported a distro with --import, without creating a new user, you are likely root by default and can omit sudo from the following commands.

Update Packages

To check for available package upgrades in the repository of your distribution, run the following on Debian, Ubuntu, Pengwin, Kali, and other Debian family distributions. This will download the latest package metadata from the repository, compare it to the installed packages in your distro, and determine which packages, if any, can be upgraded.

```
sudo apt update
```

If package upgrades are available, a message will report how many can be upgraded (Figure 4-2).

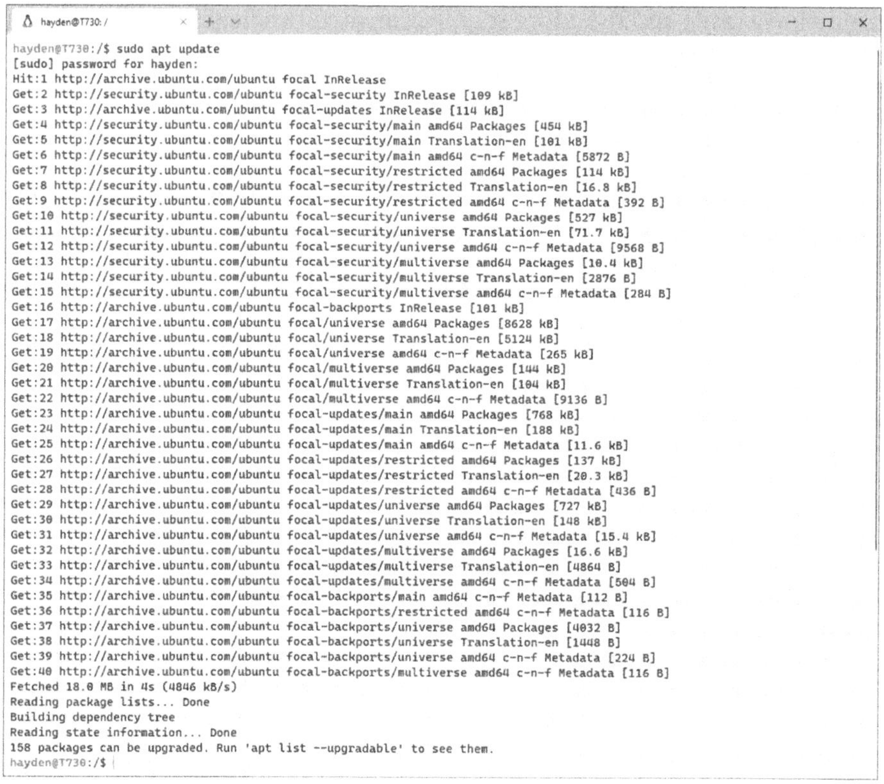

Figure 4-2. *Updating package metadata from the Ubuntu archive repository with sudo apt update*

Upgrade Packages

To apply available upgrades, run the following. Apt will examine the installed package state, calculate upgrade changes, and then inform you of what changes will be made. These changes can include upgraded packages, new packages, and packages that may no longer be necessary:

```
sudo apt upgrade
```

In the following example (Figure 4-3), we see 158 installed packages have new versions available in the Ubuntu archive, and they have 12 new dependencies, which will be installed at the same time.

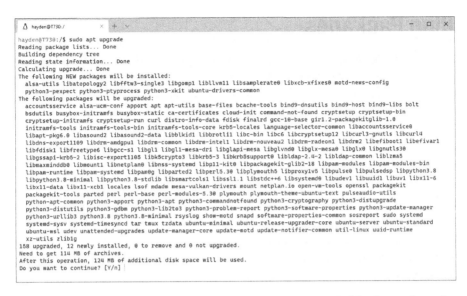

Figure 4-3. *Upgrading packages with new versions available from the Ubuntu archive with sudo apt upgrade*

Before upgrading, you will be prompted to confirm the upgrade by pressing Enter (the default is Y, the capital letter in the [Y/n]) or entering Y yourself and pressing Enter.

If you would like to upgrade without being prompted, you can automatically accept the prompt by adding the -y flag to your command (Figure 4-4):

```
sudo apt -y upgrade
```

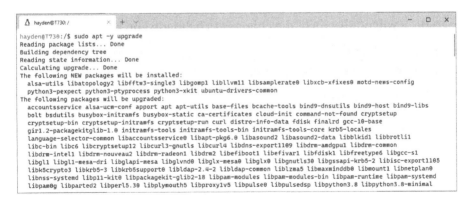

Figure 4-4. *Upgrading packages with new versions available from the Ubuntu archive automatically with sudo apt -y upgrade*

77

Installing Packages

To install an individual package, use the apt install command. For example, Ubuntu ships with the nano text editor, but perhaps you prefer the neovim text editor. To install neovim, we use

```
sudo apt install <package name>
```

Example:

```
sudo apt install neovim
```

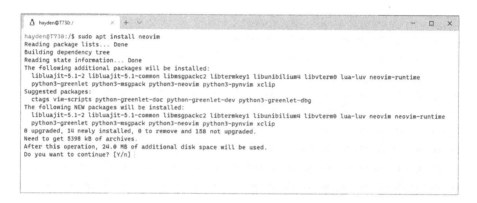

Figure 4-5. *Installing the neovim text editor with sudo apt install neovim*

This will install the text editor neovim as well as dependencies (Figure 4-5). Like on apt upgrade, it will notify you of the changes to be made and request permission to continue. To automatically approve changes on install, you can add the -y flag to the command, and the install process will complete automatically (Figure 4-6):

```
sudo apt -y install neovim
```

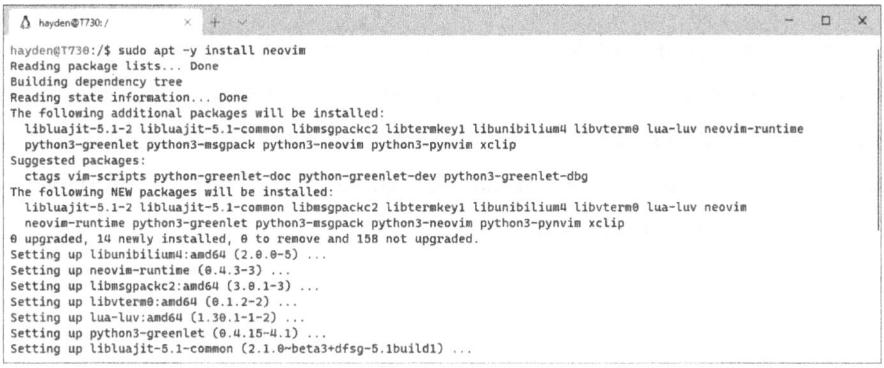

Figure 4-6. *Installing the neovim text editor noninteractively with sudo apt -y install neovim*

Tip   If you do not know what package you would like to install or the name of the package, see the following on how to find packages.

Uninstalling Packages

Packages can be removed with the apt remove function (Figure 4-7):

```
sudo apt remove <package name>
```

Example:

```
sudo apt remove neovim
```

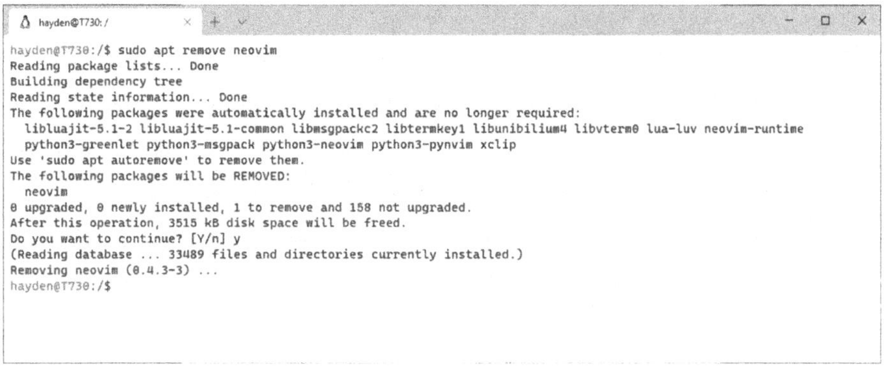

Figure 4-7. *Removing the neovim text editor with sudo apt remove neovim*

Tip   Caution is warranted when uninstalling packages that may be dependencies of other applications you may run. Uninstalling a dependency of several applications will uninstall all those applications that rely on that dependency. If run interactively, apt will warn you of all the packages that will be removed or abandoned by removing the package you specified.

You will see in the preceding example removing neovim will leave behind a handful of packages that will no longer be required.

Abandoned Dependencies

Occasionally, you will remove a package, and it will leave behind a dependency that no other application relies upon (or you will upgrade a package that no longer relies on a specific dependency). Apt will detect when this occurs, and you can automatically remove those unneeded dependencies (Figure 4-8) with the apt autoremove function:

```
sudo apt autoremove
```

Example:

```
sudo apt autoremove
```

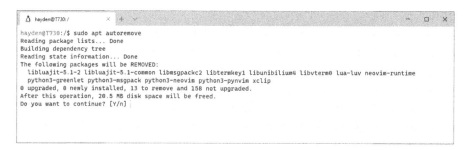

Figure 4-8.   *Automatically removing unnecessary dependency packages with sudo apt autoremove*

Here, we see several dependencies of neovim that were left behind when we removed neovim will now be cleaned up.

Finding Packages

Installing any distro on WSL gives you access to a vast library of free and open source packages to begin tinkering and developing with, including development tools, libraries, databases, web servers, document processing suites, scientific tools, games, and productivity tools.

Sometimes locating those packages can be daunting from a command line. First, it is not clear what is available out there. The average Linux distro has tens of thousands of available packages. Second, you do not always know what that application's package name is. The name of packages can vary from distro to distro or be nonobvious.

For example, the web browser GNOME Web was previously known as Epiphany. Running `sudo apt install epiphany` will install an open source clone of the game Boulder Dash. To install GNOME Web, run `sudo apt install epiphany-browser`.

There are several ways to identify and locate the packages you need.

From the Terminal

If you know the name of the software you are looking for, but perhaps not the exact package name, you can search from the terminal using apt (Figure 4-9):

```
apt search <keyword>
```

Example:

```
apt search lynx
```

Figure 4-9. *Searching for a package named lynx from the terminal using apt*

If there are too many results from the search, you can use the | character, a pipe, to pipe the results to the less command. Piping the results to less will allow you to browse the results page by page (Figure 4-10).

```
apt search <keyword> | less
```

Example:

```
apt search gnome | less
```

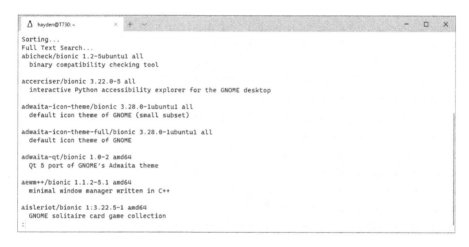

Figure 4-10. *Paging through the output of apt-cache search gnome with less*

Simple text stream management tools, like less, tail, cat, sed, and grep, can become enormously powerful for you as you become more comfortable on the Linux terminal. A manual for each of these tools is always close by, which can be accessed with the man command (Figure 4-11):

```
man <name of application>
```

Example:

```
man tail
```

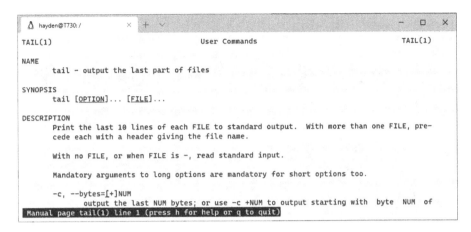

Figure 4-11. *The manual page of tail, opened by running man tail*

Using a Terminal User Interface (TUI)

If you cannot locate the application you are searching for by searching with the apt command, you can use aptitude in Ubuntu, Debian, Pengwin, and Kali distros, a terminal user interface with menus and mouse functionality to search, install, upgrade, and remove packages. Aptitude is installed like any other package:

```
sudo apt -y install aptitude
```

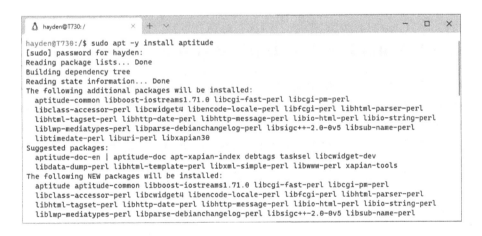

Then start aptitude as an elevated user:

```
sudo aptitude
```

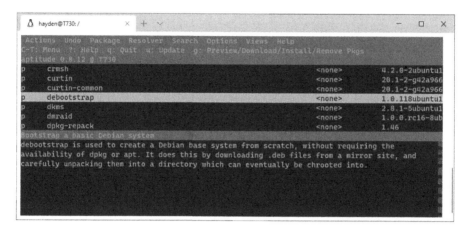

Figure 4-12. *Browsing aptitude on Ubuntu. Now that Windows Terminal has mouse support, you can use your mouse in aptitude*

Tip   If you ever get "stuck" in a Linux application you cannot seem to escape, try the following:

- :q

- <Ctrl>-C

- <Ctrl>-X

Using a Graphical User Interface (GUI)

If you are new to the Linux terminal using apt and aptitude will have a learning curve, you may wish to start with the traditional graphical user interface. Getting a graphical user interface started on WSL is not a small feat by itself; it requires setting up and configuring an X server, at least until official GUI support lands in WSL 2 later in 2021. You can read more on setting up your own X server for now in Chapter 7 "Customizing WSL."

Once an X server is configured and running on Windows, you can install a GUI apt package manager called synaptic (Figure 4-13):

```
sudo apt install synaptic
```

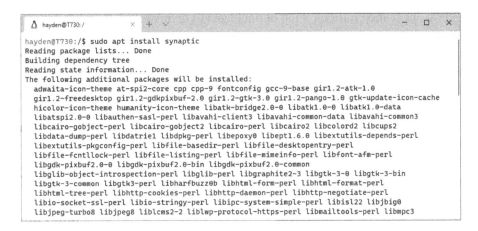

Figure 4-13. Installing the synaptic GUI package manager with apt

Once synaptic is installed, you must run as an elevated user just as you would apt or aptitude on the command line:

```
sudo synaptic
```

Within synaptic, you can search for packages by name or description, browse by category or installation status, and select packages to install or remove (Figure 4-14).

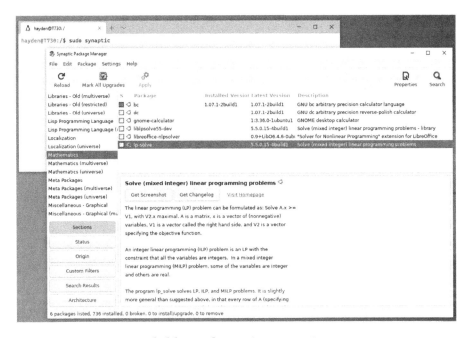

Figure 4-14. Browsing available packages in synaptic

When you apply the changes, a list of packages to be installed, upgraded, or removed will be presented for confirmation (Figure 4-15).

Figure 4-15. *Confirming the changes installing lp-solve using synaptic*

The changes will then be applied:

Figure 4-16. *Synaptic installing packages selected for installation*

Once the changes have been applied, you will be notified (Figure 4-17), and you may then exit synaptic.

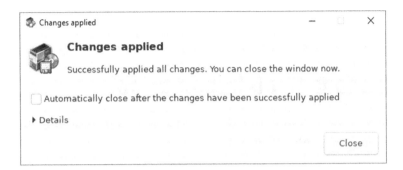

Figure 4-17. *Synaptic changes applied confirmation dialog box*

Build Your Own Ubuntu WSL Image

Canonical, the publisher of Ubuntu, makes standardized images of Ubuntu available for WSL on the Microsoft Store, its cloud images website, and through wsl.exe --install. These images contain a base set of packages which will meet most users' initial needs. They closely track the default packages on an Ubuntu server in the cloud, have been extensively tested by internal Canonical QA processes, and have paid support options for enterprise organizations.

However, there may be circumstances where you want to build your own image of Ubuntu with a custom set of packages. For example, if you are the administrator of a university computer lab with a focus on geographic information systems (GIS) and want Ubuntu WSL in your lab to come preloaded with specific GIS-related packages, you can generate a custom Ubuntu WSL image with those packages, export the image, and distribute to students or systematically apply to all the computers in your GIS lab.

This is accomplished by

1. Installing an Ubuntu image bootstrapping tool

2. Creating a temporary folder in which we will bootstrap our image

3. Bootstrapping a very basic Ubuntu image in that folder from the minimum packages to run Ubuntu

4. Customizing the Ubuntu image in that folder by running commands "inside" the image using chroot, installing packages we want for our image, and setting custom options

5. Building a tarball archive of the Ubuntu image from the temporary folder and copying it to the Windows file system

6. Importing that Ubuntu image tarball into WSL as a custom WSL image

Install an Image Bootstrapping Tool

To begin, install debootstrap, which will allow us to bootstrap an Ubuntu image from packages in the Ubuntu archive (Figure 4-18):

```
sudo apt -y install debootstrap
```

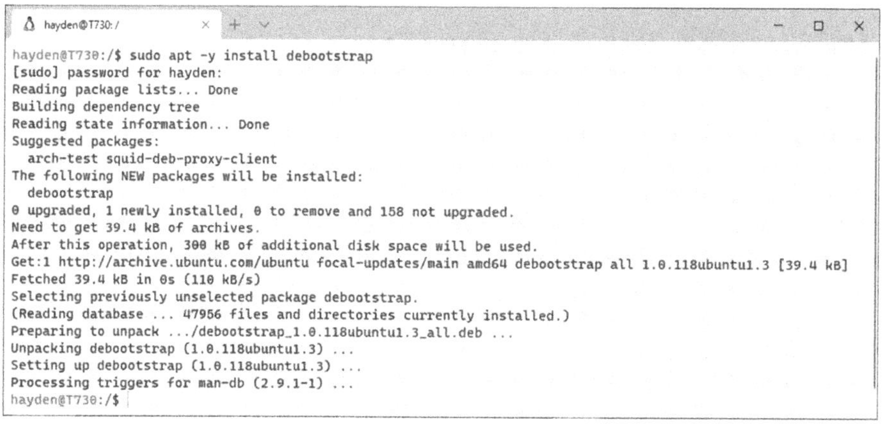

Figure 4-18. Installing debootstrap to build our Ubuntu image

Build Our Base Image

Next, we create a folder in which we will build our Ubuntu image. After the next step, this folder will contain the complete Ubuntu file system of our image in its own directory before we pack it up into a tarball archive that we can then import as its own WSL distro.

We create a folder with (Figure 4-19)

```
mkdir /tmp/wslchroot
```

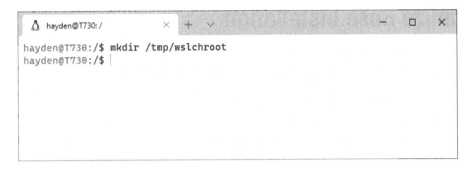

Figure 4-19. *Creating a folder to build our Ubuntu image inside*

Next, we will run debootstrap (Figure 4-20) to create a base Ubuntu image. debootstrap has several required settings. First, we specify our system architecture with --arch "amd64". The --include setting specifies the base image should also include the sudo and python3 packages in the bootstrapped image. The remaining settings specify the image will be built from Ubuntu release code-named focal (equivalent to Ubuntu 20.04 LTS), in our folder at /tmp/wslchroot, from the main Ubuntu archive repository URL:

```
sudo debootstrap --arch "amd64" --include=sudo focal /tmp/wslchroot http://
archive.ubuntu.com/ubuntu/
```

For more help with debootstrap, remember you can always run man debootstrap.

You can tweak debootstrap settings to build for arm64 (though cross-compilation of images between different architectures gets more complicated); build from different Ubuntu releases, such as the Ubuntu release code-named hirsute for Ubuntu 21.04; or use a local Ubuntu archive mirror.

```
hayden@T730:/$ mkdir /tmp/wslchroot
hayden@T730:/$ sudo debootstrap --arch "amd64" --include=sudo,python3 focal /tmp/wslchroot http://archive.u
buntu.com/ubuntu/
I: Retrieving InRelease
I: Checking Release signature
I: Valid Release signature (key id F6ECB3762474EDA9D21B7022871920D1991BC93C)
I: Retrieving Packages
I: Validating Packages
I: Resolving dependencies of required packages...
I: Resolving dependencies of base packages...
I: Checking component main on http://archive.ubuntu.com/ubuntu...
I: Retrieving adduser 3.118ubuntu2
I: Validating adduser 3.118ubuntu2
I: Retrieving apt 2.0.2
I: Validating apt 2.0.2
I: Retrieving apt-utils 2.0.2
I: Validating apt-utils 2.0.2
I: Retrieving base-files 11ubuntu5
I: Validating base-files 11ubuntu5
I: Retrieving base-passwd 3.5.47
```

Figure 4-20. *Bootstrapping our Ubuntu image with debootstrap into /tmp/wslchroot*

Customize Base Installation

Once the bootstrap is complete, we have a complete minimal Ubuntu image in our folder at /tmp/wslchroot. We can run commands inside that folder; they are being run natively on that image using the chroot command.

As an elevated user, as root or with sudo, run the chroot command, specify the chroot folder (here being /tmp/wslchroot), and follow it by the command to be run inside the image.

For example, we can clean up the apt metadata cache inside the Ubuntu image we just created as follows (Figure 4-21):

```
sudo chroot /tmp/wslchroot/ apt clean
```

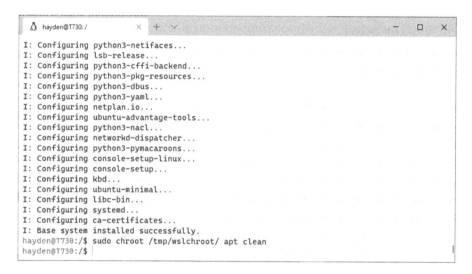

Figure 4-21. *Running commands inside our Ubuntu image using chroot to clean the apt package cache*

Tip   Cleaning the apt metadata cache inside the image is useful if you would tend to reuse it or share it as this information will expire and will just take up space in your image.

As this is a new image, it does not have default language settings set, which should be set as follows:

```
sudo chroot /tmp/wslchroot/ dpkg-reconfigure locales
```

You will then be asked what language and text encoding settings to generate in your base image. For American English, select en_US as the language and UTF-8 encoding (Figure 4-22). You can select another language here if your preferred is not American English and even select more than one language. Some non-Latin alphabets will require distinct ISO encodings to render correctly, which you can also specify here.

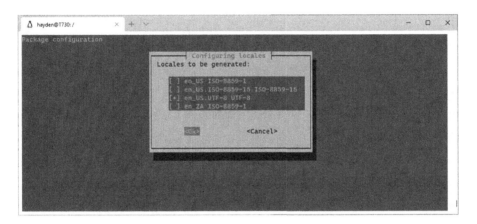

Figure 4-22. *Specifying which languages and text encodings to be installed on our Ubuntu image*

You will then be prompted to select the default language and encoding for the system environment (Figure 4-23). Again, for American English, you will want to specify en_US.UTF-8.

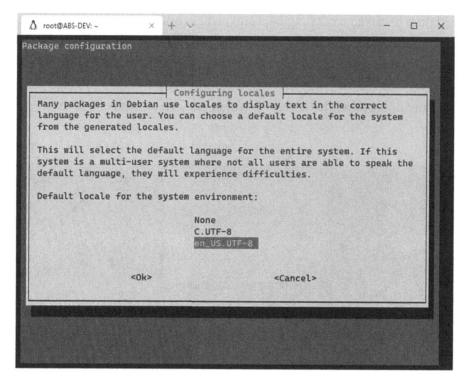

Figure 4-23. *Select the default language and text encoding for the system environment in our Ubuntu image*

The selected languages and text encodings will be generated, and the default will be set (Figure 4-24).

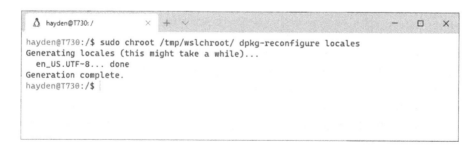

Figure 4-24. *Selected languages and text encoding settings generated and applied in our Ubuntu image*

We can now do some more customization of our image before packing it up into a tarball file for import into WSL as its own distro.

For example, we can install additional packages, such as `software-properties-common,` which contains `add-apt-repository` to easily enable additional Ubuntu repositories, like universe and multiverse, which, in turn, grants us access to even more packages for our distro, including third-party software.

We install software-properties-common into the image as follows (Figure 4-25):

```
sudo chroot /tmp/wslchroot/ apt install software-properties-common
```

Figure 4-25. *Installing software-properties-common in our Ubuntu image*

Now, using the `add-apt-repository,` we can enable the Ubuntu universe and multiverse repositories to get access to additional packages from apt, aptitude, or synaptic from our Ubuntu image. We do this with (Figure 4-26)

```
sudo chroot /tmp/wslchroot/ add-apt-repository universe && sudo chroot /
tmp/wslchroot/ add-apt-repository multiverse
```

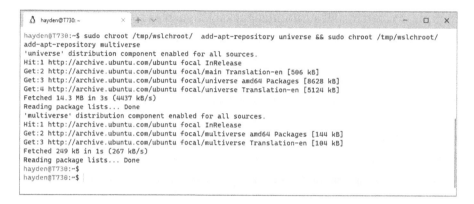

Figure 4-26. *Enabling universe and multiverse Ubuntu repositories in our Ubuntu image*

Tip   Linux commands can be combined and run sequentially by separating them with &&.

Finally, let's install some packages we want for our hypothetical Ubuntu GIS WSL distro image. The `gis-workstation` meta-package is an Ubuntu package that uses the dependencies capability in apt to install dozens of GIS-related tools without the need to install each one individually. It is installed as follows (Figure 4-27):

```
sudo chroot /tmp/wslchroot/ apt install gis-workstation
```

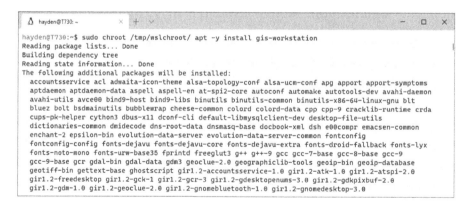

Figure 4-27. *Installing the gis-workstation metapackage in our Ubuntu image containing dozens of GIS-related applications*

Create rootfs tar

Once we are done building our Ubuntu image in /tmp/wslchroot, it is time to pack it up as a tarball archive file for export and then import to WSL as its own WSL distro.

Here's how to set the proper file structure for our image, drop down into our image folder (Figure 4-28):

```
cd /tmp/wslchroot/
```

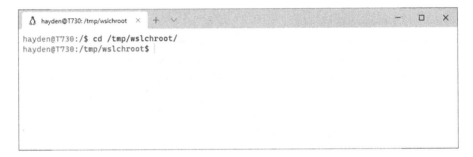

Figure 4-28. *Dropping down into our Ubuntu image folder at /tmp/wslchroot before we archive the folder as a tarball*

If you take a quick look in this folder before proceeding with ls, you will see we have built a complete Ubuntu installation in this folder that resembles the root file system of any Ubuntu Linux image (Figure 4-29):

```
ls -a
```

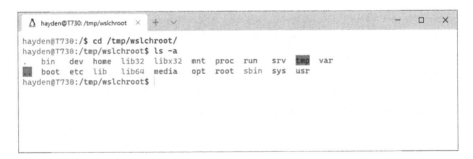

Figure 4-29. *Viewing the Ubuntu image folder contents of /tmp/wslchroot*

Now, we will compress our bootstrapped and customized Ubuntu image folder as a tarball archive file for export and then import to WSL as its own WSL distro.

Run tar to compress the Ubuntu image folder into a rootfs tar file called /tmp/ubuntu-gis-wsl.tar.gz (Figure 4-30). Depending on the size of the Ubuntu image you created, and your system's performance capabilities, this can take a few minutes. In our example, gis-workstation installed about 3 GB of additional packages, which will take some time to compress.

```
sudo tar --ignore-failed-read -czf /tmp/ubuntu-gis-wsl.tar.gz *
```

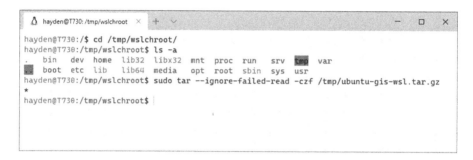

Figure 4-30. *Compressing our Ubuntu image folder into a tarball at /tmp/ubuntu-gis-wsl.tar.gz*

Now, we must move the tarball to our Windows file system so that we can import it into WSL as its own distro. I prefer to create a handy WSL folder at C:\WSL for custom WSL-related files and folders, but it can be anywhere your Windows user has write permission. This can be done from WSL as follows (Figure 4-31):

```
mkdir /mnt/c/WSL
```

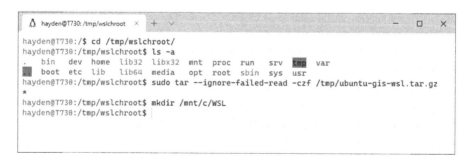

Figure 4-31. *Creating a folder at C:\WSL to store our tarball and later to unpack our custom Ubuntu GIS image*

Next, we move our tarball. You could use cp or mv, but I prefer to use rsync here to move the file as it gives us a nice progress status (Figure 4-32).

```
sudo rsync --progress --remove-source-files /tmp/ubuntu-gis-wsl.tar.gz
/mnt/c/WSL/
```

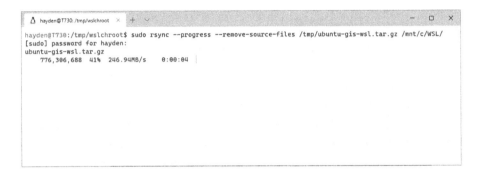

Figure 4-32. *Moving ubuntu-gis-wsl.tar.gz to C:\WSL\ on our Windows file system using rsync*

Import into WSL

Now, we follow the standard procedure for importing a WSL image file discussed in Chapter 2 "Installing WSL."

First, we drop down into a Windows Command Prompt from our current WSL session with cmd.exe (Figure 4-33):

```
cmd.exe
```

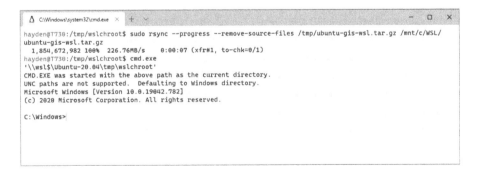

Figure 4-33. *Launching a Windows Command Prompt from our current WSL session*

Then, we call wsl.exe with --import to import our Ubuntu image, naming our new custom WSL distro "Ubuntu-GIS," storing the VHDX file containing the WSL file system in C:\WSL\Ubuntu-GIS, and set it as a WSL 2 distro (Figure 4-34):

```
wsl.exe --import "Ubuntu-GIS" C:\WSL\Ubuntu-GIS C:\WSL\ubuntu-gis-wsl.tar.
gz --version 2
```

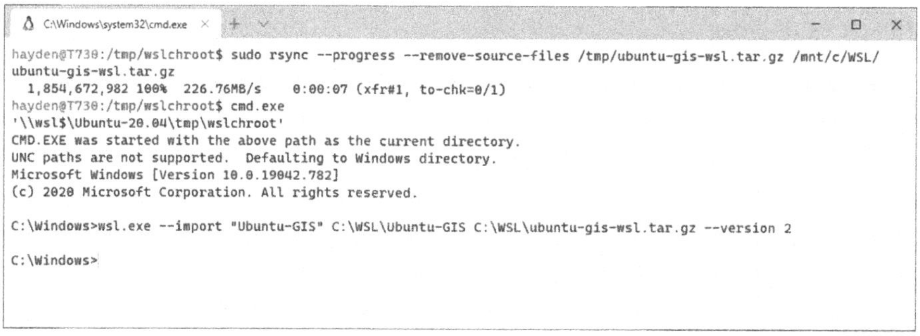

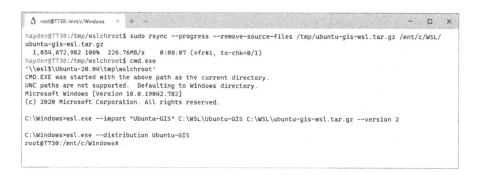

Figure 4-34. *Importing our custom Ubuntu GIS image using wsl.exe --import*

We can test that the distro was properly imported by running wsl.exe --distribution Ubuntu-GIS (Figure 4-35). If we are successful, we will be root user in our new distro.

```
wsl.exe --distribution Ubuntu-GIS
```

Figure 4-35. *Launching our custom Ubuntu GIS WSL distro to test if it was properly loaded*

We can test to make sure everything is in place and working with a few commands:

cat /etc/os-release verifies we are running an Ubuntu 20.04 LTS focal image (Figure 4-36).

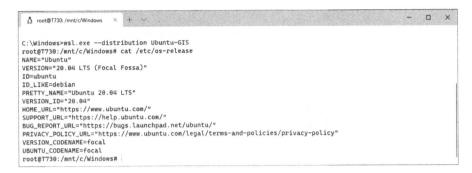

Figure 4-36. *Verifying the base OS of our custom Ubuntu GIS WSL distro*

After closing and reopening Windows Terminal, our custom Ubuntu GIS WSL distro will now be auto populated in the shell drop-down box (Figure 4-37).

Figure 4-37. *Verifying Ubuntu-GIS is visible in Windows Terminal*

With a properly configured third-party X server, as discussed in Chapter "Customizing WSL," or in the forthcoming native GUI support for WSL 2, we can test the GIS applications we built into our Ubuntu GIS WSL distro, for example, qgis (Figure 4-38):

```
qgis
```

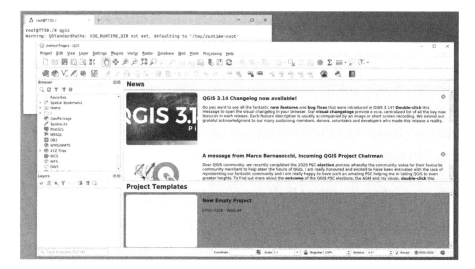

Figure 4-38. *QGIS running from our custom Ubuntu GIS WSL distro*

This chapter discussed maintaining your WSL Linux distro, including the distro-specific package management tools. We covered upgrading packages, various ways to find and install specific packages, and removing packages on Ubuntu, Debian, Kali, Pengwin, and other apt-based Linux distros. The chapter concluded with a guide on generating your own custom special-purpose Ubuntu WSL image.

CHAPTER 5

Configuring WSL Distros

Once you have a WSL distro installed, there are several settings unique to WSL that you do not find in a standard Linux distribution and unique ways to continue them. These settings are divided into "per-distro" settings, which are adjusted in each individual distro installation, and "global" WSL settings, which affect all WSL distros on a single device.

Setting Per-Distro Settings

Per-distro settings are set in /etc/wsl.conf in each respective distro. This file is read on "boot" by WSL. Some distro publishers publishing images for WSL include a wsl.conf file with default settings. But if it is not present in your distro, then you may manually create or edit this file if you want to override the default WSL settings. The default settings are represented here (Figure 5-1).

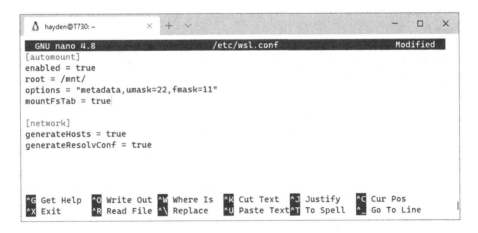

Figure 5-1. /etc/wsl.conf with common default settings

© Hayden Barnes 2021
H. Barnes, *Pro Windows Subsystem for Linux (WSL)*, https://doi.org/10.1007/978-1-4842-6873-5_5

Automount Settings

The automount settings include the ability to mount Windows drives, such as the C drive under /mnt/c to provide file system interoperability.

Enabling

Automount is enabled by setting the "enabled" Boolean value to true in /etc/wsl.conf:

```
[automount]
enabled = true
```

The **default is true**, to mount Windows drives automatically. If you wish to isolate your WSL instance from the Windows file system, you should set this to false:

```
[automount]
enabled = false
```

Root

The root folder for mounting Windows drives is set in /etc/wsl.conf with the "root" string value:

```
[automount]
enabled = true
root = /mnt/
```

The **default is /mnt/**. If you wish to mount your Windows drives in another folder, you can specify where here. For example, to mount them at /windrives/, set

```
[automount]
enabled = true
root = /windrives/
```

Keep in mind that the root folder must exist; if not, you need to create it:

```
sudo mkdir /windrives
```

File System Tab

/etc/fstab is the traditional Linux file system configuration file. The option to load it or not on WSL boot can be set in /etc/wsl.conf with the "mountFsTab" Boolean value:

```
[automount]
enabled = true
mountFsTab = true
```

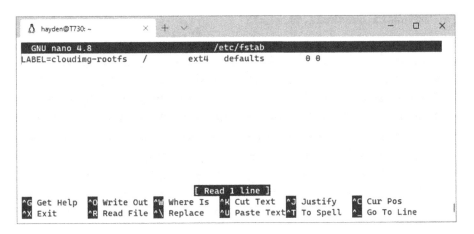

Figure 5-2. */etc/fstab default in Ubuntu*

The **default is true**.

You can configure /etc/fstab (Figure 5-2) to perform more advanced mounting functions on WSL boot. This can include virtual disks and network file shares.

If you do not want WSL to parse this file, for example, for greater isolation of the WSL environment, you can set this value to false:

```
[automount]
enabled = true
mountFsTab = false
```

Keep in mind, however, the root file system will be automatically mounted on boot, and without parsing /etc/fstab, it will be mounted with the default WSL settings. It can be useful to enable or disable this for troubleshooting advanced mounting settings.

Mount Options

DrvFs is the file system that allows WSL to mount Windows drives. This allows WSL to access files on the Windows file system and handle permissions.

These options are set in /etc/wsl.conf with the "options" string value, for example:

```
[automount]
enabled = true
mountFsTab = true
options = "metadata,umask=22,fmask=11"
```

A note on how file permissions work on WSL:

On the Linux file system in WSL, the file permissions follow common Linux standards, with read, write, and execute settings for the user, group, and other. When accessing the Windows file system from WSL, the file permissions are interpreted from NTFS into those common Linux permissions. New files and folders created in WSL on the Windows system will inherit the parent folder permissions.

This can be altered, however, with the metadata option.

Metadata

By specifying the metadata option in mount options, it is possible to read and store Linux file system permissions separate from NTFS permissions in extended file attributes on NTFS files and folders. This is useful if you want to restrict access to make a file or folder read-only from WSL without changing the permissions in Windows. New files and folders created in WSL on the Windows system will inherit the permissions stored by umask in WSL.

By default, WSL will mount the Windows file system with the UID and GID of the default distro user, usually 1000 and 1000, respectively.

We can achieve the same result by running the following command:

```
sudo mount -t drvfs C: /mnt/c -o metadata,uid=1000,gid=1000,umask=22,
fmask=11
```

If you are familiar with the Linux mount command, you may recognize some of these settings.

In addition to altering how NTFS and Linux system permissions are handled, it is also possible to alter how case sensitivity is handled between Linux and Windows.

Case Sensitivity

One big difference users may notice between Linux and the Windows Terminal is the handling of case sensitivity of files.

On Linux file systems, FILE.TXT and file.txt would be considered separate files that can coexist in the same directory. Linux file systems would therefore be considered case sensitive.

On Windows file systems, by default, Windows would not allow you to create a file called file.txt in a directory with a file already called FILE.TXT, because it would consider them the same file; the case of the filename is disregarded. The default on Windows file systems would therefore be considered case insensitive. Windows 10, as a descendant of Windows NT, which aimed for a degree of POSIX compatibility, has the native capability to treat files with case sensitivity, like Linux; it is simply disabled for backward compatibility with Windows 98 applications and other tools that have come to expect case insensitivity from Windows.

This setting can be modified globally, for all of Windows, via a setting in the Windows Registry, but note that changing this setting can result in unusual behavior in third-party applications, including breakage and data loss. So how does WSL handle case sensitivity when mounting Windows folders? It uses another mechanism that bypasses the registry key, allowing WSL distros to access files that differ only by case and therefore behave in the standard "Linux" way.

When dealing with files accessed from both WSL and Windows, this can still cause issues though, particularly for Windows programs accessing case-sensitive files in folders modified from WSL. Rather than forcing users to change the aforementioned global registry key, potentially breaking third-party applications, the WSL team introduced per-directory case sensitivity in Windows 10 build 17107.

If a folder is shared between WSL and Windows programs, for example, C:\WSLworkspace and /mnt/c/WSLworkspace, where case sensitivity is expected by WSL programs but an issue for Windows programs, it is possible to enable case sensitivity in Windows just for C:\WSLworkspace. The functionality is built into fsutil.exe.

To check the status of this per-directory case sensitivity from Windows, open PowerShell, and run (Figure 5-3)

```
fsutil.exe file queryCaseSensitiveInfo <path>
```

For example, on our sample directory C:\WSLworkspace:

```
fsutil.exe file queryCaseSensitiveInfo C:\WSLworkspace\
```

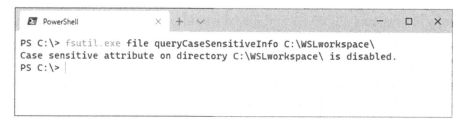

Figure 5-3. *Checking per-directory case sensitivity in Windows using fsutil*

To enable case sensitivity for a Windows directory, open PowerShell as Administrator, and run (Figure 5-4)

```
fsutil.exe file setCaseSensitiveInfo <path> enable
```

For example:

```
fsutil.exe file setCaseSensitiveInfo C:\WSLworkspace\ enable
```

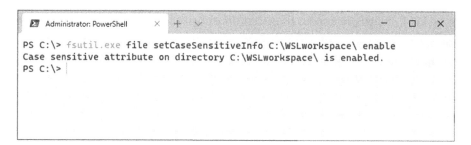

Figure 5-4. *Enabling per-directory case sensitivity in Windows using fsutil*

To disable case sensitivity for a Windows directory, open PowerShell as Administrator, and run (Figure 5-5)

```
fsutil.exe file setCaseSensitiveInfo <path> enable
```

For example:

```
fsutil.exe file setCaseSensitiveInfo C:\WSLworkspace\ disable
```

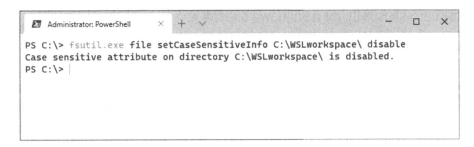

Figure 5-5. *Disabling per-directory case sensitivity in Windows using fsutil*

Applying per-directory case sensitivity in Windows using fsutil is not inheritable, meaning the case sensitivity of any new of existing subdirectories will not be modified by the setting of the parent directory.

Case sensitivity can also be managed as an automount options setting with the case setting, for example:

```
[automount]
enabled = true
mountFsTab = true
options = "metadata,case=off,umask=22,fmask=11"
```

Setting case=dir is the **default**, and new directories created by WSL on Windows file systems will be case sensitive.

Setting case=off means new directories created by WSL on Windows file systems will be case insensitive and follow the traditional Windows method.

In practice, there are very few situations in which you will be creating a lot of directories from WSL on Windows systems that will need to be case insensitive to work with Windows programs, but the need could arise.

Note   In WSL 1, on Windows builds 17692+, it is also possible to change the per-directory Windows case sensitivity from WSL. In this implementation, the case sensitivity was inheritable. However, this feature was deprecated in WSL 2. Check the status of per-directory case sensitivity with

```
getfattr -n system.wsl_case_sensitive <path>
```

To enable case sensitivity for a Windows directory:

```
setfattr -n system.wsl_case_sensitive -v 1 <path>
```

To disable case sensitivity for a Windows directory

```
setfattr -n system.wsl_case_sensitive -v 0 <path>
```

Changing the UID and GID of a Mount

If you do not want the Windows file system to be mounted with the UID and GID of default WSL distro user, it is possible to override this in mount options, to limit ownership of the mounted Windows file system to specific users, groups, or none.

You can do this by setting values for the following options in the options string:

> uid – A unique user number linked to each user on a Linux device. Root will have UID 0. UID 1–500 are commonly reserved by Linux for system-related accounts. Distros will create new users beginning at UID 1000, but some create new users starting at UID 500. UIDs are stored in the /etc/passwd file.

> gid – A unique group number linked to groups of users on a Linux device. Root will have GID 0, and GID 1–100 will be reserved by Linux for system-related groups. Normal user accounts are created at GID 100 or 1000. GIDs are stored in the /etc/groups file. Note a user will have a primary GID but often as several secondary GIDs, as it is not uncommon for a user to belong to multiple groups.

To check your user's UID and primary GID (Figure 5-6), use

```
id
```

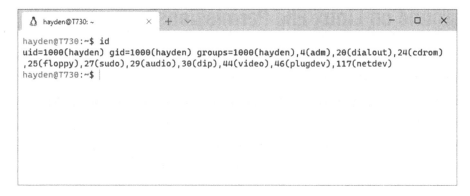

Figure 5-6. *Checking your uid and gid with id*

To check the UID and GID of another user (Figure 5-7), use

id <username>

Example:

id root

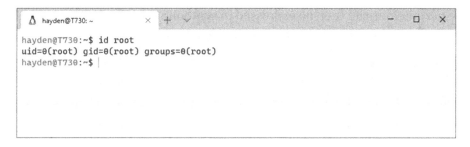

Figure 5-7. *Checking root's uid and gid with id*

Changing the UID and GID on the mounted device will affect the accessibility of existing files and folders.

It is also possible to customize the permissions on newly created files and folders, by setting the user file creation mask. The user file creation mask is the template for permissions on new files and folders. The purpose of the mask is to strip away extraneous permissions and set a secure standard set of permissions for new files. The mask is a shortened form of the longer Linux octal format for permissions, which you may have used before.

Background on Linux File Permissions

Every file on Linux has three classes of permissions associated with it; those are the permissions of a

> User – By default the user who created the file, unless modified

> Group – Users in a group with assigned access to the file

> Other – All other users, who are not the owner or in the group associated with the file

The permissions can consist of a combination of the following permissions for each class:

> **Read** or r

> **Write** or w

> **Execute** or x

> **No permissions** or -

These permissions can then be expressed in symbolic or numeric form.

Symbolic Form

In symbolic form, permissions are represented as a nine-character string, consisting of r, w, x, and -.

Example:

```
rwxr-xr--
```

> rwx – The first three characters correspond to **owner** permissions. Here, we see rwx. The owner of this file has read, write, and execute permissions.

> r-x – The next three characters correspond to **group** permissions. Here, we see r-x. Users in the group for this file are assigned to have read and execute permissions, but not write.

> r-- – The final three characters correspond to permissions for **all other users**. Here, we see r--. Other users can only read this file.

rwxr-xr-- in summary is

rwx permissions for the **owner**

r-x permissions for members of the **group**

r-- permissions for **all other users**

Checking a File's Permissions

You can find a file's symbolic form permissions with the ls -l command (Figure 5-8):

```
ls -l
```

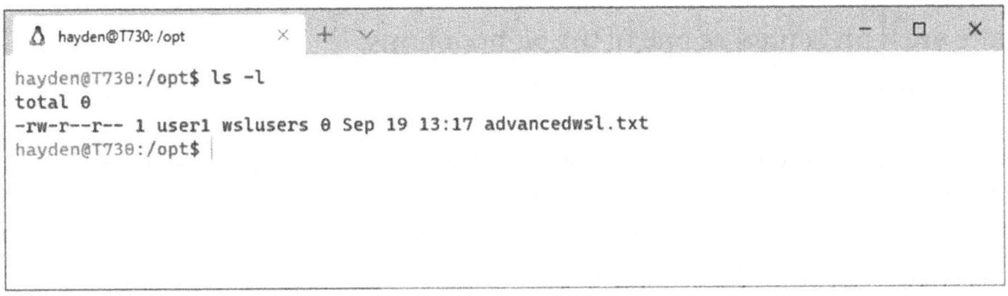

Figure 5-8. *Checking a file's permissions*

The preceding permissions are

```
rw-r--r--
```

rw permissions for owner, "user1"

r for members of the assigned group, "wslusers"

r for all other users

Additional details before and after the symbolic notation can also tell us

d is appended – This is a directory.

<user> – The user who owns the file.

<group> – The group to which the user is assigned.

4096 – The file or folder size. In the case of a folder, this is not
the size of the folder's contents; it is the content of the folder's
metadata, the minimum of which is 4096 bytes on ext4.

111

<date> – The date the file or folder was created.

<time> – The date the file or folder was created.

Other useful information here could include

l – Indicates a symbolic link

b – Indicates a block device

c – Indicates a serial device

Numeric Form

Permissions can also be represented in number form, using octal notation. Read, write, and execute are represented as one of the eight options:

0 – No permissions or ---

1 – Execute only or --x

2 – Write only or -w-

3 – Write and execute or -wx

4 – Read only or r--

5 – Read and execute or r-x

6 – Read and write or rw-

7 – Read, write, and execute or rwx

Our permissions from the preceding example, `rwxr-xr--`, then become

rwx for the owner = 7

r-x for members of the group = 5

r-- for all other users = 4

or simply = 754

In many places, the octal permissions will have a digit prefix. You may see 754 expressed as 0754. This prefix contains the setting for suid, sgid, and "sticky" bits, which are advanced Linux permissions that are outside of the scope of this book, but give you the option, among other things, to prevent writes or deletion of a file even if a user has permission, but is not the file's owner.

File Mask

The user file creation mask or umask helps define a standard for permissions on newly created files and folders.

By default, Linux assigns all new files the octal permissions 666 and all new folders the octal permissions 777.

The file mask is then subtracted from the octal permissions to set the permissions applied by the system.

umask is a bitmask; its bits are subtracted from "masking" the default Linux permissions.

Example:

A umask of 022 is the default for Ubuntu.

In this case, a new file would be created starting with octal permissions of 666 and then subtracting the "mask" of 022 resulting in permissions of 644.

All new files would be created as 644 or

6 – rw- for the owner

4 – Read or r-- for members of the group

4 – Read or r-- for all other users

> **umask** – The standard umask, for example, 022, for both new files and new folders

> **fmask** – The umask permissions to use just for new files

> **dmask** – The umask permissions just for new folders

Fmask and dmask exist for setting different umask settings for files and folders, separately.

As discussed earlier, files start at 666 and have umask subtracted. Folders start at 777 and have umask subtracted.

Umask only allows you to subtract the same level of permissions from both, for example, 022. However, using fmask or dmask, you can set separate masks, distinct delta from the standard 777/666 permission levels, for new files and folders.

Changing umask and fmask of a Mount

In our example from earlier

```
[automount]
enabled = true
mountFsTab = true
options = "metadata,umask=22,fmask=11"
```

new files and folders would be created with permissions starting at 666 and 777, respectively.

Then applying the umask of 22 would result in permissions of 644 for files and 755 for folders.

However, by applying the fmask of 11, which overrides the umask for new files, you would get permissions of 666 minus 11 or 655 for new files.

New folders would be created with the system-wide umask of 22, resulting in 777 minus 22 or 755 for new directories.

You could override this too with dmask if you choose.

You may want to adjust different masks for files and folders if you want to heavily limit read access in other directories (a high dmask) but give broad access in user's own directories (a low fmask).

Other mount settings

Note that other mount settings that would usually be set by additional flags using mount cannot be inserted here. For additional fine-grained control, you must edit /etc/fstab. See section "File System Tab" on the setting to ensure /etc/fstab is being read.

Cross-Distro Mounting

```
[automount]
crossDistro = true
```

Cross-distro mounting enables a space, /mnt/wsl, where any folder mounted by any one distro is visible to all other distros.

The **default is true**.

This is useful for sharing files between distros.

For example, with crossDistro enabled in both distros, you could mount a folder from your Ubuntu WSL distro to be accessible from your Fedora Remix distro (Figure 5-9).

```
△  hayden@T730: /            ×    △  hayden@:/mnt/c/Users/Hayden  ×  +  ∨        —   □   ×
hayden@T730:/$ mkdir ~/ubuntufolder
hayden@T730:/$ touch ~/ubuntufolder/helloworld
hayden@T730:/$ mkdir /mnt/wsl/sharedfolder
hayden@T730:/$ sudo mount --bind ${HOME}/ubuntufolder /mnt/wsl/sharedfolder
hayden@T730:/$ |
```

Figure 5-9. *Creating a folder, inserting a file, and mounting it to /mnt/wsl to be shared across distros*

In Ubuntu WSL:

```
mkdir ~/ubuntufolder
touch ~/ubuntufolder/helloworld
mkdir /mnt/wsl/sharedfolder
sudo mount --bind ${HOME}/sharedfolder /mnt/wsl/sharedfolder
```

Then, in Fedora Remix for WSL, you can view the file (Figure 5-10) at

```
ls /mnt/wsl/sharedfolder/
```

```
△  hayden@T730: /            ×    △  hayden@:/mnt/c/Users/Hayden  ×  +  ∨        —   □   ×
[hayden@T730 Hayden]$ ls /mnt/wsl/sharedfolder/
helloworld
[hayden@T730 Hayden]$ |
```

Figure 5-10. *Viewing the file in the shared folder from the cross-distro mount*

Alternatively, in an enterprise environment, you may wish to disable cross-distro mounting to isolate your WSL distros for security purposes.

ldconfig

Libraries, which are collections of common tasks and subroutines relied upon by applications, are "located" in a cache generated from a set of paths specified in ldconfig settings.

The primary ldconfig settings file is located at /etc/ld.so.conf but in most distros, that file directs ldconfig to load additional paths from multiple configuration files located in /etc/ld.so.conf.d/.

/etc/ld.so.conf will point to /etc/ld.so.conf.d/* which will, for example, contain /etc/ld.so.conf.d/libc.conf which contains the path to the default GNU C Library path /usr/local/lib (Figure 5-11). The configuration files in /etc/ld.so.conf.d/* are loaded alphabetically.

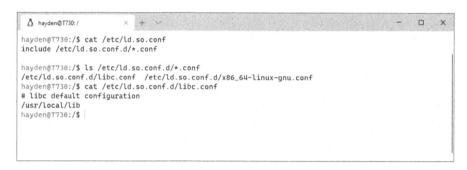

Figure 5-11. *Examining how /etc/ld/so.conf loads all *.conf files in /etc/ld.so. conf.d/ which point to library paths, such as /usr/local/lib*

Beginning in Windows 10 build 20150, WSL automatically inserts an additional file in /etc/ld.so.conf.d/ called ld.wsl.conf which adds the path to libraries at /usr/lib/wsl/lib to ldconfig (Figure 5-12).

This enables access to WSL-specific libraries for CUDA, DirectML, and other GPU compute functions (the ones located in %SystemRoot%\system32\lxss\lib).

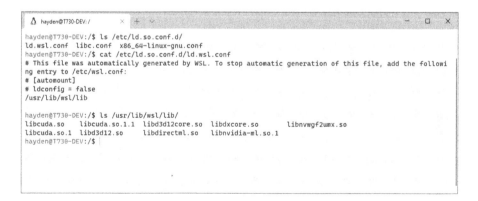

Figure 5-12. ld.wsl.conf *in /etc/ld.so.conf.d/ adding /usr/lib/wsl/lib to the list of directories for ldconfig to cache*

Generally, you will want WSL to load these directories to enable GPU compute. The setting to load them is set as an automount setting:

```
[automount]
ldconfig = true
```

The **default is true**.

However, there may be circumstances in which you want to disable GPU compute functionality, perhaps to benchmark performance with and without GPU enabled, or you want to substitute other drivers. In this case, you can specify

```
[automount]
ldconfig = false
```

to disable insertion of ld.wsl.conf. Note that after disabling ld.wsl.conf, you will want to regenerate your ldconfig cache with

```
sudo ldconfig
```

Network

Generate Hosts File

A hosts file, on both Windows and Linux, is a file that allows you to manually configure the resolution of domain names on your device.

When your computer resolves a domain name, like ubuntu.com, it will first consult the hosts file, then a local cache of recently resolved domains, and then finally issue the request to your network DNS server.

You can manually set a host name in your hosts file if you want to easily reach other devices on your network by their host name but do not want to set up your own DNS server.

If you are building and testing a website locally, you could edit your hosts file so that links on your test site resolve back to your test site on your device and not the live website on the Web.

By default, WSL will copy your Windows hosts file at `C:\Windows\System32\drivers\etc\hosts` over your WSL distro hosts file at `/etc/hosts` on each launch. Yes, Windows and Linux hosts files are compatible.

The option to copy your Windows hosts file (Figure 5-13) to your WSL distro (Figure 5-14) is set in /etc/wsl.conf with the "generateHosts" Boolean value:

```
[network]
generateHosts = true
```

The **default is true.**

You may wish to set generating hosts to false if you want to maintain a separate Linux hosts file for your own WSL distro. Note that while additions to the Windows hosts file (Figure 5-14) will be copied to WSL, additions to the WSL distro hosts file will not be synchronized back to Windows. The WSL distro hosts file will be overwritten from the Windows hosts file on each new launch.

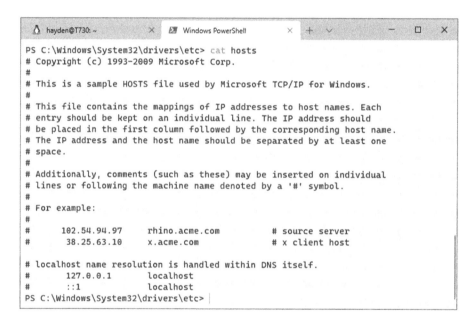

Figure 5-13. *Viewing the contents of Windows hosts*

```
△  hayden@T730: ~              ×    ⚙ Windows PowerShell    ×  +  ∨         −  □  ×

hayden@T730:~$ cat /etc/hosts
# This file was automatically generated by WSL. To stop automatic generation of t
his file, add the following entry to /etc/wsl.conf:
# [network]
# generateHosts = false
127.0.0.1        localhost
127.0.1.1        T730.localdomain        T730

# The following lines are desirable for IPv6 capable hosts
::1      ip6-localhost ip6-loopback
fe00::0 ip6-localnet
ff00::0 ip6-mcastprefix
ff02::1 ip6-allnodes
ff02::2 ip6-allrouters
hayden@T730:~$
```

Figure 5-14. *Viewing the contents of /etc/hosts in Ubuntu*

Generate DNS File

resolv.conf, located at /etc/resolv.conf, is a file that allows you to manually configure where your device will look to resolve domain names that are not in the hosts file or the local DNS cache:

[network]
generateHosts = true
generateResolvConf = true

> The **default is true**.

> Like your hosts file, resolv.conf is automatically generated for your distro by WSL from your Windows networking settings.

> The WSL environment networking is managed by the Host Networking Service, a Windows Service, on a virtual Ethernet adapter, like other Hyper-V network adapters.

> The IP address of the nameserver will be the same as the IP address of the virtual network adapter. For example, compare the IP address in /etc/resolv.conf (Figure 5-15) to the IPv4 address of the adapter itself (Figure 5-16).

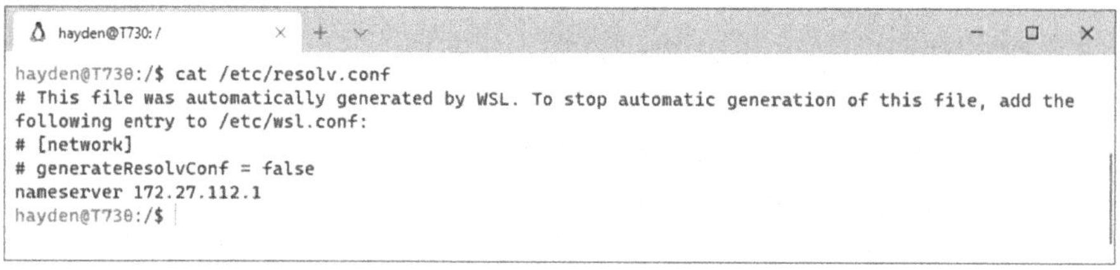

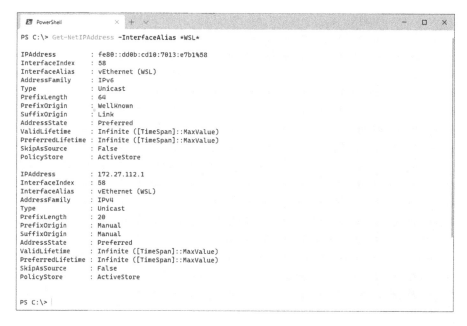

Figure 5-15. *Viewing the contents of /etc/resolv.conf in Ubuntu*

Figure 5-16. *Viewing the IP address of the WSL virtual network adapter*

In limited circumstances, you may wish to override this; one example may be if you have connected windows through a VPN and need to manually set a DNS server.

Hostname

Traditionally, your WSL instance inherits the device name of your Windows device. WSL overwrites /etc/hostname in your distro with your Windows hostname on "boot," like how /etc/hosts is overwritten.

On Windows 10 builds 20180 and greater, it is also possible to configure this behavior and set a custom hostname for your WSL instance:

```
[network]
generateHosts = true
generateResolvConf = true
hostname = Biswa96
```

The **default is to inherit the device name of your Windows device**. However, customizing your WSL instance hostname can be useful for specific advanced networking functions. By altering the hostname for your WSL distro (or distros), you can have separate hostnames for each WSL distro and Windows.

Interoperability

Enabling

WSL interoperability includes the ability to run Windows programs from Linux (Figure 5-17), Linux programs from Windows, and shared environment variables. The interop setting in wsl.conf allows you to enable or disable the ability to run Windows programs from Linux. Beginning in Windows build 20190, it is also possible to run Windows app execution aliases, such as those for UWP apps, from WSL. See Chapter 9, "Maximizing Windows Interoperability," for more tricks on how to get the most out of this unique feature of WSL.

```
[interop]
enabled = true
```

Tho **dofault io truc**.

Figure 5-17. *Launching Notepad from WSL*

You may wish to disable this to confine your WSL distro, for example, if you have git and python installed on Windows that can sometimes cause issues if you also have git and python installed on WSL.

It is also possible to enable or disable this feature in a single session, without altering wsl.conf. To temporarily disable Windows programs in Linux, run

```
echo 0 > /proc/sys/fs/binfmt_misc/WSLInterop
```

To reenable Windows programs in Linux, run

```
echo 1 > /proc/sys/fs/binfmt_misc/WSLInterop
```

Note that this setting will not persist between sessions. To permanently disable WSL interop, you will need to make the needed change to your wsl.conf file.

Appending Windows Path

Another feature of WSL interoperability is the appending of the Windows path variable to the WSL distro path variable. This adds all directories in your Windows path variable to your Linux distro's existing path variables, making binaries in both platforms accessible from WSL (Figure 5-18).

```
[interop]
enabled = true
appendWindowsPath = true
```

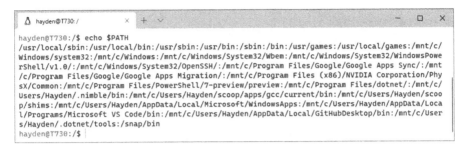

Figure 5-18. *Viewing the $PATH variable in WSL with appendWindowsPath set to true*

The default is true. Although you may disable this, leave interop enabled so that you limit Windows programs accessible to WSL to programs discoverable with your WSL distro PATH.

WSLENV

While not specific to this config file, now is a good place to mention WSLENV. WSLENV is a special meta environment variable that exists in both Windows and WSL. WSLENV defines which environment variables are shared between Windows and WSL. WSLENV contains a list of these other environment variables, separated by a colon in WSL or a semicolon in Windows, with flags for how each of the environment variables should be interpreted.

Windows environment variables can be viewed by searching for "Edit the system environment variables" from the Windows Start Menu (Figure 5-19).

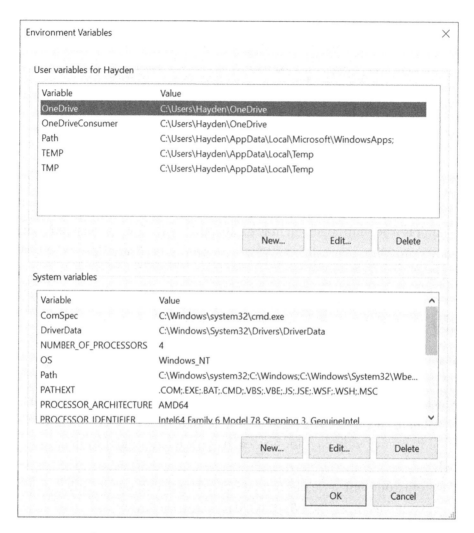

Figure 5-19. *Windows environment variables*

Linux environment variables can be viewed with the printenv command (Figure 5-20).

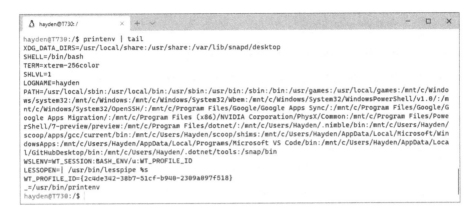

Figure 5-20. *Output of printenv on WSL showing Linux environment variables*

Why is sharing environment variables between Windows and WSL useful? The same reason WSL is generally useful, you get the best of both Linux and Windows. You might also end up having a project you want to work on from both Linux and Windows. Let us say you wanted to share a path, set as PATHTOPROJECT, from a WSL to Windows.

We define PATHTOPROJECT in WSL:

```
export PATHTOPROJECT=~/project
```

Then add PATHTOPROJECT to WSLENV:

```
export WSLENV=PATHTOPROJECT/p
```

Now, switch to Windows and read it back:

```
cmd.exe
set PATHTOPROJECT
```

Windows will have PATHTOPROJECT as an environment variable (Figure 5-21).

Tip   If you are setting DISPLAY to point WSL to an X server on Windows, you can then export that DISPLAY variable to all other WSL distros with

---

```
export WSLENV=DISPLAY
```

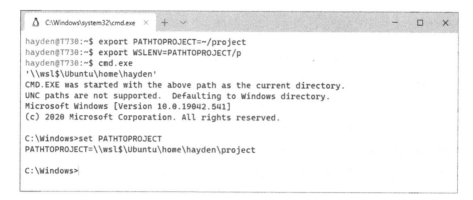

Figure 5-21. Using WSLENV to share environment variables between Windows and WSL

WSLENV Flags

What is that /p? There are four flags to define handling of variables between Windows and WSL:

> **/p** – Translates a path between Windows and WSL paths, as demonstrated earlier

> **/l** – Indicates a list of paths

Suppose you have several paths stored as a list in WSL:

export PROJECTLIST=/opt/project1:/opt/project2/

To make this accessible in Windows, we would

export WSLENV=PROJECTLIST/l

> **/u** – Shares the variable only from Windows to WSL

> **/w** – Shares the variable only from WSL to Windows

Tip   WSL variables are only propagated when executing a Windows command from the WSL session through interop. Likewise, the inverse only occurs when crossing the boundary in the other direction – be that via opening a new terminal or executing a command with wsl.exe.

What if you already have something defined in WSLENV and do not want to overwrite it, but instead append to it? In WSL, you would export that variable, adding one of the four flags mentioned earlier as needed, and then append the existing $WSLENV as follows:

```
export WSLENV=PROJECTLIST/l:$WSLENV
```

Default User

When WSL "boots," you will be running as the default user.

Here, you can set the default user:

```
[user]
default = root
```

The default built into WSL is root, but most distros, including Ubuntu, will create a new user with sudo privileges on installation from the Microsoft Store and set it as the default user.

Boot

Speaking of boot, beginning in Windows 10 build 21286, the ability to run startup commands was added to WSL:

```
[boot]
command = <string>
```

For example:

```
[boot]
command = apt update && apt upgrade -y
```

This brand-new feature, as of writing this book, unlocks new potential for running tasks at WSL "boot" time. This can replace clunky scripts previously stored in ~/.bashrc or /etc/profile. The commands are executed as root, allowing high-level changes to the environment. These commands are only run when the WSL is manually launched from the Start Menu or Windows Terminal, so it does not replace the ability to use a Windows Service to run WSL tasks in the background or automate tasks on WSL using Windows Task Scheduler, but it does complement those.

## CHAPTER 6

Configuring WSL 2

WSL 2 brings several new settings to WSL because of its architecture. As a lightweight VM, some of these settings may be familiar to users of other virtualization software, such as Hyper-V or VirtualBox, where you can define the amount of memory or processors for a specific VM. In WSL 2, you can define these parameters for the WSL 2 environment. The following settings require WSL 2 and are available in Windows 10 build 18980 or higher.

.wslconfig

WSL 2-specific settings are defined in a separate file. It is located in your Windows user home folder in a file named .wslconfig. The settings are global for all WSL 2 distros, unlike /etc/wsl.conf, which are distinct for each WSL distro. If this file does not exist, then the defaults for WSL 2 are applied. So, in general, you only need this file if you wish to override the default WSL 2 settings.

Kernel

WSL 2 ships with a kernel that is stored in Windows 10 at `%SystemRoot%\system32\lxss\tools\kernel` and is updated through Windows Update automatically or manually with

```
wsl.exe --update
```

This is the officially supported kernel for WSL 2 from Microsoft, which contains a handful of optimizations specifically for WSL 2, such as memory compaction discussed in the "Page Reporting" section.

It is, however, possible to replace this kernel with your own kernel, using `kernel=` in .wslconfig. I would recommend one built and modified from the official WSL 2 kernel, which carries over the optimizations Microsoft has made. However, it is possible to

© Hayden Barnes 2021
H. Barnes, *Pro Windows Subsystem for Linux (WSL)*, https://doi.org/10.1007/978-1-4842-6873-5_6

take most common Linux kernels and use one here. Note, though, if you do not use the official WSL 2 kernel, you may lose some of those WSL-specific optimizations. The good news is that the WSL 2 kernel is open source, available at `https://github.com/microsoft/WSL2-Linux-Kernel`, and can be easily tailored to your needs, if the default, for example, doesn't contain support for a specific file system or other kernel features. Note that adding kernel drivers to the WSL 2 kernel will not necessarily enable support for that hardware in WSL 2, which is still contained in a lightweight virtualization container. In other words, even with certain hardware drivers, the kernel cannot "see" those devices.

WSL 2 will default to the built-in kernel. You only need to specify a kernel here if you wish to override this default:

```
[wsl2]
kernel=C:\\Users\\Hayden\\bzImage
```

Note that the path to the kernel must be absolute, so you should avoid using environmental variables here. You should also use escaped backslashes \\ in your path to the compiled kernel.

Tip   bzImage is the commonly used filename for a compressed Linux kernel. You may also see kernel files in their commonly used uncompressed filename vmlinux. WSL 2 can boot either.

Kernel Command Line

The kernel command line is a way to configure advanced elements of the Linux kernel, such as enabling specific security features like AppArmor, debugging features, or tuning driver options. Because WSL 2 operates in a VM, some of those driver options are limited regarding hardware (which WSL 2 cannot directly reach from inside the lightweight Hyper-V container), but optimizations regarding threading, syscall handling, networking, and use of a RAM disk are available. The available options will depend on what is enabled in the kernel, either built-in or added as a module.

By default, the built-in command line options will load the default kernel and init. You only need to specify a `kernelCommandLine=` to set additional kernel parameters, for example, `vsyscall=emulate,` to support older Linux distributions:

```
[wsl2]
kernel=C:\\Users\\Hayden\\bzImage
kernelCommandLine= vsyscall=emulate
```

Quotes around the Linux command line are not required; simply type the command line you wish to pass after the =.

Processors

WSL 2 will take advantage of all available cores on your computer's processor. Most consumer- and office-grade computers have one processor with between 4 and 8 cores. This is sufficient for most use cases, even compiling and debugging software. However, some high-performance workstations intended for AI/ML, CAD, or video rendering have as many as 16 or 32 cores per processor and can support multiple processors, such as the Lenovo ThinkStation P900 series. Recent high-end AMD Ryzen Threadripper-branded processors have as many as 64 cores. Regardless of whether you have 4 or 32 cores, you can configure WSL 2 to balance core usage against other tasks you might be running.

You can see the number of cores your device has on the Performance tab of Windows Task Manager (Figure 6-1).

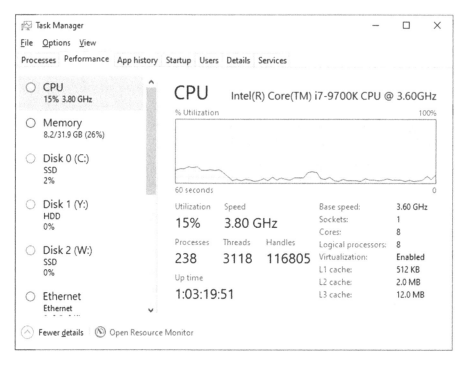

Figure 6-1. *Viewing the number of CPUs and cores in Windows Task Manager*

WSL 2 will default to using all the cores available on the Windows device.

You can limit the number of cores that WSL 2 utilizes with `processors=`, such as if you wish to assign a specific number of cores to WSL and keep the others free for Windows-based tasks.

```
[wsl2]
kernel=C:\\Users\\Hayden\\bzImage
kernelCommandLine= vsyscall=emulate
processors=4
```

You can see here in Figure 6-2 on the same system used in Figure 6-1, with 8 cores, we have limited the number of cores in WSL to 4 with `processors=` and confirmed (after a wsl.exe --shutdown and reopening Ubuntu) by grepping `/proc/cpuinfo`.

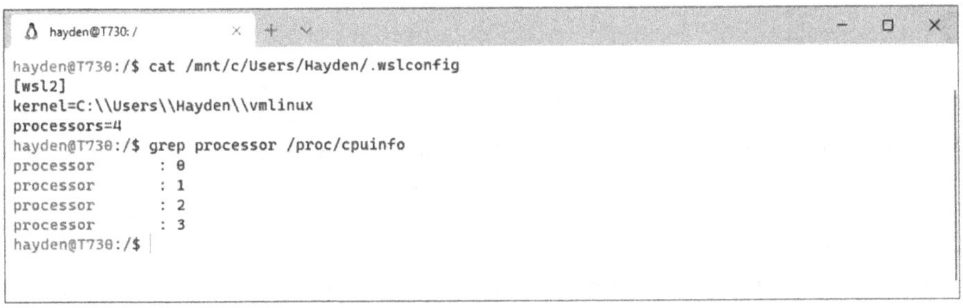

Figure 6-2. *Limiting the number of available cores to 4 with .wslconfig and confirming with* grep processor /proc/cpuinfo

Memory

WSL 2 automatically assigns memory to the WSL distro as needed and reclaims it as it is freed from tasks. Beginning in Windows build 20175, WSL 2 will default to assigning up to 50% of your available RAM or 8 GB, *whichever is less*. This means if you are in a workstation with 32 GB of RAM and you want to make 16 GB available to WSL 2, you will need to set the memory= option in .wslconfig. Doing this will maximize the amount of performance you can get from your workstation and WSL.

Conversely, if you are on a low-resource machine, you may want to restrict the RAM usage even further. A small shell and some terminal tasks are very usable at just 1 GB of RAM on a low-power machine. Note, though, applications like GUI apps, developing with larger frameworks such as NodeJS or large compilation tasks, may slow down significantly or even fail with such a small amount of RAM. If you are going to compile Chromium from source, you need at least 4 GB of RAM.

```
[wsl2]
kernel=C:\\Users\\Hayden\\bzImage
kernelCommandLine= vsyscall=emulate
processors=4
memory=12GB
```

Memory is set as gigabytes or megabytes as whole number integers followed by GB or MB, respectively.

Swap

Swap storage is disk-based random access memory (RAM) the WSL distro utilizes when demand for memory exceeds the available hardware RAM, either because of setting the memory= option too low or the hardware limitations of the Windows device.

WSL 2 will default the swap file size to 25% of the available RAM of the Windows device, rounded up to the nearest whole GB. To adjust the size of the swap space, set swap= in .wslconfig:

```
[wsl2]
kernel=C:\\Users\\Hayden\\bzImage
kernelCommandLine= vsyscall=emulate
memory=12GB
processors=6
swap=6GB
```

Swap is set as gigabytes or megabytes as whole number integers followed by GB or MB, respectively.

If you are performing RAM-intensive tasks, such as compiling Chromium from source, you may need additional swap space as your available hardware RAM is consumed. This may also be necessary on devices with lower amounts of RAM, such as under 8 GB. Note that swap space, because it is written to disk, is inherently slower than hardware RAM. However, it can solve problems when you are out of available hardware RAM. You can also disable swap on WSL 2 by setting this value to zero; however, this is generally not advised, and doing so may cause out of memory problems in some applications. On the other hand, if you are doing Kubernetes-related development, where swap is not yet supported, you may wish to disable swap to better emulate your deployment environment. This is done by setting swap=0:

```
[wsl2]
kernel=C:\\Users\\Hayden\\bzImage
kernelCommandLine= vsyscall=emulate
memory=12GB
processors=6
swap=0
```

Swap File

WSL 2 will default to storing your swap file at `%USERPROFILE%\AppData\Local\Temp\swap.vhdx`.

WSL 2 automatically creates this file; there is no need to create it manually. However, you can specify where you would like the swap to be stored if necessary, with the `swapfile=` location.

Like the kernel path, this too must be absolute and use escaped backslashes:

```
[wsl2]
kernel=C:\\Users\\Hayden\\bzImage
kernelCommandLine= vsyscall=emulate
memory=12GB
processors=6
swap=4GB
swapfile=C:\\wslswap.vhdx
```

Page Reporting

WSL 2 will default to freeing unused memory by the WSL distro and returning it back to Windows. This feature relies on a patch in the WSL 2 kernel from Microsoft. This is why I recommend building a custom kernel from the official WSL 2 kernel sources, so those patches come over to your custom kernel.

The Linux kernel allocates available memory into pages, which it then maps to running processes. An API in the Linux kernel can, when running as a guest such as in WSL 2, report to the host hypervisor when pages of memory are no longer being used. This enables WSL to reclaim that memory and move it back to the pool of available memory in Windows where it can be reused by Windows applications or taken up again by another WSL process.

This only occurs when the CPU is near idle. You can see this in action when you enable the debug console (Figure 6-3). For more on the debug console, read the following.

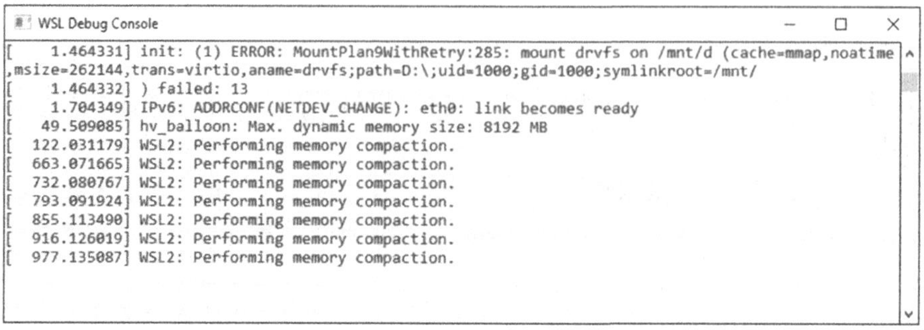

Figure 6-3. *Viewing the WSL 2 debug console*

You can manually trigger memory compaction in WSL with the following as root:

```
echo 1 | sudo tee /proc/sys/vm/compact_memory
```

You can disable the Page Reporting feature so that WSL retains all the memory it has claimed from Windows without releasing any back when it is freed in WSL:

```
[wsl2]
kernel=C:\\Users\\Hayden\\bzImage
kernelCommandLine= vsyscall=emulate
memory=12GB
processors=6
swap=4GB
swapfile=C:\\wslswap.vhdx
localhostforwarding=true
pageReporting=false
```

Localhost Forwarding

WSL 2 will default to making connections bound to localhost in the WSL 2 environment available to Windows, also on localhost. This is like the network handling in WSL 1. The difference being in WSL 1 is that there is no separate network stack; there is just localhost. In WSL 2, the WSL distro is networked on a virtual subnet with NAT and configured with DHCP. This can make some networking configuration trickier. However, with localhost forwarding, you can mimic most of that WSL 1 network experience in WSL 2.

```
[wsl2]
kernel=C:\\Users\\Hayden\\bzImage
kernelCommandLine= vsyscall=emulate
memory=12GB
processors=6
swap=4GB
swapfile=C:\\wslswap.vhdx
localhostforwarding=true
```

Nested Virtualization

Nested virtualization allows you to run virtual machines (VMs) inside of WSL 2, most commonly using KVM, the native virtualization tooling built into the Linux kernel. It specifically allows the needed processor extensions for virtualization to pass through to the lightweight virtualization container that WSL 2 runs in and makes them available to the kernel there to then run other virtual machines, hence "nested." This was my first request of the WSL team when I first learned of WSL 2, because it allows the creation of Linux VMs, from different distros, and even other operating systems, such as Windows, Haiku, BSDs, and legacy operating systems. Because this is one of my favorite features, I will go more in depth about it in Chapter 8 "Going Further with WSL 2."

```
[wsl2]
kernel=C:\\Users\\Hayden\\bzImage
kernelCommandLine= vsyscall=emulate
memory=12GB
processors=6
swap=4GB
swapfile=C:\\wslswap.vhdx
localhostforwarding=true
nestedVirtualization=true
```

Nested virtualization requires at least Windows 10 build 19645 and is enabled by default as of build 20175.

Debug Console

When WSL 2 boots the kernel, where are those logs? How do you debug the kernel and kernel command line issues? With the debugging console. Debug console provides a window in which kernel messages are printed. It is spawned each time the WSL 2 kernel is loaded. Having this enabled will also tell you how often the kernel gets reloaded and when, in some surprising circumstances, it is, for example, when opening File Explorer if you have WSL folders mounted.

This is particularly useful when building and testing your own kernel. You can monitor this and watch memory compaction at work (Figure 6-4). If a large WSL 2 task is stalling, you can check debug to see if perhaps you've run out of RAM and need to assign more or add swap space.

```
[wsl2]
kernel=C:\\Users\\Hayden\\bzImage
kernelCommandLine= vsyscall=emulate
memory=12GB
processors=6
swap=4GB
swapfile=C:\\wslswap.vhdx
localhostforwarding=true
nestedVirtualization=true
debugConsole=true
```

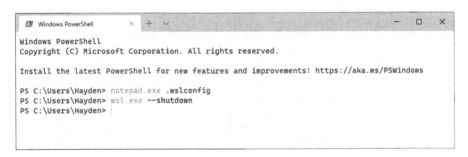

```
WSL Debug Console                                                    —   □   ×
[    1.562026] hv_pci d84f1991-0818-4307-bc7a-a95280f7719d: PCI VMBus probing: Using version 0x10002
[    1.562706] 9pnet_virtio: no channels available for device drvfs
[    1.566977] WARNING: mount: waiting for virtio device...
[    1.600456] hv_pci d84f1991-0818-4307-bc7a-a95280f7719d: PCI host bridge to bus bc7a:00
[    1.602991] pci_bus bc7a:00: root bus resource [mem 0xe00004000-0xe00006fff window]
[    1.605790] pci bc7a:00:00.0: [1af4:1049] type 00 class 0x010000
[    1.608535] pci bc7a:00:00.0: reg 0x10: [mem 0xe00004000-0xe00004fff 64bit]
[    1.611055] pci bc7a:00:00.0: reg 0x18: [mem 0xe00005000-0xe00005fff 64bit]
[    1.613644] pci bc7a:00:00.0: reg 0x20: [mem 0xe00006000-0xe00006fff 64bit]
[    1.617989] pci bc7a:00:00.0: BAR 0: assigned [mem 0xe00004000-0xe00004fff 64bit]
[    1.620703] pci bc7a:00:00.0: BAR 2: assigned [mem 0xe00005000-0xe00005fff 64bit]
[    1.623294] pci bc7a:00:00.0: BAR 4: assigned [mem 0xe00006000-0xe00006fff 64bit]
[    1.654245] IPv6: ADDRCONF(NETDEV_CHANGE): eth0: link becomes ready
[    1.672456] hv_pci 2b8fd587-6a88-403f-8331-f5d11386b17c: PCI VMBus probing: Using version 0x10002
[    1.711299] hv_pci 2b8fd587-6a88-403f-8331-f5d11386b17c: PCI host bridge to bus 8331:00
[    1.713912] pci_bus 8331:00: root bus resource [mem 0xe00008000-0xe0000afff window]
[    1.716687] pci 8331:00:00.0: [1af4:1049] type 00 class 0x010000
[    1.719399] pci 8331:00:00.0: reg 0x10: [mem 0xe00008000-0xe00008fff 64bit]
[    1.722089] pci 8331:00:00.0: reg 0x18: [mem 0xe00009000-0xe00009fff 64bit]
[    1.724168] init: (1) ERROR: MountPlan9WithRetry:285: mount drvfs on /mnt/d (cache=mmap,noatime,msize=26214
4,trans=virtio,aname=drvfs;path=D:\;uid=1000;gid=1000;symlinkroot=/mnt/
[    1.724170] ) failed: 13
[    1.724628] pci 8331:00:00.0: reg 0x20: [mem 0xe0000a000-0xe0000afff 64bit]
[    1.735308] pci 8331:00:00.0: BAR 0: assigned [mem 0xe00008000-0xe00008fff 64bit]
[    1.738044] pci 8331:00:00.0: BAR 2: assigned [mem 0xe00009000-0xe00009fff 64bit]
[    1.740886] pci 8331:00:00.0: BAR 4: assigned [mem 0xe0000a000-0xe0000afff 64bit]
[   49.514446] hv_balloon: Max. dynamic memory size: 8192 MB
[   62.086124] WSL2: Performing memory compaction.
```

Figure 6-4. *Observing WSL 2 memory compaction on the WSL debug console*

Tips

When editing .wslconfig, you must shut down the WSL 2 environment for settings to take.

You can do this with wsl.exe --shutdown.

```
Windows PowerShell          ×   + ∨                              —   □   ×
Windows PowerShell
Copyright (C) Microsoft Corporation. All rights reserved.

Install the latest PowerShell for new features and improvements! https://aka.ms/PSWindows

PS C:\Users\Hayden> notepad.exe .wslconfig
PS C:\Users\Hayden> wsl.exe --shutdown
PS C:\Users\Hayden> |
```

Figure 6-5. *Shutting down WSL from PowerShell using wsl.exe --shutdown*

While it is possible to edit WSL config from WSL, you should convert the line endings to CRLF Windows-style line endings.

If you create the file with notepad.exe, then nano and other editors should preserve the CRLF Windows-style line endings.

Figure 6-6. *Editing .wslconfig in nano. Note the "Converted from DOS format" message*

You can also easily switch back and forth between line ending styles in VS Code by clicking CRLF or LF in the status bar of Microsoft VS Code.

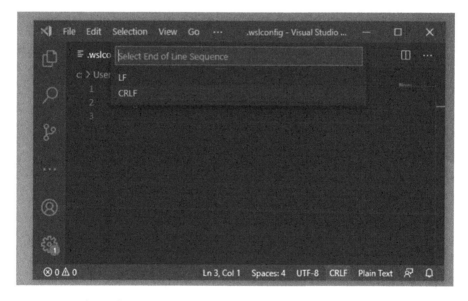

Figure 6-7. *Switching between Linux LF line endings and Windows CRLF line endings in VS Code*

WSL Registry Settings

It is possible to configure some WSL settings from the Windows Registry. I would recommend using the settings available from wsl.exe, .wslconfig, and wsl.conf before using the registry. However, in a pinch, it can suffice. All the requisite warnings regarding editing your registry go here as well.

WSL-related settings are found at

`\HKEY_CURRENT_USER\Software\Microsoft\Windows\CurrentVersion\Lxss`

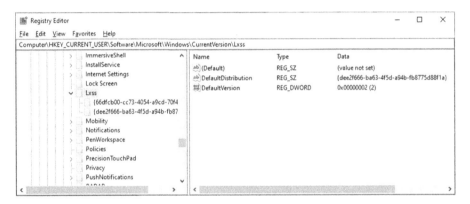

Figure 6-8. *Viewing WSL distributions in the Windows Registry*

`DefaultDistribution` contains the GUID of your default WSL distro.

`DefaultVersion` contains the default version of WSL, either 1 or 2.

Each WSL distro installed is then listed by GUID, which resembles `{66dfcb00-cc73-4054-a9cd-70f4149c8209}`.

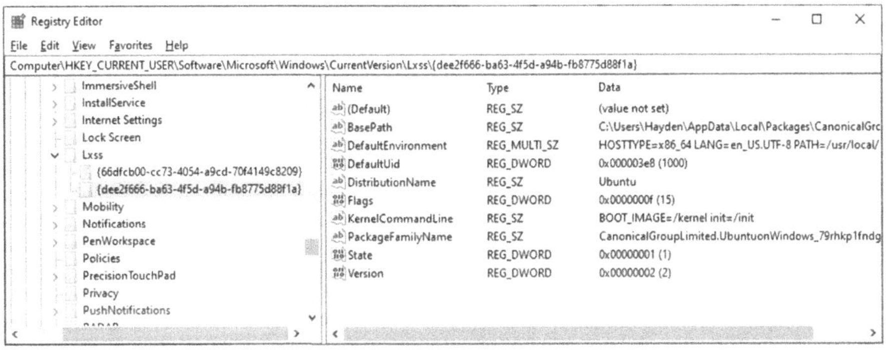

Figure 6-9. *Viewing individual WSL distribution settings in the Windows Registry*

Each distro will have a `BasePath` containing the location of the WSL distro installed, a `DistributionName`, and `Version`, either WSL 1 or 2.

Distros installed from the Microsoft Store will have more details stored in the registry.

Distros installed manually, with wsl.exe --import, will have fewer details (Figure 6-10).

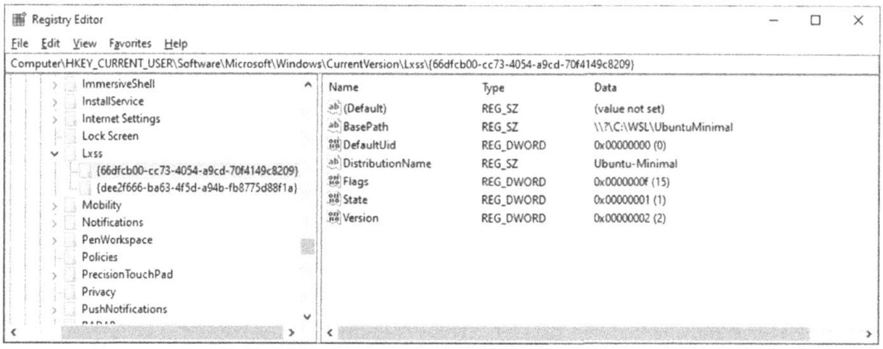

Figure 6-10. *Viewing the individual WSL distribution settings of a manually installed distro in Windows Registry*

Again, it is generally not recommended that you edit these values manually. Doing so while the WSL distro is running could leave the distro in an unstable state, and this could cause data loss.

However, since you are reading this book and reading about Windows Registry settings, you probably understand the risk here, and seeing some of these values, you may think of something you might want to tweak. Go for it. Just make sure you keep backups.

## CHAPTER 7

Customizing WSL

Now that you know the architecture of WSL and are familiar with setting it up and configuring it, let us talk about some things you can do to customize WSL.

Using Graphical Applications with X

Official support for installing graphical Linux applications on WSL, called WSLg, is currently in preview in the Windows Insider Dev Channel and to be released in versions of Windows later. It is possible to use graphical Linux applications on WSL in released versions of Windows today, though. For now, it requires a third-party X server running on Windows and a bit of configuration to point the WSL distro at the X server on the Windows side.

If you install graphical applications in your WSL distro, they will often bring in the distro's X server as a dependency, but we are not actually using that X server. Instead, we will be forwarding the X output from each application to the X server running on Windows over a local port.

Install an X Server on Windows

First, you will need to select and install an X server on Windows. Any of the following should work:

- VcXsrv

- X410

- Xmanager

- Xming

- Cygwin/X

- MobaXterm

© Hayden Barnes 2021
H. Barnes, *Pro Windows Subsystem for Linux (WSL)*, https://doi.org/10.1007/978-1-4842-6873-5_7

The two most common X servers you will find in the WSL community are X410 and VcXsrv. VcXsrv is free, open source, and built from the upstream Xorg code base. It can be slightly more challenging to get running correctly, though. X410 is paid and only available through the Microsoft Store, but it is nicely polished and requires less manual configuration.

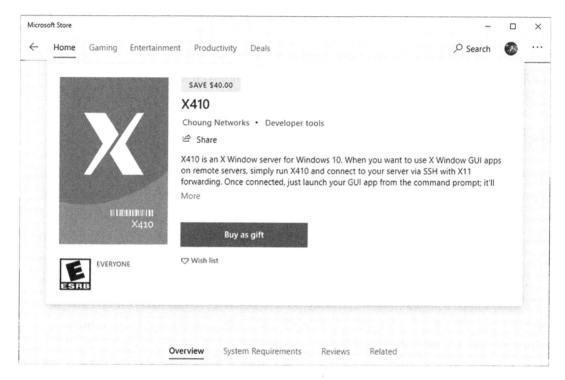

Figure 7-1. *Microsoft Store listing for X410, a Windows X server*

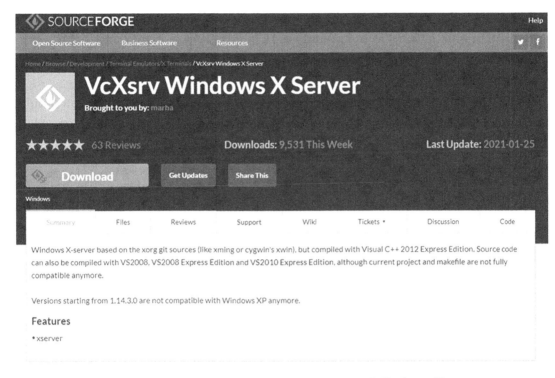

Figure 7-2. *VcXsrv project page on SourceForge.net, a Windows X server*

Configure WSL to Forward X to Your Windows X Server

Once your X server is installed and running on Windows, you will need to forward your distro's X output to the X server on Windows.

This is very straightforward in WSL 1:

```
export DISPLAY=127.0.0.1:0.0
```

In WSL 2, we must forward to the IP address of our host Windows environment. We can grab this IP address from the DNS settings that WSL has configured in /etc/resolv.conf:

```
export DISPLAY=$(awk '/nameserver/ {print $2}' /etc/resolv.conf 2>/dev/null):0
```

If you have overridden the autogeneration of resolv.conf in wsl.conf, it may not be updated with your host Windows environment IP address; in this case, you will need to script a way to grab that from your Windows system, such as

```
export DISPLAY= $ (powershell.exe -c "(Get-NetIPAddress -InterfaceAlias '*wsl*' -AddressFamily IPv4).ipaddress + ':0.0'")
```

If you intend to run GUI applications on a regular basis, you should place this command in your .bashrc file, or in Windows 10 builds 21286 or higher, as a [boot] command option in /etc/wsl.conf. Read the following for more on the .bashrc file if you're not familiar.

If the GUI application you are running offers libGL graphics acceleration, you should also set the following, which will offload the rendering from WSL to your Windows-side X server:

```
export LIBGL_ALWAYS_INDIRECT=1
```

This will accelerate rendering of OpenGL 1.4 and older graphics.

WSL 2, GUI Apps, and Windows Firewall

On WSL 2, you will need to open access in your Windows Firewall for the Windows-side X server.

In X410, right-click the tray icon, select "Allow Public Access," check "Public networks" on the Windows Firewall prompt, and then restart X410.

Figure 7-3. *Allowing public access to enable X410 on WSL 2*

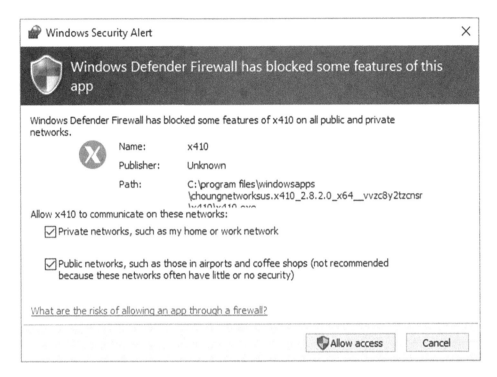

Figure 7-4. *Check "Public networks" on the Windows Firewall prompt to enable X410 on WSL 2*

In VcXsrv, check "Disable access control" when configuring XLaunch and, like X410, check "Public networks" on the Windows Firewall prompt.

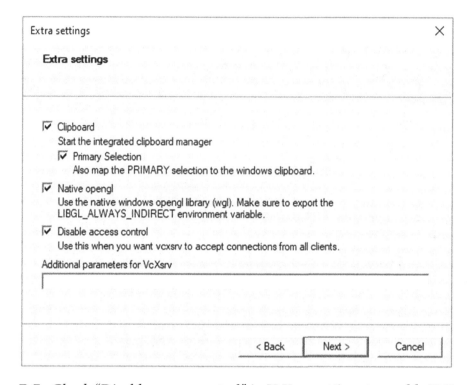

Figure 7-5. *Check "Disable access control" in VcXsrv settings to enable VcXsrv on WSL 2*

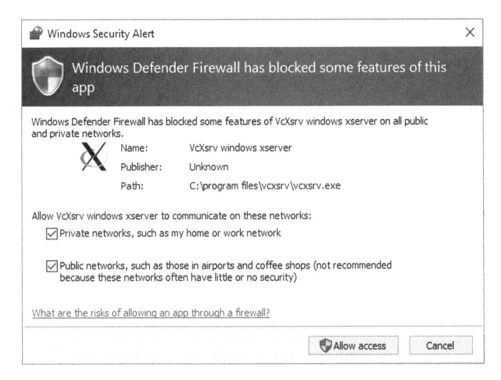

Figure 7-6. *Check "Public networks" on the Windows Firewall prompt to enable VcXsrv on WSL 2*

You may ask yourself, isn't opening a service in my firewall on public networks a security risk? Absolutely it is.

There are two things you can do about this. Never use a GUI app when connected to a public network, like at a café or on an airplane. Alternatively, you can configure a Windows Firewall rule that limits your exposure by only allowing TCP public access to your X server from your local WSL distro's subnet.

From WSL, open your advanced Windows Firewall settings:

```
cmd.exe /C wf.msc
```

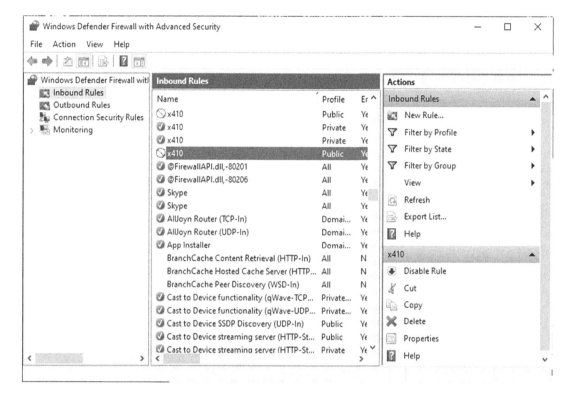

Figure 7-7. *Locating your Windows X server, in this case X410, in Windows Firewall settings*

In the "Inbound Rules" tab, find your X server in the list of applications. There will be rules for public and private networks and TCP and UDP protocols. We are editing the public network TCP protocol rule.

Inbound Rules

Name	Profile	Enabled	Action	Override	F
⊘ x410	Public	Yes	Block	No	(
✅ x410	Private	Yes	Allow	No	(
✅ x410	Private	Yes	Allow	No	(
⊘ x410	Public	Yes	Block	No	(

Figure 7-8. *Locating "public" inbound Firewall rules for our Windows X server, in this case X410*

You may have to scroll over to the "Protocol" column to see the TCP/UDP distinction.

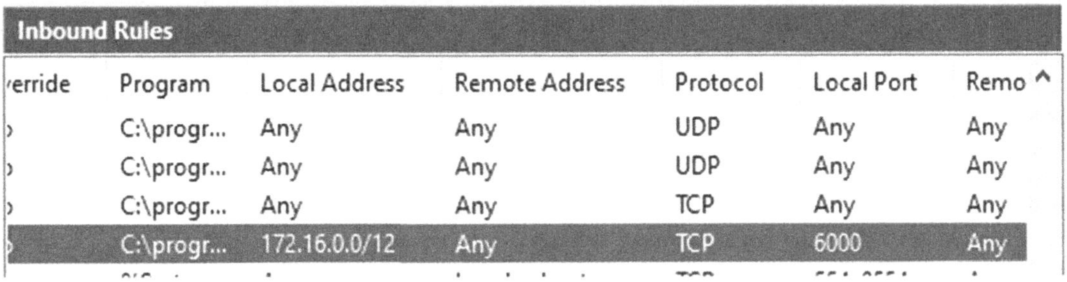

Inbound Rules
erride
Program
Local Address
Remote Address
Protocol
Local Port
Remo
C:\progr... Any Any UDP Any Any
C:\progr... Any Any UDP Any Any
C:\progr... Any Any TCP Any Any
C:\progr... 172.16.0.0/12 Any TCP 6000 Any

Figure 7-9. *Locating the "public" TCP inbound Firewall rule for our Windows X server*

Open the public TCP inbound rule for your X server by right-clicking and selecting "Properties."

Under "General," select "Allow the connection."

x410 Properties
Protocols and Ports
Scope
Advanced
Local Principals
Remote Users
General
Programs and Services
Remote Computers
General
Name:
x410
Description:
x410
Enabled
Action
Allow the connection
Allow the connection if it is secure
Customize...
Block the connection

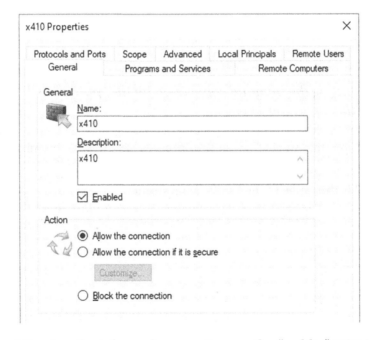

Figure 7-10. *Allowing the inbound connection on the "public" TCP inbound Firewall rule*

Next, go to the "Protocols and Ports" tab, set "Protocol type" to "TCP," and in "Local port" select "Specific Ports" and enter port 6000.

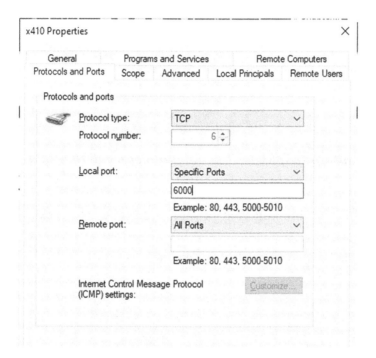

Figure 7-11. *Limiting the inbound connection on the "public" TCP inbound Firewall rule to the X port, port 6000*

Go to the "Scope" tab, select "These IP addresses" ➤ "Add…," and paste in `172.16.0.0/12`.

172.16.0.0/12 is the range of the WSL virtual subnet.

Figure 7-12. *Limiting the inbound connection on the "public" TCP inbound Firewall rule to the IP address range of the WSL virtual subnet*

Click "OK" and "Apply."

Finally, you can set or leave the public UDP rule for your X server as "Block the connection," as the X protocol does not normally use UDP.

Your X server is now more secure.

Install a GUI Application

Once the X server is installed, firewall ports are open for WSL 2, and we have configured redirection for the WSL distro, it is time to install a GUI application. This will likely bring in several Xorg-related dependencies, including an X server, but we will not be running the X server from the WSL distro:

```
sudo apt -y install synaptic
```

If everything is configured correctly, you should be able to run your GUI application now:

```
sudo synaptic
```

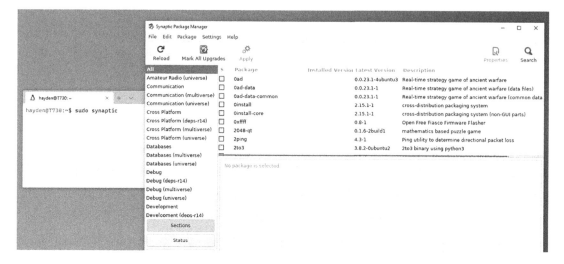

Figure 7-13. *Synaptic, a simple GUI package manager for Ubuntu, Debian, and other apt-based Linux distributions*

Debugging GUI Applications

The most common error encountered when trying to run GUI applications on WSL 2 is something like "cannot open display:" or "Unable to init server: Could not connect: Connection refused". This is because your WSL distro cannot connect to your Windows environment X server.

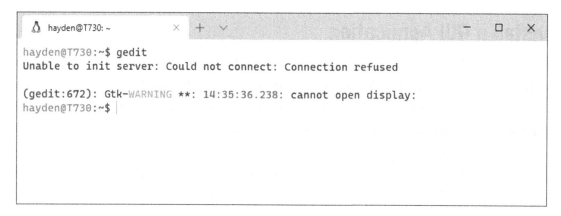

Figure 7-14. *An example of a GUI app failing to start because it cannot open the display*

Checklist:

- X server installed, such as VcXsrv or X410

- X server running – check your tray area

- DISPLAY variable set properly depending on whether you are running WSL 1 or WSL 2

dbus

Occasionally a Linux GUI application will not launch because it cannot reach the bus. dbus is a device messaging service for the Linux desktop. If X is properly configured and you can run other GUI applications, but one application is failing, it may be worth trying to set up and configure dbus, particularly if you see dbus mentioned in the error message.

Install dbus as you would any other Linux package:

```
sudo apt install dbus-x11
```

Generate a dbus device ID, which you will only need to do once per WSL distro installation:

```
sudo dbus-uuidgen –ensure
```

Then run `dbus-launch` before starting your GUI application:

```
dbus-launch --exit-with-x11
```

Rolling Your Own init System

WSL does not have a traditional init like SysVinit, systemd-init, or OpenRC. It does have an init program that handles some basic tasks, like Windows interoperability, file sharing, and networking. But it does not start services, nor is it addressable by most Linux applications looking for an init.

If you would like to start services every time WSL is opened, you have two basic options. You may script it as part of the shell, or you may run a command using Windows Task Scheduler.

.bashrc

Adding shell commands to your bash config file is the simplest way to automate commands that you want to run on each launch. Bash will execute this file every time a new window is opened, either in the traditional console or in the new Windows Terminal.

.bashrc is a good place to set environmental variables, such as the display variable for using an external X server (Figure 7-15).

It usually contains some boilerplate configuration set by your WSL distro; just append what you need underneath that.

Figure 7-15. *A sample .bashrc file in Ubuntu*

.bashrc is located in your user home folder at ~ or /home/<username>. It can be opened with the nano text editor as follows:

```
nano ~/.bashrc
```

.bashrc is Bash specific. If you change to an alternate shell, such as fish, zsh, csh, or ksh, you will need to specify the command you want to run in each launch in the respective config files for each of those shells.

.bashrc is user specific. If you create another user and launch WSL as that user, for example, by using wsl.exe -u or by changing the default user, you will need to add these commands to the .bashrc for that user, in their respective home directory.

If you would like to make a script execute on launch for all users, you will need to create a new script in /etc/profile.d/ such as

sudo nano /etc/profile.d/displayvar.sh

Then copy and paste:

```
#!/bin/bash
export DISPLAY=$(awk '/nameserver / {print $2; exit}' /etc/resolv.conf 2>
/dev/null):0
export LIBGL_ALWAYS_INDIRECT=1
```

Exit nano (Ctrl+X and then "Y"), confirming changes, and make the script executable:

sudo chmod /etc/profile.d/displayvar.sh

Note that /etc/profile.d/ scripts are only executed in interactive shells; those are shells launched on the terminal. It will not execute when you launch WSL in the background with the VS Code WSL remote extension. In these cases, you should add the needed scripting to /etc/bash.bashrc and then set a Windows environmental variable for WSL to read /etc/bash.bashrc on each launch:

export WSLENV="BASH_ENV/u"

Non-POSIX-compatible shells, like fish, may not read /etc/profile.d/* or /etc/bash.bashrc files on launch; you will need to consult the documentation for those shells on how to properly script launch behavior.

If you have a script that starts an application or service in the background (Figure 7-16), it will be triggered every time you open a new terminal; this could result in duplicate applications running or hangs.

```
△  hayden@T730: ~            ×  +  ∨                          —  □  ×

hayden@T730:~$ ps -A
  PID TTY          TIME CMD
    1 ?        00:00:00 init
    8 ?        00:00:00 init
    9 ?        00:00:00 init
   10 pts/0    00:00:00 bash
 1701 ?        00:00:00 init
 1725 ?        00:00:00 apache2
 1728 ?        00:00:00 apache2
 1729 ?        00:00:00 apache2
 1796 pts/0    00:00:00 ps
hayden@T730:~$
```

Figure 7-16. *apache2 running on a WSL distro*

Therefore, you may need to add some scripting that first checks if an application is running before trying to start it, such as

```
#!/bin/bash
SERVICE="dbus-daemon"
if pgrep -x "$SERVICE" >/dev/null
then
    echo "$SERVICE is running"
else
    echo "$SERVICE stopped"
    sudo /etc/init.d/dbus start
fi
```

You could place this script in your bashrc file or create a new script in your /etc/ profile.d/ folder for all users, but be sure to append a prefix to a new script with the proper shebang, for example, #!/bin/bash, and make it executable with chmod.

Even though there is no traditional init in WSL, the classic init scripts located in /etc/init.d/ can still be very useful for starting and stopping services on WSL. The service command also works on WSL. Even though it is commonly associated with systemd, service is actually a helper script that will default to the init.d scripts if necessary.

Experienced shell users may notice a problem in the preceding script; it calls sudo. This would require a user to enter their administrative password on each launch. This can be onerous, so what can we do about it? We can add an exception for this specific command to the sudoers file.

Sudoers, for those unfamiliar, is the file that controls what escalation is permitted with the sudo command (Figure 7-17). To edit the sudoers file, you must use visudo. Do not manually edit this file with another editor; it will break your sudoers configuration and could prevent further changes requiring you to reset your WSL distro or resulting in potential data loss.

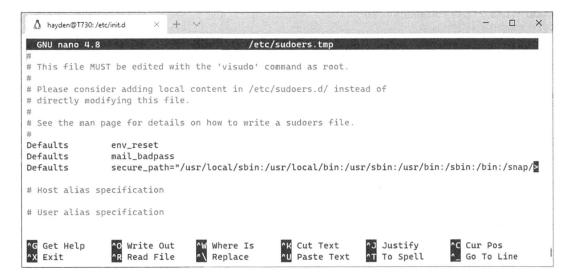

Figure 7-17. *Editing the sudoers file with the* visudo *command*

Thankfully, visudo no longer uses the vi editor but defaults to nano on Ubuntu, which is much easier to use. Open the sudoers file:

```
sudo visudo
```

And then append

```
ALL ALL=NOPASSWD: /etc/init.d/dbus start
```

Exit nano (Ctrl+X and then "Y"), and confirm changes.

Windows Services

What if you wanted to start a Linux application or service when you logged into Windows, without launching the Windows Terminal or opening WSL in the background in an IDE like Code?

The best way to do this, currently, is to create a Windows Service that launches WSL and runs the commands in the background.

For this example, we will use the Apache web server.

Install Apache:

```
sudo apt -y install apache2
```

Create a shell script:

```
sudo nano /opt/runapache.sh
```

Copy and paste the shell script, customizing as needed to the service you would like to start (Figure 7-18):

```
#!/bin/bash
SERVICE="apache2"
if pgrep -x "$SERVICE" >/dev/null
then
    echo "$SERVICE is running"
else
    echo "$SERVICE stopped"
    sudo /etc/init.d/apache2 start
fi
```

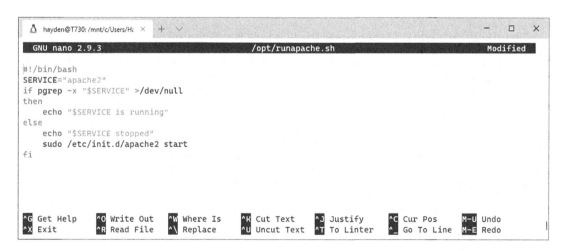

Figure 7-18. *Editing the script to launch Apache in nano*

Make the shell script executable:

```
sudo chmod /opt/runapache.sh
```

Change the owner of the shell script to our primary user:

```
sudo chown hayden /opt/runapache.sh
```

Create a Windows batch file in your Windows home directory to call the shell script (Figure 7-19):

```
nano $(wslpath $(wslvar USERPROFILE))/runapache.bat
```

Copy and paste as follows, customizing as needed:

```
@echo off
wsl.exe /opt/runapache.sh
```

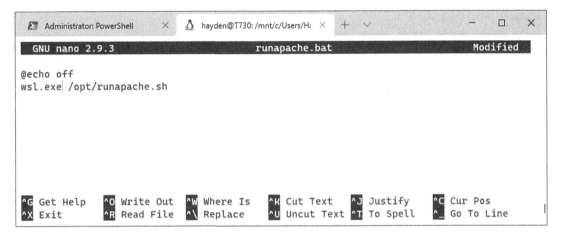

Figure 7-19. *Editing a Windows batch file to call our script*

Note wsl.exe, without any specific parameters, will call your default distro, as set with `wsl.exe --setdefault <distribution>`.

If you want to use another distro, you can substitute its .exe alias, such as `ubuntu1804.exe` if it was installed from the Store or a sideloaded .appx, or use `wsl.exe –d Ubuntu2004` followed by your command:

```
wsl.exe -d Ubuntu-20.04 sudo /etc/init.d/apache2 start
```

If you want to run the application as another user, you can specify that with -u:

```
wsl.exe -u apacheuser sudo /etc/init.d/apache2 start
```

You will see this command has a `sudo` prefix, meaning you will need to add the command to the sudoers file for your default user or the user specified with -u.

Run

```
sudo visudo
```

And add

```
ALL ALL=NOPASSWD: /etc/init.d/apache2 start
```

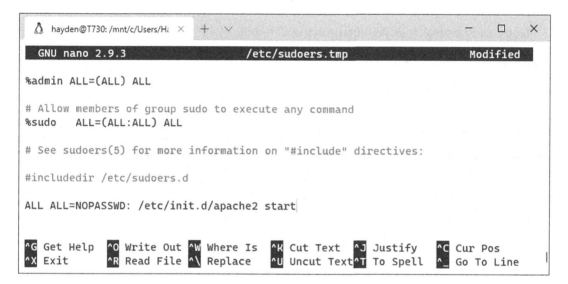

Figure 7-20. Adding /etc/init.d/apache2 start to the sudoers file

It is possible to specify -u root and bypass the need for a sudoers file addition, but this is not recommended. Running network services, which are potentially accessible from the web, as root, is a bad idea.

Next, test the Windows batch file we created. Open PowerShell, and make sure apache2 is not running:

```
wsl.exe --exec ps -A
```

You should not see any apache2 processes; if you do, run

```
wsl.exe --exec sudo killall apache2
```

Then run the batch file as follows:

```
C:\Users\Hayden\runapache.bat
```

```
PS C:\> wsl.exe --exec ps -A
  PID TTY          TIME CMD
    1 ?        00:00:00 init
   12 ?        00:00:00 init
   13 ?        00:00:00 init
   14 pts/0    00:00:00 bash
  182 ?        00:00:00 init
  183 ?        00:00:00 init
  184 pts/1    00:00:00 ps
PS C:\> C:\Users\Hayden\runapache.bat
apache2 stopped
 * Starting Apache httpd web server apache2
 *
PS C:\>
```

Figure 7-21. *Testing the batch file that calls our shell script to start apache2*

If successful, we should see that apache2 is detected as not running and then started. We should then be able to see the apache2 default landing page in any browser at localhost.

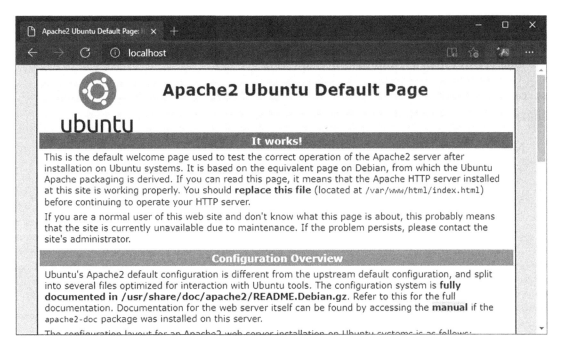

Figure 7-22. *Testing apache2 batch file/script file worked by opening localhost in a web browser*

Note, if you run the batch file immediately again, it will detect apache2 is already running and not launch a second instance.

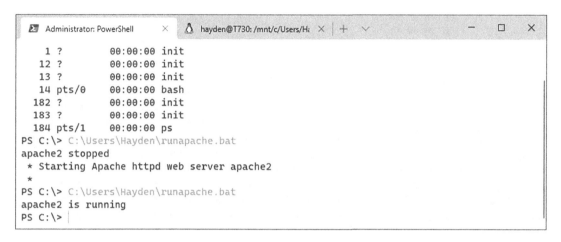

Figure 7-23. *Running apache2 batch/script file again, which detects apache2 is already running*

Finally, use the Windows Service Control Manager, sc.exe, to schedule the Windows batch file to run on Windows boot.

Open PowerShell as Administrator, and run

```
sc create 'Apache in WSL' binpath= C:\Users\Hayden\runapache.bat type=
share start= auto displayname= 'Apache in WSL'
```

Note the space after the "=" in the sc create command.

This service can now be controlled from the Windows Services pane.

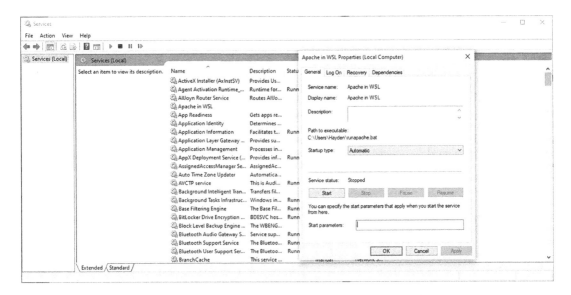

Figure 7-24. *Managing the Apache on WSL service from the Windows Services pane*

Windows Task Scheduler

If editing bash scripts and batch files seems like overkill to automate some WSL commands from Windows, there is a simpler option: using Windows Task Scheduler.

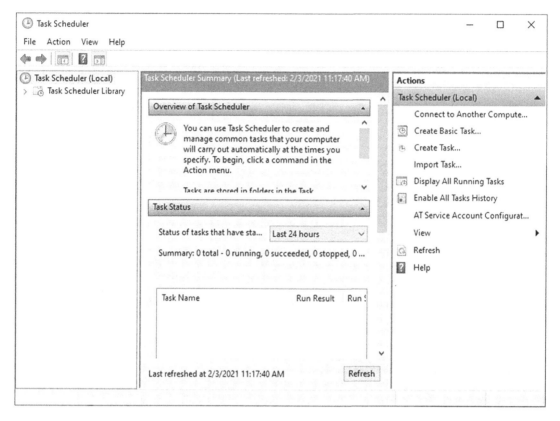

Figure 7-25. *Windows Task Scheduler*

Windows Task Scheduler is a friendlier way to automate tasks in Windows and can run commands in WSL.

Open Windows Task Scheduler in Windows, and click "Create Basic Task…." In our example, we are going to implement unattended upgrades in Ubuntu.

For the Name field, type "Unattended Upgrades in Ubuntu."

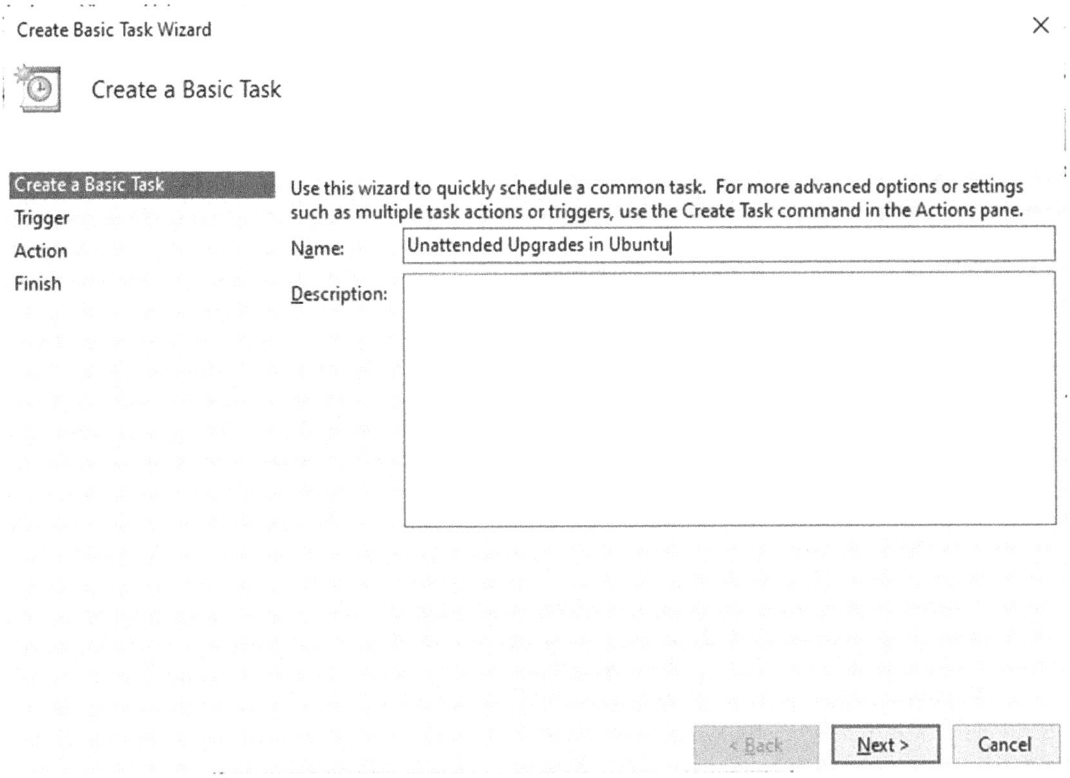

Figure 7-26. *Naming our new task*

Set the trigger for the task; in our example, we will run "Daily."

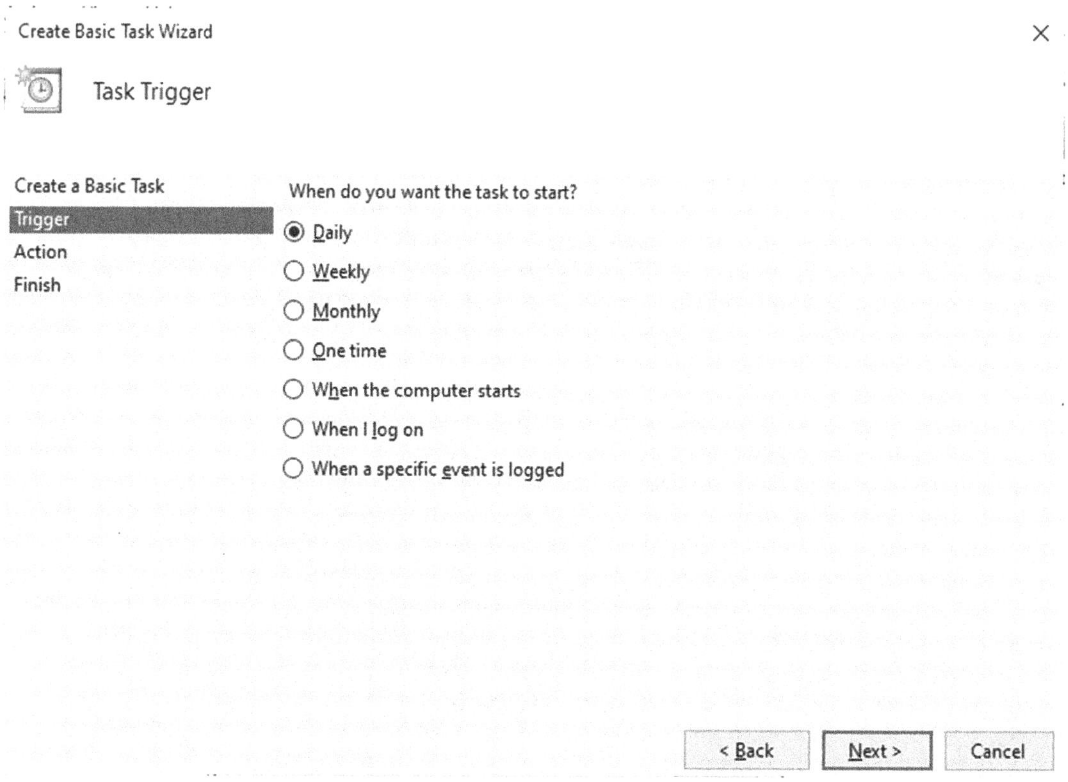

Create Basic Task Wizard   ×

Task Trigger

Create a Basic Task   When do you want the task to start?
Trigger
Action   ◉ Daily
Finish   ○ Weekly
                             ○ Monthly
                             ○ One time
                             ○ When the computer starts
                             ○ When I log on
                             ○ When a specific event is logged

                                              < Back   Next >   Cancel

Figure 7-27. *Setting the task to run daily*

And then set the task to run at 1 AM.

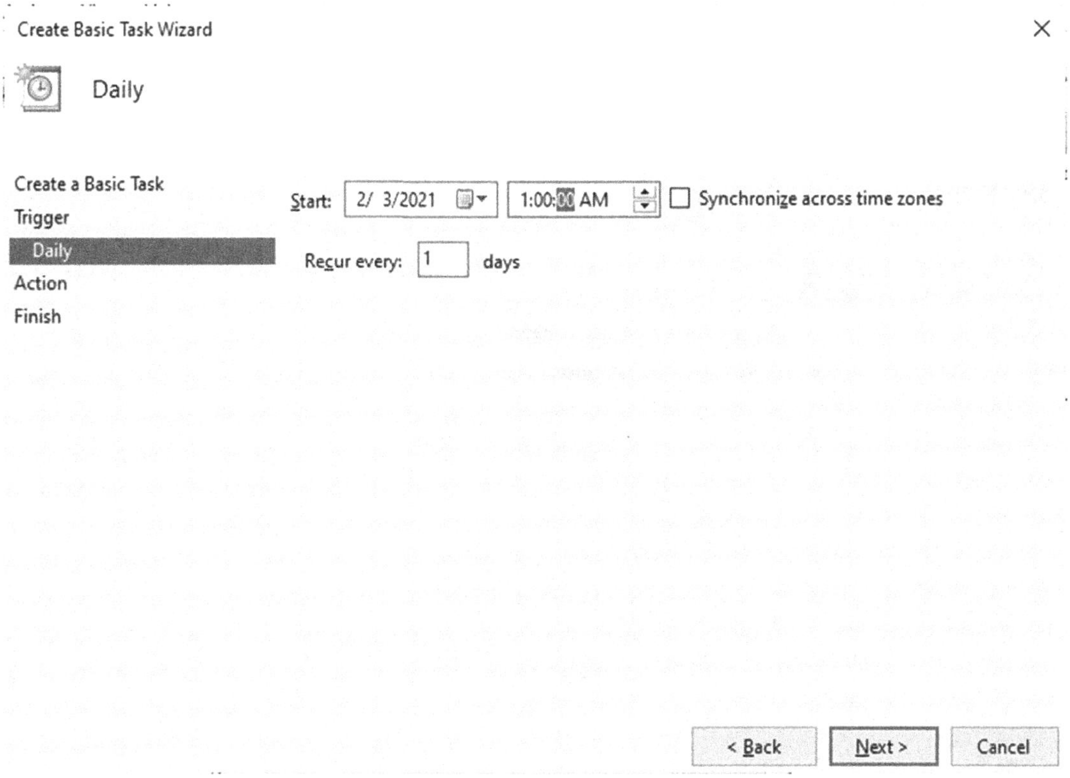

Figure 7-28. *Setting the time to run the task*

We will want our task to "Start a program."

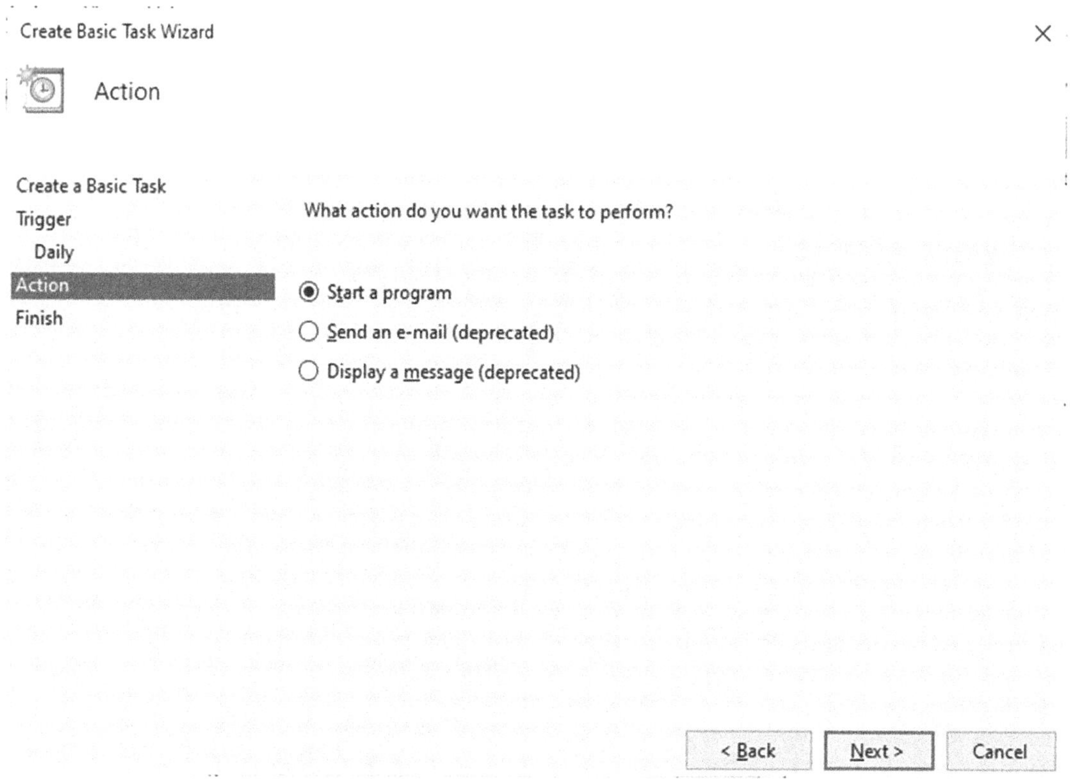

Figure 7-29. *Specifying the task will start a program*

We are going to start `wsl.exe` with the arguments:

`-u root -e apt update.`

This will have apt check for package updates from the Ubuntu repository as root.

Note that this will execute in the default WSL distro; if you have multiple WSL distros installed and want to run on a specific distro, specify the distro with -d, such as `-d Ubuntu`, as necessary.

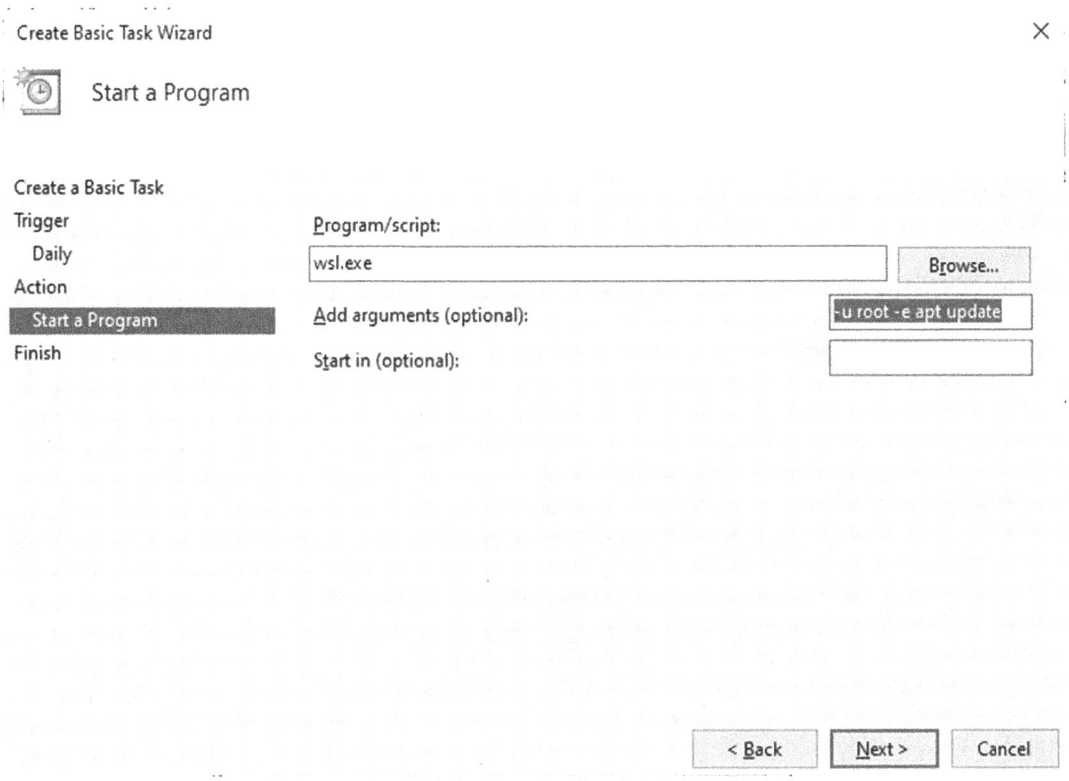

Figure 7-30. *Specifying the program to run,* `wsl.exe`, *and arguments,* `-u root -e apt update`

Finalize the new task, checking "Open the Properties dialog for this task when I click Finish" because we are not done yet (Figure 7-31). We have, so far, created an action to check for package updates from the Ubuntu repository. However, we still need to add the next step, which will apply the available upgrades.

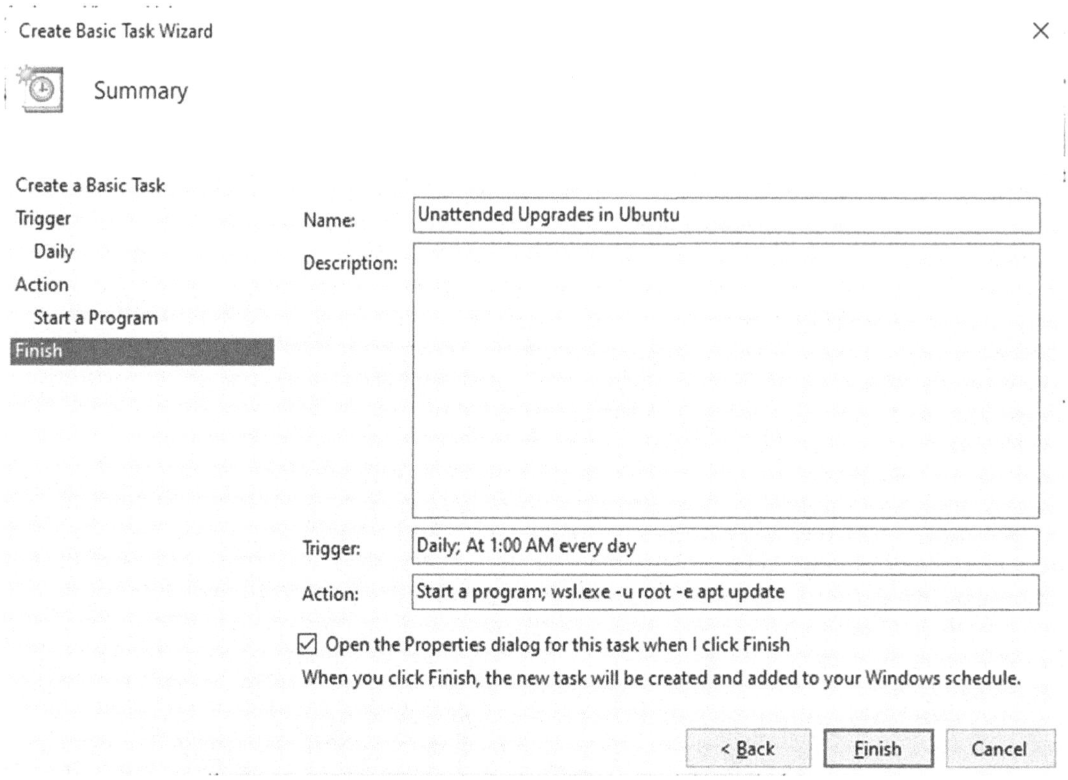

Figure 7-31. *Finishing creating our new task*

In Properties, click the "Actions" tab (Figure 7-32), and then click "New" because now we are going to add the apt package upgrade command after checking for package updates from the Ubuntu repository.

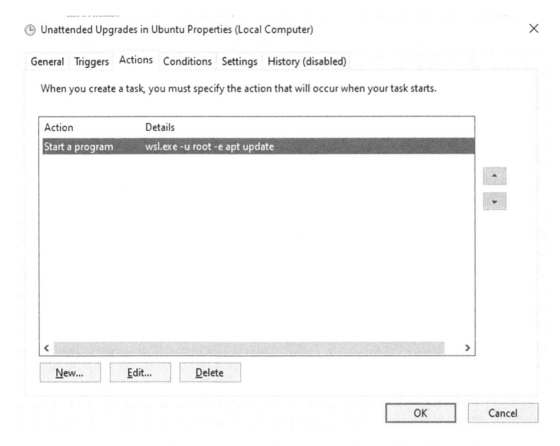

Figure 7-32. *Opening the Actions tab of our new task to add additional steps*

In the New Action window, we are going to run `wsl.exe` with the arguments:

`-u root -e apt -y upgrade`

This will run the apt package upgrade command noninteractively as root.

The Actions pane will now show both commands in this task (Figure 7-33).

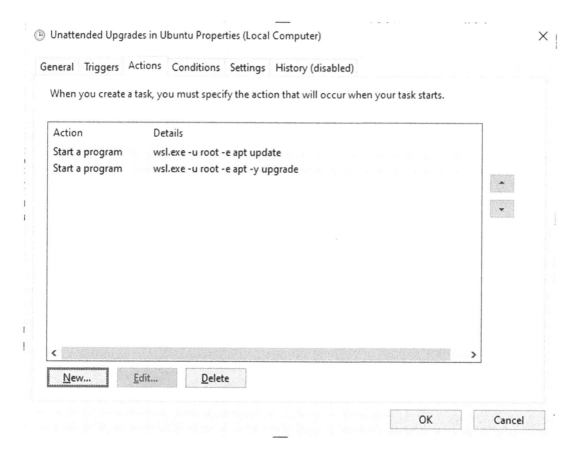

Figure 7-33. *Our two actions in our task, checking for updates and then applying available upgrades*

By running the apt update action first, we check for available package updates, and then we run the apt upgrade action to apply those available upgrades.

Click "OK," and you are done.

You can now find the task we created in Task Scheduler under "Active Tasks."

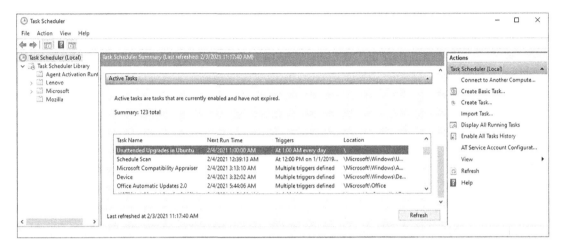

Figure 7-34. *Locating the task under Active Tasks in Task Scheduler*

To test the task we just created, double-click the task, and then click "Run" under "Selected Item" on the right (Figure 7-35).

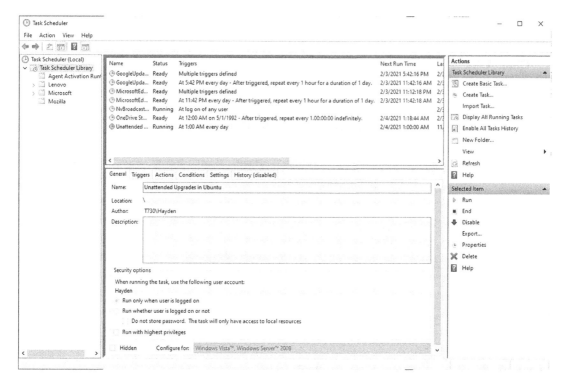

Figure 7-35. *Opening and, if necessary, editing the task, by double-clicking it in Active Tasks. We can also run the task by clicking Run under Selected Item on the right-hand side*

Boot Command

In Windows 10 builds 21286 or higher, it is now possible to manually enable startup commands in your WSL distro in /etc/wsl.conf.

These commands are executed as root. This can function as a minimal init system when launching WSL as a terminal.

It will not start services automatically in the background, like a scheduled Windows Service, or run as a scheduled task like with Task Scheduler, but only when opening a WSL distro in a terminal. However, it may fit your needs if you simply need a service launched that is more complicated than you would fit in a .bashrc file.

For more on this option, see Chapter 5, "Configuring WSL Distros," where options for /etc/wsl.conf are discussed in detail.

## CHAPTER 8

Going Further with WSL 2

Now that we have set up graphical user applications and started our own services at launch, we are ready to go a bit deeper into the things we can do with WSL, specifically WSL 2.

These steps require some familiarity with Linux in general, but if these are new to you, we will do our best to tell you what you need to know to make them work on WSL.

Running systemd

systemd is a lot of things. At its core, it is a set of tools between the kernel and your applications on Linux, to handle all the messy stuff in the middle. systemd is most known for its init system, which starts and stops background services on Linux. It replaces legacy init systems such as Upstart and SysVinit. When a traditional Linux distro boots, systemd figures out the services you need to be started and in what order so that you land on a working desktop or server.

systemd has many modular components, and not all Linux distros make use of all the available components. One of my favorite components is systemd-nspawn, which is a replacement for the traditional chroot and in my experience handles cross-platform containers better than some of the other options.

Many applications can still run without systemd, and there are several distributions of Linux that do not rely on systemd, such as Devuan, which still uses SysVinit or replacements such as OpenRC.

Systemd is comparable in some ways to the Solaris Service Management Facility or SMF. systemd is a relatively new development in the world of Linux, becoming standard in Ubuntu in 2015, but it has since been widely adopted and become a common dependency by some advanced Linux applications.

The future of mainstream Linux is going to be based on systemd at least until a future replacement comes along.

© Hayden Barnes 2021
H. Barnes, *Pro Windows Subsystem for Linux (WSL)*, https://doi.org/10.1007/978-1-4842-6873-5_8

Currently, WSL does not support systemd. WSL has its own simplified init process that allows environmental variable interoperability and mounts your Windows drives within the WSL environment at /mnt/c. It also enables file sharing along with some other environmental housekeeping. If you have a dependency on systemd, you will need to start it manually. One problem you may face here is that systemd cannot run as the primary Linux process known as PID 1, which is where many applications that rely on systemd expect to find it.

Instead, you will need to start systemd manually and then spawn a new environment in which systemd will operate as PID 1. This can be accomplished in a couple of different ways, as with everything in Linux. There are a handful of projects, listed as follows, that handle this for you as of this writing:

- one-script-wsl-systemd, `https://github.com/diddledan/one-script-wsl2-systemd`

- Genie, `https://github.com/arkane-systems/genie`

- Subsystemctl, `https://github.com/sorah/subsystemctl`

A Simple Approach to systemd

To enable systemd (Figure 8-1) in your active terminal, without using one of the preceding projects, we will start a new process namespace with systemd running as PID 1 and then switch the terminal session into that namespace.

First, we install the daemonize utility:

```
sudo apt -y install daemonize
```

Then, we use daemonize and unshare to set up a process namespace, calling systemd to run inside that specific namespace:

```
sudo daemonize unshare --fork --pid --mount-proc /lib/systemd/systemd &
```

Next, we get the process ID of the systemd process from outside the process namespace so that we can enter the namespace correctly:

```
SYSTEMD_PID="$(ps -eo pid=,args= | awk '$2=="/lib/systemd/systemd" {print $1}')"
```

Finally, we move our user session into the process namespace with nsenter, so that we can control system and systemd will appear as PID1:

```
sudo /usr/bin/nsenter --all --target "$SYSTEMD_PID" -- su - "$USER"
```

```
hayden@T440:~$ sudo /usr/bin/daemonize /usr/bin/unshare --fork --pid --mount-proc /lib/systemd/systemd
hayden@T440:~$ SYSTEMD_PID="$(ps -eo pid=,args= | awk '$2=="/lib/systemd/systemd" {print $1}')"
hayden@T440:~$ echo $SYSTEMD_PID
409
hayden@T440:~$ sudo /usr/bin/nsenter --all --target "$SYSTEMD_PID" -- su - "$USER"
[sudo] password for hayden:
Welcome to Ubuntu 20.04.1 LTS (GNU/Linux 5.4.72-microsoft-standard-WSL2 x86_64)

 * Documentation:  https://help.ubuntu.com
 * Management:     https://landscape.canonical.com
 * Support:        https://ubuntu.com/advantage

  System information as of Fri Feb 12 15:17:50 GMT 2021

  System load:  0.1              Processes:          28
  Usage of /:   0.6% of 250.98GB  Users logged in:    0
  Memory usage: 15%              IPv4 address for eth0: 172.17.19.98
  Swap usage:   0%


162 updates can be installed immediately.
71 of these updates are security updates.
To see these additional updates run: apt list --upgradable


This message is shown once once a day. To disable it please create the
/home/hayden/.hushlogin file.
hayden@T440:~$ ps -eo pid=,args=
    1 /lib/systemd/systemd
   44 /lib/systemd/systemd-journald
   62 /lib/systemd/systemd-udevd
   70 /lib/systemd/systemd-networkd
  254 /lib/systemd/systemd-resolved
  257 /usr/lib/accountsservice/accounts-daemon
  258 /usr/bin/dbus-daemon --system --address=systemd: --nofork --nopidfile --systemd-activation --syslog-on
  261 /usr/bin/python3 /usr/bin/networkd-dispatcher --run-startup-triggers
  262 /usr/sbin/rsyslogd -n -iNONE
  265 /lib/systemd/systemd-logind
  279 /usr/lib/policykit-1/polkitd --no-debug
  294 /usr/sbin/cron -f
  297 /usr/bin/python3 /usr/share/unattended-upgrades/unattended-upgrade-shutdown --wait-for-signal
  298 /usr/sbin/atd -f
  310 sshd: /usr/sbin/sshd -D [listener] 0 of 10-100 startups
  690 snapfuse /var/lib/snapd/snaps/snapd_8542.snap /snap/snapd/8542 -o ro,nodev,allow_other,suid
  834 /usr/lib/snapd/snapd
 1043 snapfuse /var/lib/snapd/snaps/core18_1880.snap /snap/core18/1880 -o ro,nodev,allow_other,suid
 1196 snapfuse /var/lib/snapd/snaps/lxd_16558.snap /snap/lxd/16558 -o ro,nodev,allow_other,suid
 1705 /sbin/agetty -o -p -- \u --noclear tty1 linux
 1732 su - hayden
 1734 /lib/systemd/systemd --user
 1735 (sd-pam)
 1740 -bash
 1800 ps -eo pid=,args=
hayden@T440:~$
```

Figure 8-1. *Creating and entering a process namespace running systemd*

Building Your Own Kernel for WSL 2

Microsoft provides a Linux kernel optimized for WSL 2. This optimized kernel contains patches for the WSL 2 environment including device support and memory management. You can use any other kernel from third parties, or you built yourself from upstream, but it will lack these specific WSL 2 patches.

There may be times when you would like to use a kernel feature that is not enabled by default in the WSL 2 kernel. You can either port the patches for WSL by Microsoft from their WSL 2 kernel into your own kernel or rebuild the Microsoft kernel with your needed optimizations. The latter is my recommendation unless you are familiar with handling patches between different kernels and can reconcile any differences.

One such example of a feature that I have enabled in WSL 2 kernel is acceleration for KVM guests in WSL. This requires downloading and tweaking the kernel configuration and rebuilding the kernel. It also requires Windows 10 build 20175 or higher and an Intel CPU. I will show you how it is done here. The purpose of this exercise is to get you more familiar with different methods of kernel configuration, including editing the raw configuration file and using the kernel menu configuration tool.

The Microsoft WSL 2 kernel can be found on GitHub at `https://github.com/microsoft/WSL2-Linux-Kernel/`

Let us use git in WSL to clone the WSL 2 kernel source code, with a depth of 1, a "shallow clone" because we do not need the entire commit history for the Linux kernel for our purposes (Figure 8-2):

```
git clone --depth 1 https://github.com/microsoft/WSL2-Linux-Kernel
```

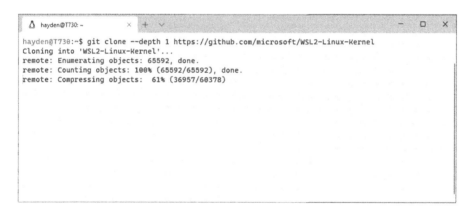

Figure 8-2. *Cloning the Microsoft WSL 2 kernel from GitHub*

Install needed dependencies for building our kernel using apt (Figure 8-3):

```
sudo apt -y install build-essential libncurses-dev bison flex libssl-dev libelf-dev
```

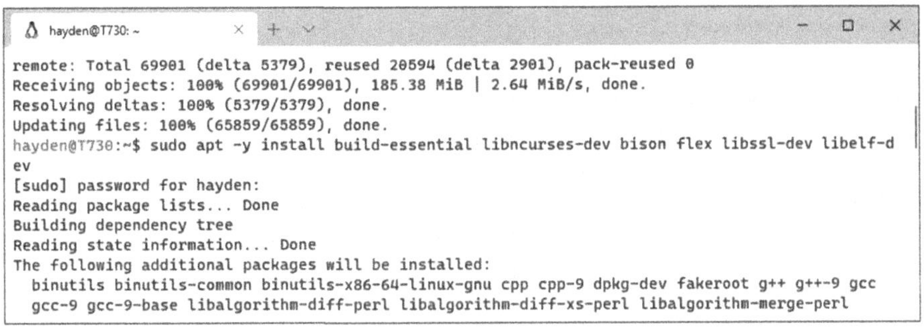

Figure 8-3. *Installing the dependencies needed for building a kernel on Ubuntu*

Change directories, dropping down into the Git project folder (Figure 8-4):

```
cd WSL2-Linux-Kernel/
```

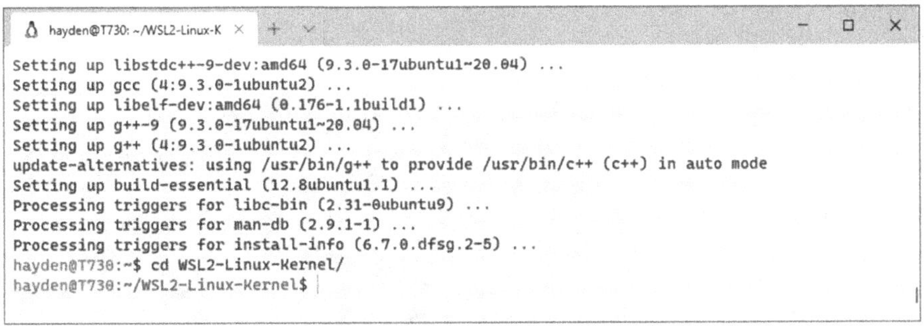

Figure 8-4. *Entering the WSL2-Linux-Kernel directory we cloned from GitHub*

We are then going to start from Microsoft's kernel config file as a starting point, which we will copy into the root project folder as .config (Figure 8-5):

```
cp Microsoft/config-wsl .config
```

Hint   Use the Microsoft/config-wsl-arm64 file if you are building for an ARM64 device.

```
Setting up libstdc++-9-dev:amd64 (9.3.0-17ubuntu1~20.04) ...
Setting up gcc (4:9.3.0-1ubuntu2) ...
Setting up libelf-dev:amd64 (0.176-1.1build1) ...
Setting up g++-9 (9.3.0-17ubuntu1~20.04) ...
Setting up g++ (4:9.3.0-1ubuntu2) ...
update-alternatives: using /usr/bin/g++ to provide /usr/bin/c++ (c++) in auto mode
Setting up build-essential (12.8ubuntu1.1) ...
Processing triggers for libc-bin (2.31-0ubuntu9) ...
Processing triggers for man-db (2.9.1-1) ...
Processing triggers for install-info (6.7.0.dfsg.2-5) ...
hayden@T730:~$ cd WSL2-Linux-Kernel/
hayden@T730:~/WSL2-Linux-Kernel$ cp Microsoft/config-wsl .config
hayden@T730:~/WSL2-Linux-Kernel$
```

Figure 8-5. *Copying Microsoft's default kernel config file to the root project folder as .config*

If you prefer to manually edit your kernel config file, you can now open the config file in nano, VS Code (Figure 8-6), or even Notepad and make those manual changes:

```
code .config
```

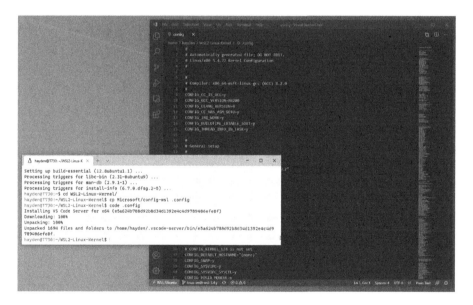

Figure 8-6. *Manually editing the kernel config file in VS Code*

The manual changes to make are

```
KVM_GUEST=y
CONFIG_KVM=y
CONFIG_KVM_INTEL=m
CONFIG_VHOST=y
```

I am somewhat "old-school" and prefer the traditional terminal menu interface for editing kernel options; this can be launched with the appropriate make command:

```
make menuconfig
```

After a bit of compilation, you will arrive at the Linux kernel configuration menu (Figure 8-7). Use the up and down arrow keys to move up and down the options, space to select between build options for each item (on, off, and module, if module is available for that option), and enter to enter a subdirectory as indicated by the ---> symbol. Use the left and right arrow keys to select functions at the bottom, including Exit to go up one level in the menu to the top menu, where Exit will then prompt you to save before exiting the configuration tool. You can also save and load different config files.

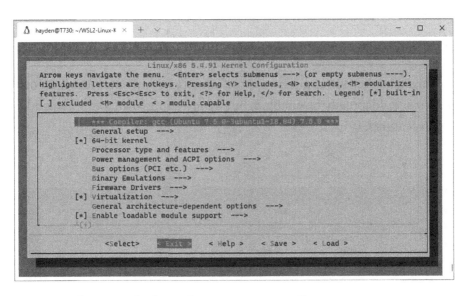

Figure 8-7. *Configuring the kernel using menuconfig*

First, navigate to the "Processor type and features" directory (Figure 8-8), using the up and down arrow keys and then the Enter key to enter the directory.

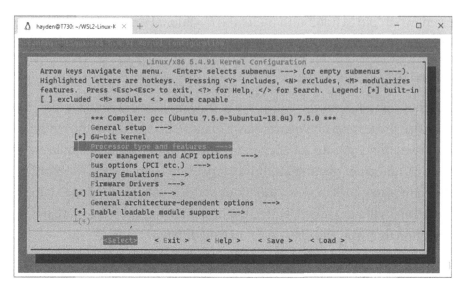

Figure 8-8. *Highlighting the Processor type and features directory*

Next, navigate to the "Linux guest support" directory, and enter the directory (Figure 8-9). It should already be enabled, but we are going to enable some additional guest support features.

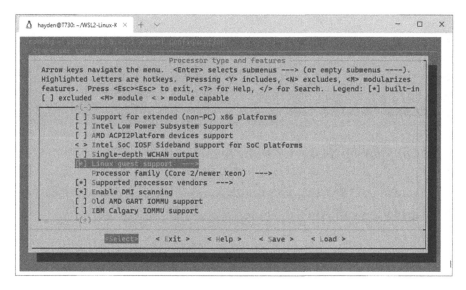

Figure 8-9. *Highlighting the Linux guest support directory*

In the Linux guest support directory, enable "KVM Guest support" by using the arrow keys to navigate to the item (Figure 8-10) and then pressing the space bar to mark the feature with a * or, alternatively, the Y key (Figure 8-11).

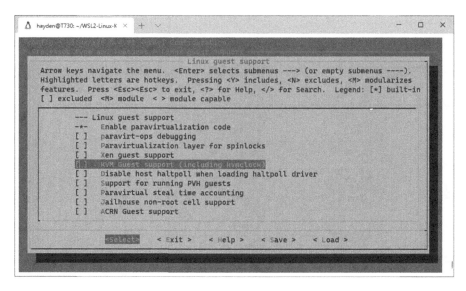

Figure 8-10.   *Selecting KVM Guest support in the Linux guest support directory*

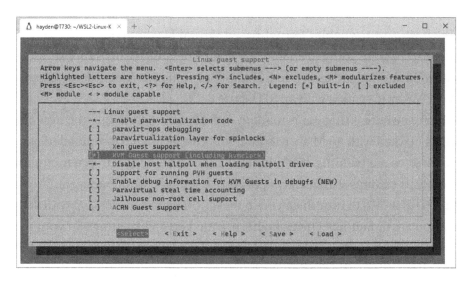

Figure 8-11.   *Enabled KVM Guest support in the Linux guest support directory*

Next, use the left and right arrow keys to select Exit, and press Enter twice to go up two levels to the top level of the configuration directory. Then scroll down to the "Virtualization" directory (Figure 8-12).

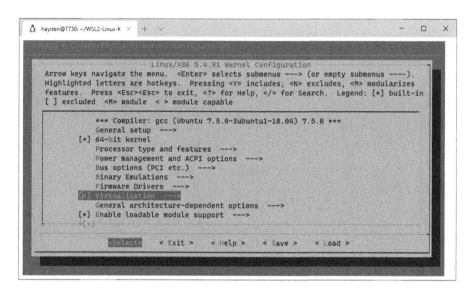

Figure 8-12. *Highlighting the Virtualization directory*

Use the Enter key to enter the "Virtualization" directory. Here, use the space bar or Y key to mark it with a * to enable "Kernel-based Virtual Machine (KVM) support." Then, for our purposes, we are going to enable "KVM for Intel processors support" as a module that we can load and unload as needed. Highlight it and press the space bar to mark it with an M or M key to mark it with an M (Figure 8-13).

The difference here is that items marked with a * will be built into the monolithic kernel. Items marked with an M are modular and can be loaded or unloaded as needed. In this exercise, we are building "KVM for Intel processors support" as a module so that we can modify its settings and quickly apply those settings by unloading and reloading the module. This is also to introduce you to these concepts and working with kernel modules if you are unfamiliar. Once you have settled on KVM settings for your use case, you may wish to return to this exercise and rebuild the kernel with this feature built in so you don't have to load the module each time you wish to work with it, or alternatively add the kernel module name to the kernel command line in .wslconfig.

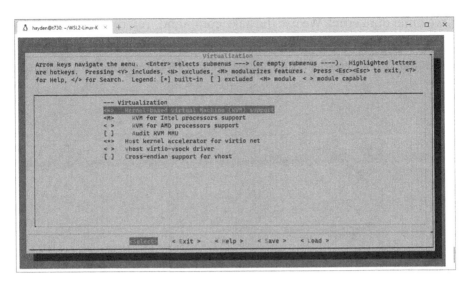

Figure 8-13. *Enabling Kernel-based Virtual Machine (KVM) support and KVM for Intel processors support as a module*

After enabling "Kernel-based Virtual Machine (KVM) support" as built-in and "KVM for Intel processors support" as a module, select Exit twice, and you will be prompted to save your new configuration (Figure 8-14). Select Yes.

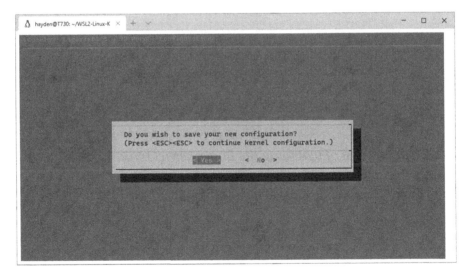

Figure 8-14. *Prompt to save your new Kernel configuration, which will be saved to .config by default*

Next, we build our kernel. We use the make command. You can dramatically speed up build time by setting the -j flag followed by the number of cores your device has (or that you have specified in .wslconfig). In this case, we have 8 cores, so we run (Figure 8-15)

```
make -j 8
```

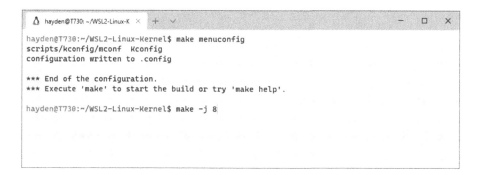

Figure 8-15. *Building our new Linux kernel using make*

Sit back and enjoy a cup of tea while your Linux kernel builds (Figure 8-16).

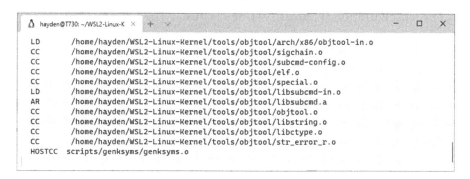

Figure 8-16. *Ah, the joys of watching the Linux kernel build*

If compilation is successful, you will be informed (Figure 8-17):

```
Kernel: arch/x86/boot/bzImage is ready
```

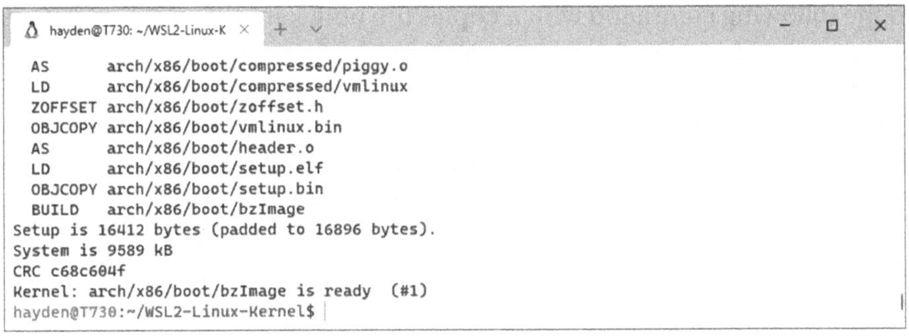

Figure 8-17. *Successful compilation of the Linux kernel*

Our monolithic kernel has been built, and it is in a subdirectory of our current directory at `arch/x86/boot/bzImage`.

But we are not done yet. Now, we must build and install those features we flagged as modules. They will be installed on our distro file system at `/lib/modules` because they are not built into the kernel. Run the make command as follows to complete building the modules, and install them in the appropriate directories (Figure 8-18):

```
sudo make modules_install
```

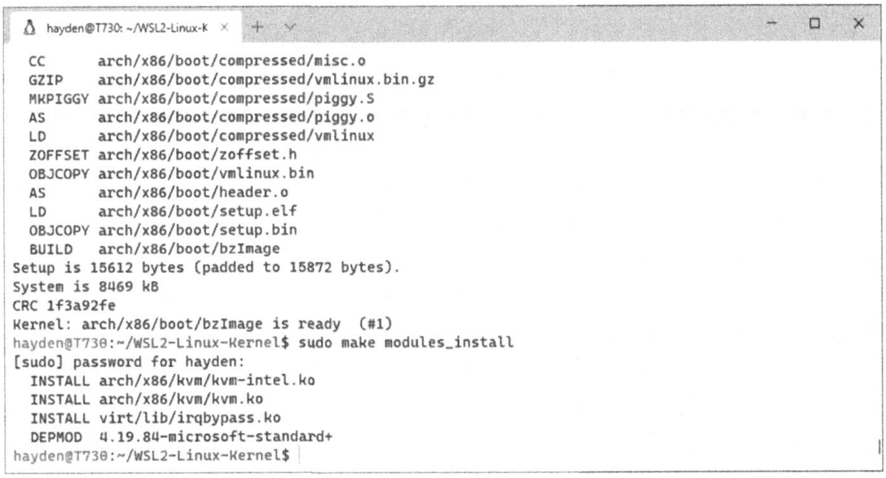

Figure 8-18. *Successful compilation and installation of Linux kernel modules*

Now, with our modules installed on `/lib/modules`, we return to our monolithic kernel file, `arch/x86/boot/bzImage`. We need to move it to our Windows file system to make it accessible to WSL 2. I recommend your Windows user home directory. We can do this in the following command which copies the built kernel there (Figure 8-19). wslvar, part of wslutilities, will retrieve the %USERPROFILE% environment variable from Windows which we then convert to Linux format with wslpath:

```
cp arch/x86/boot/bzImage $(wslpath $(wslvar USERPROFILE))
```

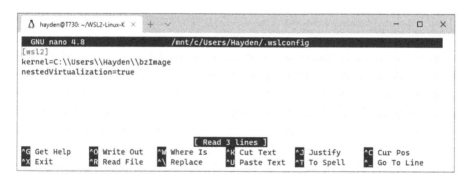

Figure 8-19. *Copying our compiled Linux kernel to our Windows user home folder*

Next, we need to configure WSL 2 to use our custom kernel. We do this with .wslconfig in our Windows user home directory. Open .wslconfig as follows (Figure 8-20):

```
nano $(wslpath $(wslvar USERPROFILE))/.wslconfig
```

Figure 8-20. *Configuring .wslconfig to use our custom Linux kernel and enable nested virtualization*

If the file does not yet exist, nano will create the file for us. Copy the following to .wslconfig, adjusting for your username in the path or the overall path if you placed your kernel somewhere besides your Windows user home directory:

```
[wsl2]
kernel=C:\\Users\\Hayden\\bzImage
nestedVirtualization=true
```

The path to our custom Linux kernel must be absolute, no variables are permitted here, and backslashes require double backslashes. Beginning in Windows 10 build 20175, nested virtualization is enabled by default, so if you are on a more recent build, this may be omitted. I still leave it on for good measure.

Next, we can set options for our "KVM for Intel processors support" module, referred to as a kvm-intel. Open/create /etc/modprobe.d/kvm-nested.conf as follows (Figure 8-21):

```
sudo nano /etc/modprobe.d/kvm-nested.conf
```

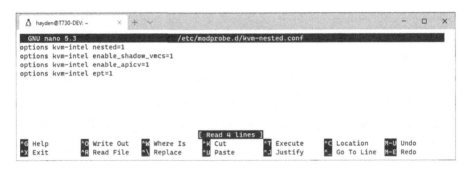

Figure 8-21. *Editing nested KVM options in /etc/modprobe.d/kvm-nested.conf*

Copy the following to /etc/modprobe.d/kvm-nested.conf, enabling nested virtualization and advanced options to optimize the speed of nested virtual machines:

```
options kvm-intel nested=1
options kvm-intel enable_shadow_vmcs=1
options kvm-intel enable_apicv=1
options kvm-intel ept=1
```

Save to /etc/modprobe.d/kvm-nested.conf, and exit.

Next, we are going to reboot our WSL environment with our new kernel. Open a new PowerShell tab, and shut down WSL as follows (Figure 8-22):

```
wsl.exe --shutdown
```

Figure 8-22. *Shutting down WSL*

If you return to your Ubuntu tab, you should see that the process has exited (Figure 8-23).

```
   GZIP    arch/x86/boot/compressed/vmlinux.bin.gz
   MKPIGGY arch/x86/boot/compressed/piggy.S
   AS      arch/x86/boot/compressed/piggy.o
   LD      arch/x86/boot/compressed/vmlinux
   ZOFFSET arch/x86/boot/zoffset.h
   OBJCOPY arch/x86/boot/vmlinux.bin
   AS      arch/x86/boot/header.o
   LD      arch/x86/boot/setup.elf
   OBJCOPY arch/x86/boot/setup.bin
   BUILD   arch/x86/boot/bzImage
Setup is 15932 bytes (padded to 16384 bytes).
System is 8685 kB
CRC d0a426c9
Kernel: arch/x86/boot/bzImage is ready  (#1)
hayden@T730-DEV:~/WSL2-Linux-Kernel$ cp arch/x86/boot/bzImage $(wslpath $(wslvar USERPROFILE))
hayden@T730-DEV:~/WSL2-Linux-Kernel$ nano $(wslpath $(wslvar USERPROFILE))/.wslconfig
hayden@T730-DEV:~/WSL2-Linux-Kernel$ sudo nano /etc/modprobe.d/kvm-nested.conf
[sudo] password for hayden:
hayden@T730-DEV:~/WSL2-Linux-Kernel$
[process exited with code 1]
```

Figure 8-23. *Confirming that WSL has been shut down*

Close that tab, and reopen a new Windows Terminal tab for our distro. This will effectively "reboot" our WSL environment, with the new kernel loaded.

Once "booted," you can confirm that you are running a new kernel by running uname and checking the build date and time, which should show the current date and the time a few minutes ago you finished building the kernel (Figure 8-24):

```
uname -ar
```

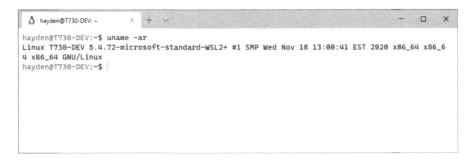

Figure 8-24. *Confirming you are running your custom kernel with uname*

Next, install a tool called kvm-ok to confirm availability of nested KVM functionality we built into the kernel, as follows:

```
sudo apt -y install cpu-checker
```

Then run kvm-ok as follows (Figure 8-25):

```
kvm-ok
```

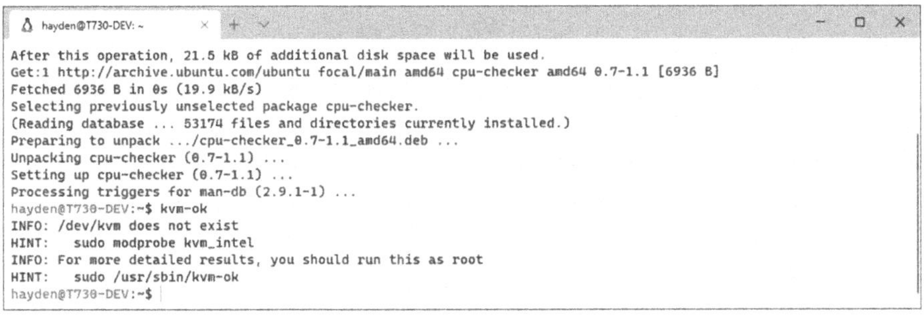

Figure 8-25. *Running kvm-ok before loading the kvm_intel kernel module results in an error message*

This will report that KVM support is not available, that /dev/kvm does not exist. We need one more step, to load the "KVM for Intel processors support" feature we built as a module, also known as kvm_intel, which we do as follows (Figure 8-26):

```
sudo modprobe kvm_intel
```

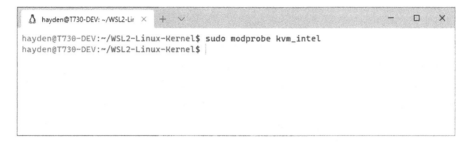

Figure 8-26. *Loading the kvm_intel kernel module. An uneventful affair when successful*

Hint   If you get the error message "Module kvm_intel not found in directory /lib/modules/4.19.84-microsoft-standard+", you forgot the preceding `sudo make modules_install` step.

Now rerun kvm-ok (Figure 8-27):

```
kvm-ok
```

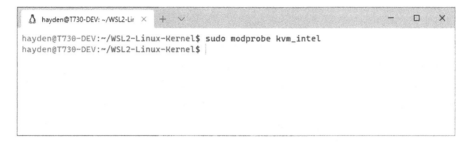

Figure 8-27. *Running kvm-ok after loading the kvm_intel kernel module results in a message /dev/kvm exists*

If you receive the message "KVM acceleration can be used," we have successfully loaded the kernel module, and KVM is now working.

We can then confirm KVM nested virtualization support by checking one of the parameters provided directly by the kvm_intel module as follows (Figure 8-28):

```
cat /sys/module/kvm_intel/parameters/nested
```

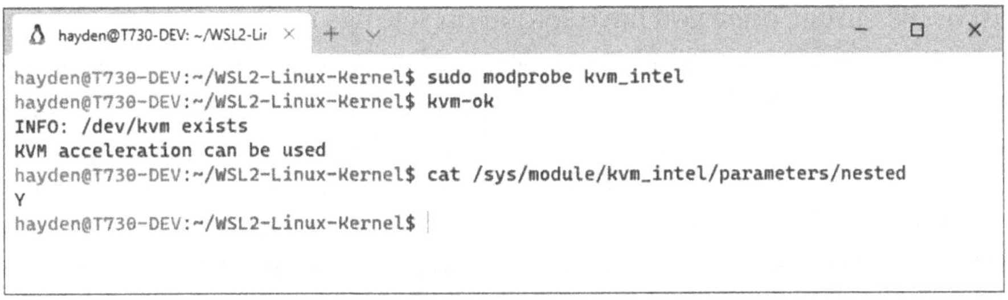

Figure 8-28. *Confirming nested virtualization support in the kvm_intel kernel module*

The final step in configuring KVM for use is making /dev/kvm accessible by setting proper access permissions for our user, which we set as follows (Figure 8-29):

```
sudo chmod 666 /dev/kvm
```

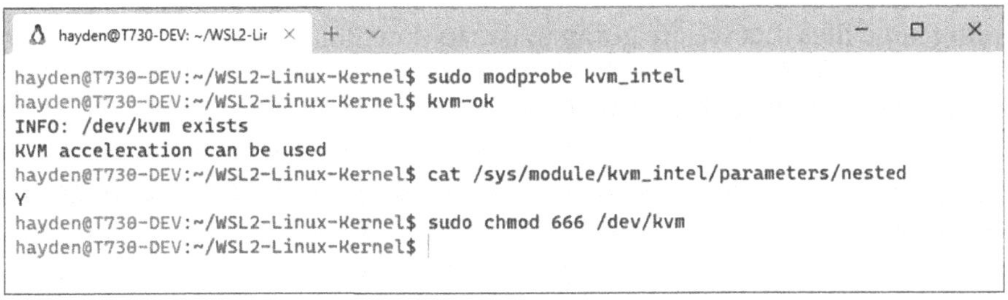

Figure 8-29. *Setting access permissions for /dev/kvm*

Because we built it as a module, you will need to manually load kvm_intel on each launch of WSL you intend to utilize KVM.

As you experiment with running different guest operating systems, you may need to edit the settings in /etc/modprobe.d/kvm-nested.conf.

The way to do this is to unload kvm_intel with

```
sudo modprobe -r kvm_intel
```

Then make the appropriate edits to /etc/modprobe.d/kvm-nested.conf and finally reload the kvm_intel module as before:

```
sudo modprobe kvm_intel
```

As discussed earlier, once you have settled on settings for kvm-nested.conf, you might then choose to rebuild your kernel with kvm_intel built-in, not as a module. This avoids the need to manually load the module on each launch of WSL. You could also add sudo modprobe kvm_intel as a [boot] command in Windows 10 builds 21286+.

Installing a Guest Operating System on KVM on WSL

We have learned how to build a custom kernel, load modules, apply custom kernel module settings, and install a custom kernel in WSL 2; what can we do with this? With nested KVM support, we can use tools like minikube that depend on KVM to run Kubernetes containers. We can also run other entire operating systems directly using QEMU, not just Linux guests but also macOS, Arca Noae, OpenIndiana, or Haiku.

Let us run through an example with Kubuntu, the KDE flavor of Ubuntu. First, install qemu-kvm, the set of tools for running guest operating systems, as well as aria2, a tool for downloading large files that we are going to use to download an ISO to boot (Figure 8-30):

```
sudo apt -y install qemu-kvm aria2
```

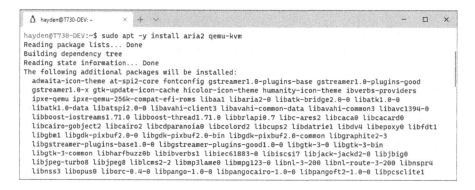

Figure 8-30. *Installing qemu-kvm for booting guest operating systems with KVM and aria2 for downloading large files, like guest operating system install ISOs*

QEMU will display a window via X, so you need to have a third-party X server configured as detailed in Chapter "Customizing WSL" or have official GUI app support in WSL when it lands. As a quick reminder, you can point your WSL instance at your running X server on Windows with

```
export DISPLAY=$(cat /etc/resolv.conf | grep nameserver | awk '{print $2;}'):0.0
```

Next, let's grab a bootable ISO (cd-rom image) of a guest operating system. ISOs tend to be large, which is why I recommend using aria2 with download multithreading vs. basic wget or curl. Download the Kubuntu install ISO torrent file with aria2 as follows (Figure 8-31):

```
aria2c -x 10 --seed-time=0 http://cdimage.ubuntu.com/kubuntu/
releases/20.04/release/kubuntu-20.04.2-desktop-amd64.iso.torrent
```

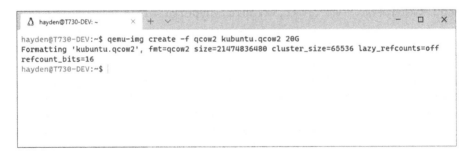

Figure 8-31. *Downloading the Kubuntu install ISO with aria2*

Next, we need to create a virtual hard drive to install Kubuntu to in QEMU, not unlike the VHDX our WSL 2 environment is stored in. To create a virtual hard drive for Kubuntu, run qemu-img create as follows creating a 20 G drive in qcow2 format, the native virtual drive format for QEMU (Figure 8-32):

```
qemu-img create -f qcow2 kubuntu.qcow2 20G
```

```
hayden@T730-DEV:~$ qemu-img create -f qcow2 kubuntu.qcow2 20G
Formatting 'kubuntu.qcow2', fmt=qcow2 size=21474836480 cluster_size=65536 lazy_refcounts=off
refcount_bits=16
hayden@T730-DEV:~$
```

Figure 8-32. *Creating a virtual hard drive for Kubuntu with qemu-img create*

Protip: qemu-img can convert images between QCOW used by QEMU, VHDX used by Hyper-V, and VMDK used by VirtualBox.

Next, we will boot Kubuntu (Figure 8-33). Do the following:

- Mount kubuntu.qcow2 as a virtual hard drive to install to.

- Mount the Kubuntu ISO as a read-only CD-ROM file.

- Enable network access with a virtual network interface card (NIC).

- Assign 5172 MB of RAM.

- Enable a virtual VGA port, which will be forwarded to our screen via an X window.

- Enable KVM acceleration.

- Assign 4 virtual CPU cores.

- Enable advanced CPU options to take advantage of the nested virtualization settings we enabled in kvm_intel discussed earlier.

Run as follows:

```
qemu-system-x86_64 \
      -drive file=kubuntu.qcow2,format=qcow2 \
      -drive file=kubuntu-20.04.2-desktop-amd64.iso,media=cdrom,readonly \
      -net nic -net user \
      -m 5172 \
      -vga qxl \
      --enable-kvm \
      -smp 4 \
      -cpu kvm64,+vmx,+vme,+msr,+x2apic,+hypervisor
```

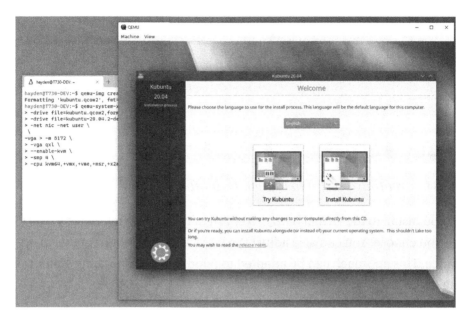

Figure 8-33. *Kubuntu install screen running in QEMU*

Provided everything was successful, you should now see a window with the Kubuntu installer window. You can now try the live image or install to the virtual hard drive we created. You can store this QEMU command in a shell script (Figure 8-34), for example:

```
nano start_kubuntu.sh
```

Copy the following:

```
#!/bin/bash
qemu-system-x86_64 \
    -drive file=kubuntu.qcow2,format=qcow2 \
    -net nic -net user \
    -m 5172 \
    -vga qxl \
    --enable-kvm \
    -smp 4 \
    -cpu kvm64,+vmx,+vme,+msr,+x2apic,+hypervisor
```

Exit, save, and do not forget to make it executable:

```
sudo chmod +x start_kubuntu.sh
```

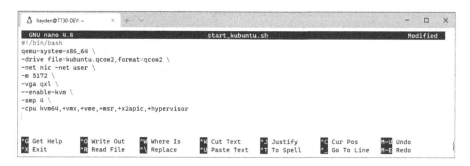

Figure 8-34. *Creating a script to launch Kubuntu*

Once you install to the virtual hard drive, you may omit the reference to the ISO and delete it if you choose. You can also adjust the RAM and core requirements to optimize performance. This approach can be adapted to booting other operating systems from their installer ISOs.

WSL 2 Advanced Networking

WSL 1 networking was relatively basic. Because WSL 1 was a system call translation layer, the WSL environment shared the same networking stack with the Windows environment. In other words, localhost was localhost.

In WSL 2, networking is a bit more complicated. The WSL 2 network has its own IP address on a DHCP NAT subnet.

This can introduce some complications. Once such complication is with X, addressed in the previous chapter setting up X on WSL 2. The second complication is accessing services running in WSL 2 from outside your device. This also requires opening a port in Windows Firewall and then forwarding the port to the WSL 2 environment IP.

In this example, we will set up an apache web server and then enable access from our LAN.

First, install apache (Figure 8-35):

```
sudo apt -y install apache2
```

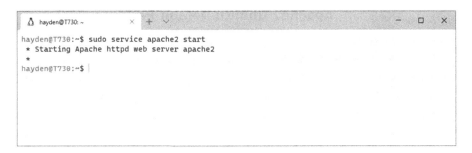

Figure 8-35. *Installing the Apache web server*

Once installed, we now start the web server using the service command as follows (Figure 8-36):

```
sudo service apache2 start
```

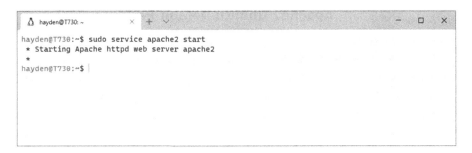

Figure 8-36. *Starting Apache using the service command*

We can now use wslview, part of wslutilities bundled in several WSL distros and available for others, to open the default landing page for Apache running on localhost (Figure 8-37):

```
wslview http://localhost
```

Figure 8-37. *Opening the default landing page for Apache using wslview*

The default landing page for Apache should be visible on localhost (Figure 8-38), but it is only accessible on localhost. How do we make it accessible to other devices on our local area network (LAN)?

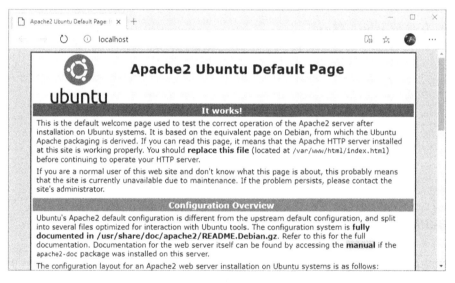

Figure 8-38. *The default landing page for Apache web server running on localhost*

First, we open PowerShell and retrieve the IP address of our Windows device's Ethernet or Wi-Fi connection. These IP addresses are visible and accessible to other devices on the LAN (Figure 8-39):

```
Get-NetIPAddress
```

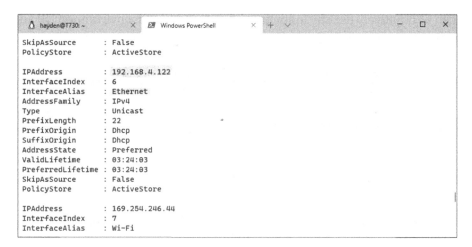

Figure 8-39. *Identifying the IP address of our Windows device using* `Get-NetIPAddress`

Next, we identify the virtual IP address that has been assigned to our WSL environment with `ip a` (Figure 8-40), specifically the eth0 device. Unlike the Windows device IP address, our WSL IP address is not accessible by default to other devices on the LAN. We need to set up forwarding to make the service running in WSL accessible to the LAN via the Windows IP address. Then we need to open the proper ports in the Windows firewall.

```
ip a
```

```
hayden@T730:~$ ip a
1: lo: <LOOPBACK,UP,LOWER_UP> mtu 65536 qdisc noqueue state UNKNOWN group default qlen 1000
    link/loopback 00:00:00:00:00:00 brd 00:00:00:00:00:00
    inet 127.0.0.1/8 scope host lo
       valid_lft forever preferred_lft forever
    inet6 ::1/128 scope host
       valid_lft forever preferred_lft forever
2: bond0: <BROADCAST,MULTICAST,MASTER> mtu 1500 qdisc noop state DOWN group default qlen 1000
    link/ether ee:1f:8f:fd:7a:dc brd ff:ff:ff:ff:ff:ff
3: dummy0: <BROADCAST,NOARP> mtu 1500 qdisc noop state DOWN group default qlen 1000
    link/ether 12:c6:4b:30:f1:e0 brd ff:ff:ff:ff:ff:ff
4: eth0: <BROADCAST,MULTICAST,UP,LOWER_UP> mtu 1500 qdisc mq state UP group default qlen 1000
    link/ether 00:15:5d:cf:7f:84 brd ff:ff:ff:ff:ff:ff
    inet 172.28.202.134/20 brd 172.28.207.255 scope global eth0
       valid_lft forever preferred_lft forever
    inet6 fe80::215:5dff:fecf:7f84/64 scope link
       valid_lft forever preferred_lft forever
5: sit0@NONE: <NOARP> mtu 1480 qdisc noop state DOWN group default qlen 1000
    link/sit 0.0.0.0 brd 0.0.0.0
hayden@T730:~$
```

Figure 8-40. *Identifying the virtual IP address assigned to our WSL environment* `ip a`

You can alternatively use the following to locate your WSL environment IP address (Figure 8-41):

```
ip addr show eth0 | awk -F'[ /]+' '$2=="inet" {print $3}'
```

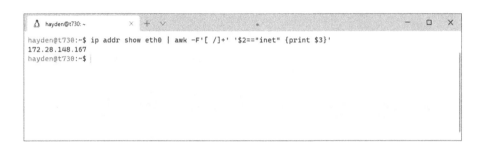

Figure 8-41. *Identifying the virtual IP address assigned to our WSL environment by parsing the output of* ip addr

If you were to attempt to access Apache from another device on the LAN at either of these IP addresses at this point, the connection would time out (Figure 8-42). The connection is not being forwarded from Windows into the WSL environment, and it is also being blocked by the Windows Firewall.

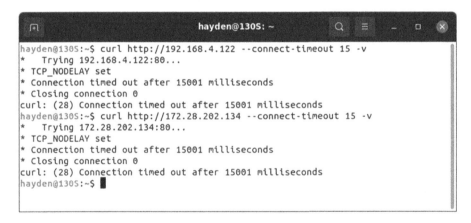

Figure 8-42. *Attempting to connect to either IP address results in a connection timeout*

Open PowerShell as Administrator on Windows, and we will create a forwarding port proxy that links our Windows IP address to our WSL environment IP address on port 80, the port used by Apache as follows (Figure 8-43):

```
netsh interface portproxy add v4tov4 listenaddress=192.168.4.122
listenport=80 connectaddress=172.28.202.134 connectport=80
```

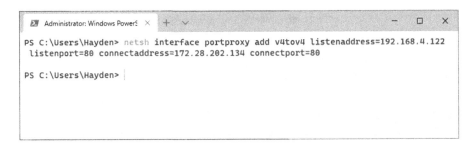

Figure 8-43. *Creating a port proxy on Windows to forward incoming traffic to our Windows IP address on port 80 to our WSL environment IP address on port 80*

While still in PowerShell as Administrator, we will open a port in our Windows Firewall to allow inbound connections on port 80 as follows (Figure 8-44):

```
netsh advfirewall firewall add rule name="Open Port 80 for WSL2" dir=in
action=allow protocol=TCP localport=80
```

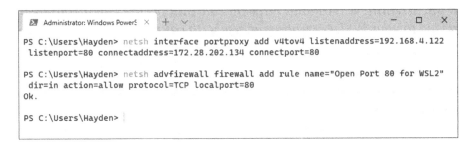

Figure 8-44. *Creating a Windows Firewall rule that allows inbound traffic on port 80 on our Windows device*

Alternatively, we can create a Windows Firewall rule that allows all incoming traffic to traverse to the virtual Ethernet adapter for WSL, but caution should be used here as this opens your WSL environment completely to the network, without the protection of the Windows Firewall. This is done as follows (Figure 8-45):

```
New-NetFirewallRule -DisplayName "WSL" -Direction Inbound  -InterfaceAlias
"vEthernet (WSL)"  -Action Allow -EdgeTraversalPolicy Allow
```

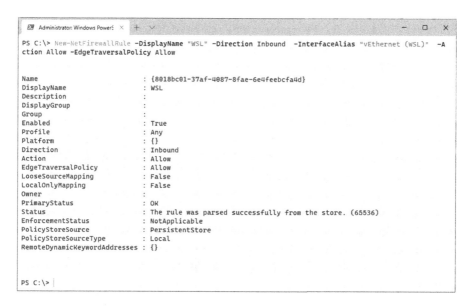

Figure 8-45.   *Creating a Windows Firewall rule that permits all incoming traffic to be forwarded to your WSL environment, use with caution*

But once we have forwarded our port and opened a port in our firewall, the Apache service now becomes accessible via our Windows IP address to other devices on our LAN (Figure 8-46).

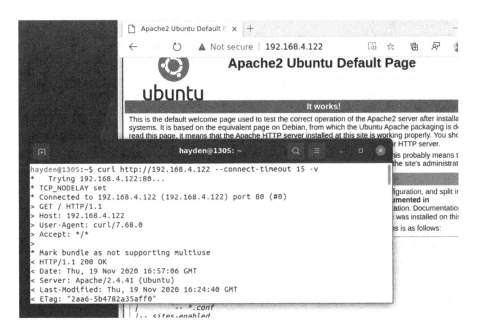

Figure 8-46. *Accessing Apache running on WSL from another device on our land after successfully configuring port forwarding and opening a port in our firewall*

One important caveat is that the IP address of your WSL environment changes every time it is launched, so on reboot, you will need to reconfigure port forwarding each time, to forward to the proper port. You can automate this with PowerShell or bash commands in your .bashrc file or using the new [boot] command= option in Windows 10 builds 21286 or higher.

For example, the following script may be called by your [boot] command= option in Windows 10 builds 21286 or later, or your .bashrc file, to configure a port forward from your physical network to your WSL instance. You can discover your network adapter's interface index by executing `Get-NetIPAddress -AddressFamily IPv4` in PowerShell (Figure 8-47).

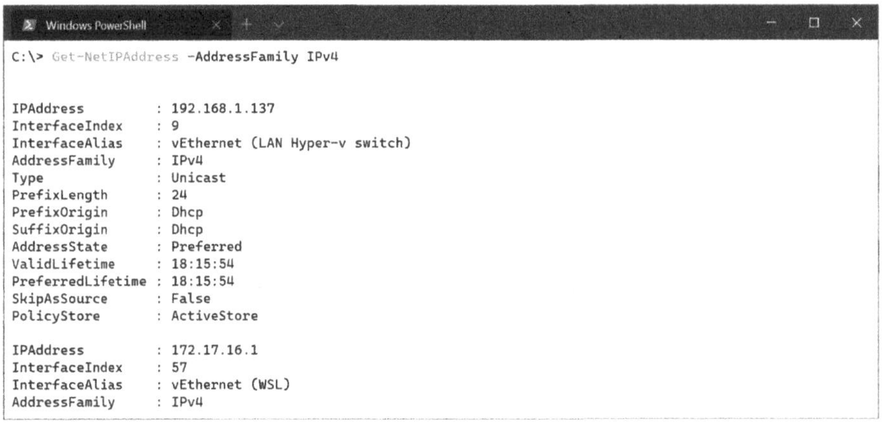

```
Windows PowerShell                                              —  □  ×

C:\> Get-NetIPAddress -AddressFamily IPv4

IPAddress         : 192.168.1.137
InterfaceIndex    : 9
InterfaceAlias    : vEthernet (LAN Hyper-v switch)
AddressFamily     : IPv4
Type              : Unicast
PrefixLength      : 24
PrefixOrigin      : Dhcp
SuffixOrigin      : Dhcp
AddressState      : Preferred
ValidLifetime     : 18:15:54
PreferredLifetime : 18:15:54
SkipAsSource      : False
PolicyStore       : ActiveStore

IPAddress         : 172.17.16.1
InterfaceIndex    : 57
InterfaceAlias    : vEthernet (WSL)
AddressFamily     : IPv4
```

Figure 8-47. *Getting the InterfaceIndex for my Windows PC's main network interface card - here it is index number 9*

```bash
#!/bin/bash

# Configuration
INTERFACE_IDX=9 # Your Windows network device's InterfaceIndex from
Get-NetIPAddress in PowerShell
PORT=80

# The script
IPADDRESS="$(ip addr show eth0 | awk -F'[ /]+' '$2=="inet" {print $3}')"

powershell.exe -Command "
\$WINIPADDR=Get-NetIPAddress -AddressFamily ipv4 -InterfaceIndex
$INTERFACE_IDX | Select-Object -ExpandProperty IPAddress

Start-Process -Verb RunAs -FilePath netsh.exe -ArgumentList @
('interface', 'portproxy', 'add', 'v4tov4', \"listenaddress=\$WINIPADDR\",
'listenport=$PORT', 'connectaddress=$IPADDRESS', 'connectport=$PORT')"
```

CHAPTER 9

Maximizing Windows Interoperability

When working with WSL, you may find you need to use utilities or files from Windows in your workflow or vice versa. Thankfully, there are several ways that you can blur the barrier between your WSL distro and Windows allowing a much more productive environment than Windows, or a Linux Distro, would provide on their own.

wslpath

wslpath is a tool built into WSL that allows for simple conversion of paths between WSL and their Windows equivalents and vice versa (Figure 9-1):

```
wslpath C:\\Users\\Hayden returns /mnt/c/Users/Hayden
wslpath -w /mnt/c/Users/Hayden returns C:\Users\Hayden
```

wslpath is useful when scripting tasks in Windows from WSL, without having to parse and rearrange the characters, particularly all those \ and /s that must be escaped in sed and grep. wslpath is particularly powerful when paired with wslenv, detailed as follows.

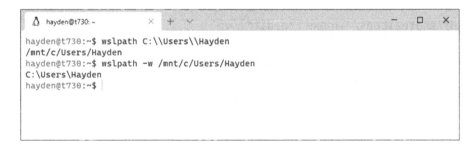

Figure 9-1. *Using* wslpath *to convert paths between WSL and Windows equivalents*

© Hayden Barnes 2021
H. Barnes, *Pro Windows Subsystem for Linux (WSL)*, https://doi.org/10.1007/978-1-4842-6873-5_9

wslutilities

wslutilities are a collection of tools by Patrick Wu that have been adopted by several WSL distros published on the Microsoft Store. Ubuntu and Pengwin include wslutilities by default. wslutilities are available for several other distros, including SUSE, Alpine, Debian, CentOS, and openSUSE. wslutilities include the following tools:

wslusc allows you to create a shortcut to Linux applications on the Windows desktop. For example, install the GNOME text editor `gedit` (Figure 9-2):

```
sudo apt -y install gedit
```

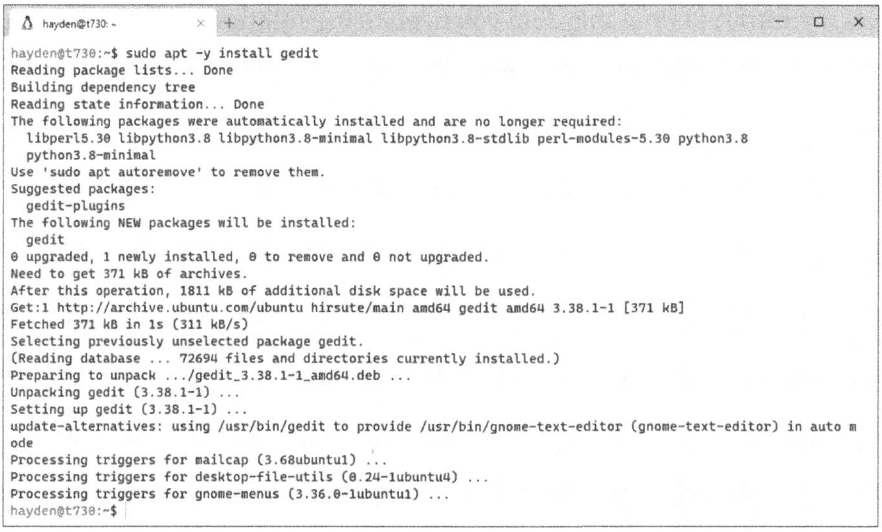

```
hayden@t730:~$ sudo apt -y install gedit
Reading package lists... Done
Building dependency tree
Reading state information... Done
The following packages were automatically installed and are no longer required:
  libperl5.30 libpython3.8 libpython3.8-minimal libpython3.8-stdlib perl-modules-5.30 python3.8
  python3.8-minimal
Use 'sudo apt autoremove' to remove them.
Suggested packages:
  gedit-plugins
The following NEW packages will be installed:
  gedit
0 upgraded, 1 newly installed, 0 to remove and 0 not upgraded.
Need to get 371 kB of archives.
After this operation, 1811 kB of additional disk space will be used.
Get:1 http://archive.ubuntu.com/ubuntu hirsute/main amd64 gedit amd64 3.38.1-1 [371 kB]
Fetched 371 kB in 1s (311 kB/s)
Selecting previously unselected package gedit.
(Reading database ... 72694 files and directories currently installed.)
Preparing to unpack .../gedit_3.38.1-1_amd64.deb ...
Unpacking gedit (3.38.1-1) ...
Setting up gedit (3.38.1-1) ...
update-alternatives: using /usr/bin/gedit to provide /usr/bin/gnome-text-editor (gnome-text-editor) in auto m
ode
Processing triggers for mailcap (3.68ubuntu1) ...
Processing triggers for desktop-file-utils (0.24-1ubuntu4) ...
Processing triggers for gnome-menus (3.36.0-1ubuntu1) ...
hayden@t730:~$
```

Figure 9-2. *Installing* `gedit`

Next, locate an acceptable icon for `gedit` by searching `/usr/share/icons` for icons containing the name gedit (Figure 9-3):

```
find /usr/share/icons/ -name "*gedit*.svg"
```

```
hayden@t730: ~                    ×    +  ∨                              —   □   ×

hayden@t730:~$ find /usr/share/icons/ -name "*gedit*.svg"
/usr/share/icons/Humanity/apps/48/gedit-icon.svg
/usr/share/icons/Humanity/apps/48/gedit-logo.svg
/usr/share/icons/Humanity/apps/24/gedit-icon.svg
/usr/share/icons/Humanity/apps/24/gedit-logo.svg
/usr/share/icons/Humanity/apps/16/gedit-icon.svg
/usr/share/icons/Humanity/apps/16/gedit-logo.svg
/usr/share/icons/Humanity/apps/32/gedit-icon.svg
/usr/share/icons/Humanity/apps/32/gedit-logo.svg
/usr/share/icons/Humanity/apps/22/gedit-icon.svg
/usr/share/icons/Humanity/apps/22/gedit-logo.svg
/usr/share/icons/hicolor/symbolic/apps/org.gnome.gedit-symbolic.svg
/usr/share/icons/hicolor/scalable/apps/org.gnome.gedit.svg
hayden@t730:~$
```

Figure 9-3. *Searching for icons for gedit in* `/usr/share/icons`

Then, run `wslusc`, specifying `gedit` is a GUI application with the -g flag; name the shortcut gedit with -n 'gedit', specifying an icon we found with -i, followed by the `gedit` command (Figure 9-4):

```
wslusc -g -n 'gedit' -i /usr/share/icons/Humanity/apps/48/gedit-icon.svg
gedit
```

Figure 9-4. *Creating a shortcut to* `gedit` *on the Windows desktop using wslusc*

And you now have a shortcut for `gedit` on your desktop (Figure 9-4). Note that GUI applications still require an X server to be running on Windows until official GUI app support lands in WSL.

wslsys provides some basic system information, useful when filing WSL-related bug reports (Figure 9-5).

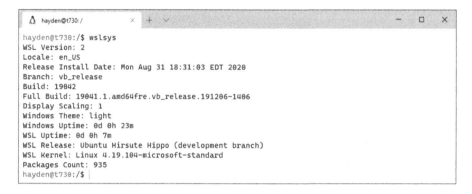

Figure 9-5. *System information provided by* `wslsys`

The output of wslsys can also be grepped for use in scripts. For example

```
wslsys | grep 'Theme' | sed 's/^.*: //'
```

will return simply "light" or "dark" for the Windows Theme.

wslfetch is like tools such as neofetch but also provides information about the host Windows 10 system, such as the Windows 10 build number (Figure 9-6).

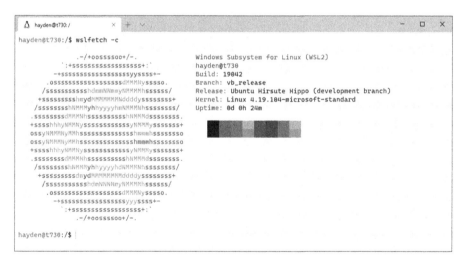

Figure 9-6. *Splash screen by* `wslfetch`

wslvar allows you to retrieve Windows environmental variables, such as %APPDATA% and %USERPROFILE%. For example, if you want to share a script that writes to a Windows user home folder, you will not want to hardcode /mnt/c/Users/ Hayden because other users' usernames and paths would be different.

You can use a combination of wslpath and $(wslvar USERPROFILE) instead to retrieve that location and then convert it to Linux path that WSL would understand, for example (Figure 9-7):

```
touch hello
cp hello $(wslpath $(wslvar USERPROFILE))
```

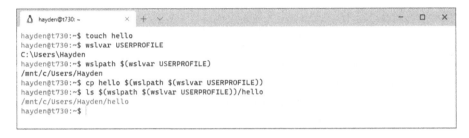

Figure 9-7. *Creating an empty file named hello and copying it to the current Windows user's home folder*

wslview registers itself as the default web browser in WSL that when run will open the corresponding URL in the default web browser in Windows. For example, the following will open the URL in Microsoft Edge, the default browser I have set on my Windows 10 (Figure 9-8):

```
wslview http://boxofcables.dev
```

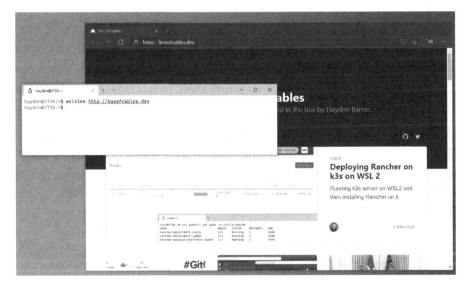

Figure 9-8. *Using wslview to open web URLs in the default web browser in Windows*

However, wslview does not stop at URLs. You can use wslview to open any file in WSL using the default application for that file type in Windows. For example, the following will open the file in Notepad, the default editor for .txt files, on Windows 10 (Figure 9-9):

```
echo 'hello Patrick' > textfile.txt
wslview textfile.txt
```

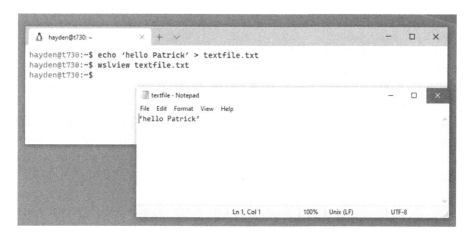

Figure 9-9. *Opening a .txt file with Notepad on Windows using* `wslview`

Redirecting Between Windows and Linux Applications

Redirection is a mechanism where you can take the output from running a command and feed it into the input for another command. This is often known as "piping" and is common to use on the command line. In a Linux shell, this is usually marked by the | character, which on most keyboard layouts is accessed with shift+\.

Another common pattern is to use the content of a file as the input for a command or write the output from a command to a file. These are usually denoted with the << and >> symbols. (Those are two < characters and two > characters, not the single guillemet characters of « and ».)

Piping

When using the pipe mechanism, commands can be created that perform complex action chains without requiring you to write a program to perform the complete process. For example, you could use `gzip` to compress a file, convert it to `base64` encoding so that it is suitable for displaying or sending in a text format, and forward the base64 text into gnupg to sign it using a "PGP" key and print the result to the terminal.

The command for the described chain of events is (Figure 9-10)

```
gzip --stdout /etc/hosts | base64 | gpg --clear-sign
```

Figure 9-10.   *Pipeline to compress a file, convert it to text, and sign it with PGP*

If you do not have a default GPG key, you can create one with

```
gpg --full-gen-key
```

If you receive the error message "`gpg: signing failed: Inappropriate ioctl for device`," then set

```
export GPG_TTY=$(tty)
```

The example shows how we take the output of the command on the left of the | character and "pipe" the output to the command on the right. Here, we use the pipe mechanism twice, where the first pipe takes the output from `gzip` and passes it into base64 and the second takes the output from the `base64` command and passes it to `gpg`. We could do this with a separate program that saves the outputs and feeds them to the inputs of the next command. We would, however, need to write that program, and the pipe mechanism is much simpler to immediately understand and can be written quickly and easily.

Piping Between Windows and WSL

With WSL on Windows, we can use the piping mechanism to redirect input and output to and from commands between Windows and WSL and vice versa. This gets powerful when you realize you can make the hop between Windows and WSL multiple times in a single pipeline.

Piping from WSL to Windows

For a simple example, we can use `clip.exe` on Windows combined with a pipe from WSL to easily put text into the Windows clipboard for use with the paste feature of your favorite programs.

```
cowsay "Hi readers!" | clip.exe
```

This gives the following in our clipboard for pasting with `Ctrl+V` (Figure 9-11):

```
 -------------
< Hi readers! >
 -------------
        \   ^__^
         \  (oo)_____
            (__)\       )\/\
                ||----w |
                ||     ||
```

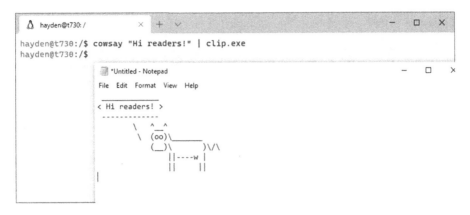

Figure 9-11. *Copying the output of piping to clip.exe into Notepad*

By default, the PATH variable from Windows is passed through to WSL so you can execute programs using the same expectation of it working as if you were executing directly from Windows' command line. For executables that are not in the locations included in the PATH, you may also use the full location.

The equivalent to the preceding, using the full location of clip.exe, could be

```
cowsay "Hi readers!" | /mnt/c/Windows/System32/clip.exe
```

Expanding on this, we can replace clip.exe with a short PowerShell script that uses Windows' "Component Object Model" (COM) API to compose a new email in Microsoft Outlook with the text from the pipeline inserted into the body.

Here, we use git format-patch to create a source code diff, sign it with our PGP key, and put the signed result into an email body in Microsoft Outlook:

```
git format-patch --stdout HEAD~1 | \
GPG_TTY=$(tty) gpg --clear-sign | \
powershell.exe '
  $M=(New-Object -ComObject Outlook.Application).CreateItem(0);
  $M.Body=$input | %{$r=""}{$r+="$_`n"}{$r}; $M.BodyFormat=1;
  $M.Display()'
```

We could save the PowerShell code to a reusable file; let us call it sendmail.ps1 and pass the path to that instead of rewriting it verbatim every time we need it (Figure 9-12).

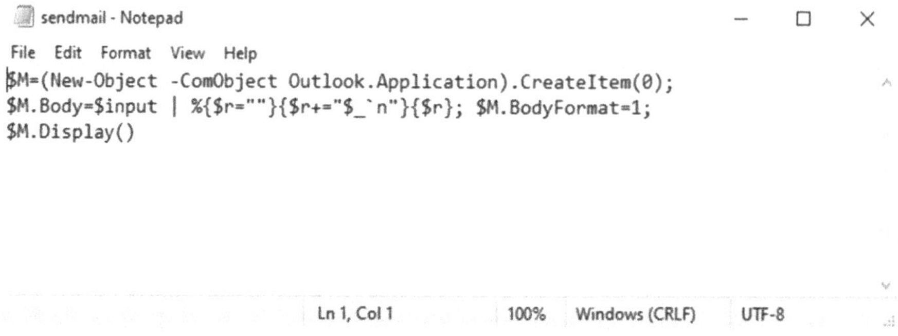

Figure 9-12. *Saving PowerShell code to a reusable file that can be called from WSL*

Note   Slashes / are used to separate the Windows file path because Bash in WSL will interpret the backslash \ as a special character requiring a double backslash \\ instead – PowerShell is fine with this, but other programs may be less forgiving.

We can then run the following to create a new Outlook message from our command output (Figure 9-13):

```
git format-patch --stdout HEAD~1 | GPG_TTY=$(tty) gpg --clear-sign |
powershell.exe -File C:/Users/Hayden/sendmail.ps1
```

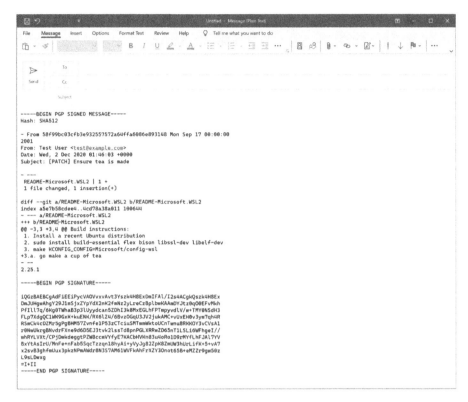

Figure 9-13. *A new Outlook email compose window with the output of "git format-patch" inserted to the email body*

Piping from Windows to WSL

Much like piping from WSL to Windows, we can perform the inverse operation. We can execute a command in Windows and pipe its output into another command in WSL. Let us consider that we want to find all the Windows Services that are Xbox related. To achieve this, we will use PowerShell's Get-Service "cmdlet" and pipe the output into grep in WSL to filter the output to only lines of text that include the word Xbox (Figure 9-14):

```
Get-Service | wsl.exe -d Ubuntu-20.04 grep Xbox
```

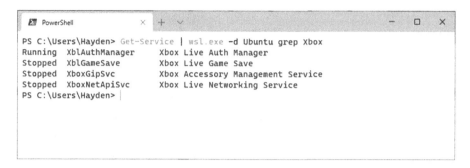

Figure 9-14. *Using PowerShell to list Windows Services and filtering the result with "grep" in WSL*

We can also take the output from the WSL command and pass it back into another PowerShell cmdlet. Replacing the grep with a similar `awk` command, which we also use to extract just the second column, we can start and stop all the services together. In the following, I show this to start and stop the `ssh-agent` service by filtering on the text `ssh` as Administrator.

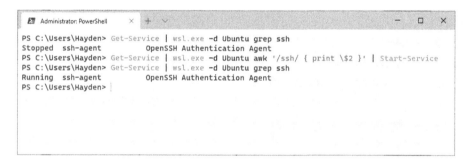

Figure 9-15. *Using PowerShell to start the ssh-agent service in Windows by filtering the list of services through AWK in WSL*

If you receive the error `"Start-Service: Service 'OpenSSH Authentication Agent (ssh-agent)' cannot be started due to the following error: Cannot start service 'ssh-agent' on computer '.'."`, then you need to enable manual launch of the ssh-agent (Figure 9-15):

```
Set-Service ssh-agent -StartupType Manual
```

File Redirection

Redirecting files allows you to save the output of a command to a file or use a file as input to a command. An input file is indicated in Bash with a < symbol followed by the filename whose content you want to use as input to the command, while an output file is, conversely, indicated with a > symbol followed by the filename of the file to save the output of the command into.

For a simple file redirection example, we use the content of /etc/hosts as the input to the base64 command; we write that as

```
base64 < /etc/hosts
```

With base64, it would be simpler to write base64 /etc/hosts without the file redirection, but this only helps with commands that allow usage of a filename as a parameter. It would also have not illustrated file redirection.

Likewise, to save the output of the tar command, which creates archives of any number of files, we write it as

```
tar c /etc/hosts > hosts.tar
```

Again, tar has a built-in parameter that is easier to perform this action with:

```
tar cf hosts.tar /etc/hosts
```

Windows' command line and PowerShell both also support the concept of file redirections, which means we can use them to redirect a file in a command line or PowerShell window to a WSL command. In the following, we take the content of the Windows hosts file and copy it verbatim into the hosts file in our default WSL distro:

```
wsl.exe -u root tee /etc/hosts < C:\Windows\System32\drivers\etc\hosts
```

Heredocs

Along with file redirection, Bash provides a feature called "heredocs." These enable you to write long multiline text input to a command without requiring to first write the text to a file. The "heredoc" is defined with << followed by any unique word that will be used to indicate the end of the input text. A heredoc needs to be at the end of the command or pipeline that it is to be the input for. The end of input indicator word needs to be on a line by itself, with no leading spaces or tabs, and can be any word you desire if it does not occur naturally in the text. A common end of input indicator is EOF.

For example, here is a simple command to print the input text back to the console to show how it works:

```
cat <<ENDOFINPUTINDICATOR
Hi readers!
The next line indicates the end of this input text
ENDOFINPUTINDICATOR
```

We can use this feature to send any arbitrary text to our commands, including those on Windows. The following is an example (Figure 9-16) using the sendmail.ps1 we used earlier in the "Piping Between Windows and WSL" section to write a new email in the terminal (Figure 9-17):

```
powershell.exe -File C:/Users/Hayden/sendmail.ps1 <<EOF
Hi, Readers

This text will be used as the body or a new email message in Microsoft
Outlook. Congratulations on learning about Heredocs.


Best regards,
Hayden
EOF
```

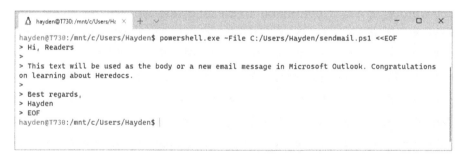

Figure 9-16. *Writing an email from WSL using PowerShell*

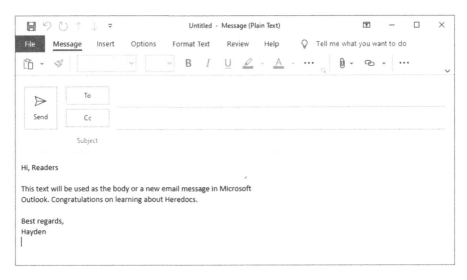

Figure 9-17. *Example new email message composer in Microsoft Outlook created with the content of a heredoc in WSL*

Environmental Variables

Windows and WSL can share environmental variables. These are small in-memory text data entries that are forwarded to and program you run. By default, the Windows environment variables and those in WSL are separate, but this can be configured with a specially named variable in called WSLENV. This variable is interrogated every time the border between Windows and WSL is crossed, so you can change it whenever it suits your workflow.

For example, you can specify that the environment variable JAVA_HOME, which points to the installed Java runtime location, transitions the border when crossing between Windows and WSL by setting the WSLENV variable to JAVA_HOME/p.

You can add any number of environment variable names to the WSLENV configuration by separating each entry with a colon. Here, we have JAVA_HOME and OneDrive specified (Figure 9-18).

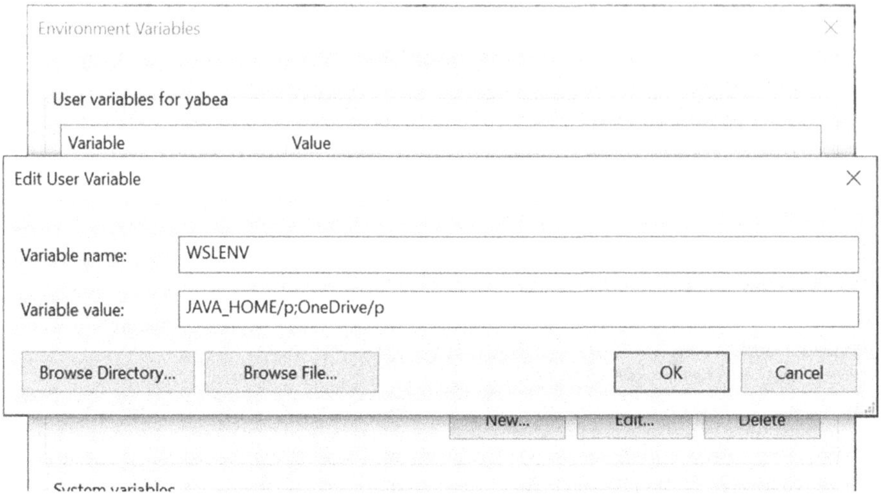

Figure 9-18. *Windows' environment variable configuration dialog with "WSLENV" set*

The /p part of each of the preceding configured variables tells WSL to translate between Windows and WSL paths in the values of each of those variables. For example, with the preceding WSLENV set in Windows, the variables in Windows look like this:

```
C:\Program Files\AdoptOpenJDK\jdk-14.0.2.12-hotspot\
C:\Users\Hayden\OneDrive
```

While in WSL, they look like this, due to the path translation indicated by the /p:

```
/mnt/c/Program Files/AdoptOpenJDK/jdk-14.0.2.12-hotspot/
/mnt/c/Users/Hayden/OneDrive
```

There are other suffixes in addition to /p. All the usable suffixes are

- /p – Indicate that the variable should have its value treated as a path and translate between Windows and WSL equivalent representations.

- /l – Indicate that the variable should be treated as a colon-delimited list of paths in WSL or a semicolon-delimited list of paths in Windows. Like /p, each individual path in the list is converted between Windows and WSL representations.

- /u – Indicate that the variable should be forwarded from Windows to WSL but not from WSL to Windows.

- /w – Indicate the inverse of /u. The variable should be forwarded from WSL to Windows but not from Windows to WSL.

You may also combine /u and /w with either /p or /l. For example, the following are some variants you may use, but not an exhaustive list:

- /pu – The variable contains a path to be translated, and the variable should only propagate from Windows to WSL.

- /lw – The variable contains a list of paths to be translated, and the variable should only propagate from WSL to Windows.

Mount File Systems in WSL 2

File systems come in many forms, and Windows does not support Linux-specific ones. We can use WSL 2 to access these previously inaccessible locations and expose them to Windows applications via the WSL-to-Windows special path \\wsl$ and the Linux node in Windows Explorer (Figure 9-19).

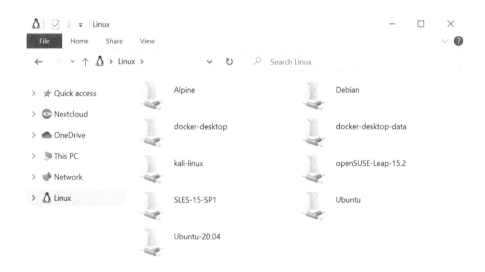

Figure 9-19. *Windows Explorer showing the Linux node with installed WSL distros*

Windows File Shares

Windows file sharing is supported via `drvfs`, which forwards locations known to Windows into the WSL environment. First, let us see how to do this with a Windows Share mapping to a Drive Letter in Windows:

1. In Windows, navigate to the Network item in Windows Explorer.

2. Navigate into the server object that holds your share.

3. Right-click your share, and choose "Map network drive."

4. In the new window, choose `Z:`, and then close the dialog.

   a. Enter your username and password for the share if prompted or you have chosen to use alternative credentials.

5. In WSL, run `sudo mkdir /mnt/z; sudo mount -t drvfs Z: /mnt/z`.

6. You will now find your network share's files accessible under the path `/mnt/z`.

7. To ensure that the drive is remounted when WSL restarts, add the following line into `/etc/fstab`: `Z: /mnt/z drvfs defaults 0 0`.

As an alternative to mapping the Share to a drive letter, we can use the "UNC" path when calling `mount`. The caveat here is that Windows will use a default set of credentials, and these cannot be overridden with this method. If you need to use different credentials, you must use the preceding drive letter mapping method.

1. In WSL, run the following, ensuring that you replace `\\server\share-name` with the UNC path of your share:

   ```
   sudo mkdir /mnt/file-share; sudo mount -t drvfs '\\
   server\share-name' /mnt/file-share
   ```

2. To ensure that the drive is remounted when WSL restarts, add the following line into `/etc/fstab`:

   ```
   \\server\share-name /mnt/file-share drvfs defaults 0 0
   ```

SSHFS and Other FUSE-Based File Systems

One of the great features of Linux that you can use with WSL 2 is the support for "FUSE"-based file systems. FUSE is an acronym for "Filesystem in User space" where the actual file system driver is run as a program rather than as a part of the kernel. This means that you can use any file system that has a FUSE driver without learning how to and using a customized rebuilt kernel. A great file system that FUSE allows is the "SSHFS," which uses Secure Shell connections to a remote PC and exposes the remote file system locally.

To mount an SSHFS file system, we must first edit the file `/etc/fuse.conf` to add a line containing `user_allow_other`. This will allow us to use the `allow_root` option when mounting the file system. Note this requires sshfs to be installed and ssh keys to be generated.

We can now call `sshfs`, after creating a folder owned by the user who executes `sshfs`:

```
sshfs -o idmap=user,uid=1000,gid=1000,allow_root server:/root/test /mnt/test
```

By using FUSE-based file systems in WSL with the `allow_root` option specified when mounting, we allow Windows Explorer to see the files using the Linux node in the sidebar. The file system is also exposed via the UNC path `\\wsl$\distro\path\to\mountpoint` (Figure 9-20).

Figure 9-20. *A mounted SSHFS file system accessed through Windows Explorer*

The magic thing this allows is for any FUSE file system, which is not supported by Windows natively such as SSHFS, to be usable from any Windows application that supports opening a UNC path. For example, we could open a file on a remote server through WSL 2 into `notepad.exe` (Figure 9-21).

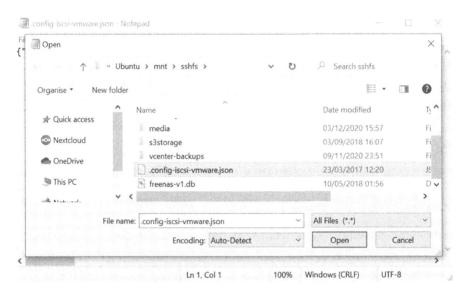

Figure 9-21. *notepad.exe window showing the ability to open a file from a mounted "sshfs" file system inside WSL 2*

Native Linux File Systems in a Disk Image or "Partition"

This is a powerful feature, so do not attempt if you are at all uncomfortable.

With that said, Linux supports a bewildering array of file systems, some more recognizable than others. The usual Linux suspects are `ext2/3/4`, XFS, and `btrfs`. With WSL 2, we can mount these file systems in our distro and then access them from Windows. This means that, through WSL 2, Windows now supports any native Linux file system.

You can find which file systems are supported by your currently running kernel by executing the following inside WSL 2:

```
cat /proc/filesystems
```

In a Partition

If you have a hard disk with native Linux partitions on it, then you can expose them to your WSL 2 distro by using the --mount parameter to wsl.exe. This has the caveat that it requires that the partition be on a disk that is currently not used by Windows, such as if the partition is a secondary partition on your Windows boot device.

You need to know the Windows internal disk path when using wsl.exe –mount, which you can find by running the following in a command line or PowerShell window:

```
wmic diskdrive list brief
```

This will show an output like the one in Figure 9-22.

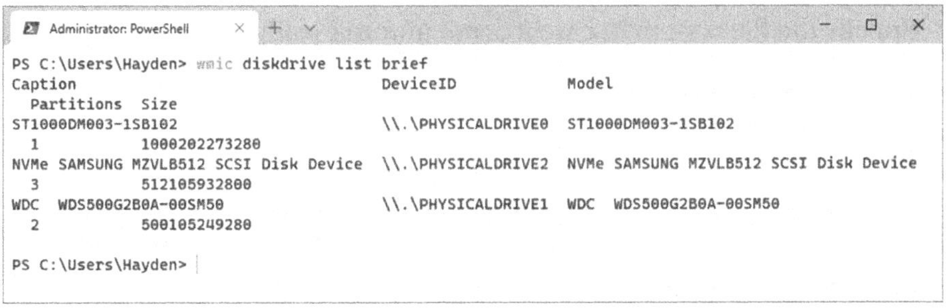

Figure 9-22. *Output of "wmic" command showing available physical disks*

Once you have found your DeviceID, which looks like \\.\PHYSICALDRIVEn where n is a number starting from 0, you can construct the wsl.exe command as follows:

```
wsl.exe --mount \\.\PHYSICALDRIVE1 --partition 2
```

In a Disk Image (VHDX File)

You can, instead of using a physical disk or partition, use a virtual hard disk image stored as a .vhdx file. These are typically created by Windows Hyper-V virtualization system, of which WSL 2 is a very specialized variant.

This method is very similar to using a physical disk or partition with the difference being that instead of physically attaching the disk, you will use PowerShell to mount the .vhdx file into Windows and then proceed the same as for a physical disk or partition.

To mount the .vhdx file in Windows, run the following in a PowerShell window, after ensuring you replace <pathToVHDX> with the full path to your .vhdx file:

```
Write-Output \\.\PhysicalDrive$((Mount-VHD -Path <pathToVHDX> -PassThru |
Get-Disk).Number)
```

This will mount the virtual disk file and then print out its \\.\PhysicalDrive name, which you can use in the wsl.exe --mount commands.

Mounting Options

You may also optionally add any of the following parameters which mirror their Linux counterparts:

1. Specify the file system in case it is not automatically detected:

   ```
   -t <FileSystem>
   ```

   For example:

   ```
   wsl.exe --mount \\.\PHYSICALDRIVE1 --partition 2 -t ext4
   ```

2. Specify any Linux file system mount options:

   ```
   -o <options>
   ```

   For example:

   ```
   wsl.exe –mount \\.\PHYSICALDRIVE1 --partition 2 -o
   noatime,uid=1000,gid=1000
   ```

3. You can also pass through the whole device instead of a single partition with

   ```
   --bare
   ```

   This requires that you omit the --partition, the -t, and the -o parameters. For example:

   ```
   wsl.exe –mount \\.\PHYSICALDRIVE1 --bare
   ```

When you have a mounted file system in WSL 2, the normal methods of accessing from Windows apply, such as the Linux node in Explorer and the \\wsl$ UNC paths.

When you are finished with your disk or disk image, you can remove it from WSL 2, with the `--unmount` command:

```
wsl.exe --unmount <DiskPath>
```

For example:

```
wsl.exe --unmount \\.\PHYSICALDRIVE1
```

Alternatively, you can unmount all disks and images by omitting the disk path parameter:

```
wsl.exe -unmount
```

## CHAPTER 10

Using WSL for Enterprise Development

With the interoperable nature of WSL, you can run your favorite IDE or editor in Windows while keeping the compatibility of running your project inside a real Linux environment. Because WSL 2 uses the Linux kernel, exciting new opportunities are opened such as the ability to run a Kubernetes distribution for developing microservices architecture systems. There is also the enticing ability to use your workstation or laptop's Graphics Processor (GPU) to accelerate machine learning tasks.

Creating a Microk8s Workstation

The computing world is abuzz with the idea of microservice development and deployment patterns. These concepts are made possible by the software Kubernetes, which is difficult to have not heard mention of. Canonical, the company behind the ever-popular Ubuntu, has packaged a distribution of Kubernetes that they call "microk8s." The great thing about microk8s is that it is fully self-contained and is installable with a single command.

Prerequisites for Microk8s

The great thing about microk8s is that it is packaged into a Snap package. Snaps are self-contained bundles that include everything an application requires to operate and are installed simply and quickly. This guide requires that you have an operational systemD-enabled distribution in WSL 2 as Snaps require systemD to operate correctly. Make sure to read Chapter 7, "Customizing WSL" for details on enabling systemd in your environment.

233

© Hayden Barnes 2021
H. Barnes, *Pro Windows Subsystem for Linux (WSL)*, https://doi.org/10.1007/978-1-4842-6873-5_10

To verify that your environment is set up correctly, run (Figure 10-1):

```
snap version
```

Figure 10-1. *Running "snap version" in WSL 2 with an operational systemd*

If your system is correctly set up, this will report your Snap and Snapd versions along with the distribution you are running and the WSL 2 kernel version.

Now that we have verified that Snapd is at least responding, try installing and running `hello-world`:

```
sudo snap install hello-world
hello-world
```

This should successfully install the `hello-world` Snap from the Snap Store and execute the new command. If everything worked, the `hello-world` command will print a welcome message (Figure 10-2).

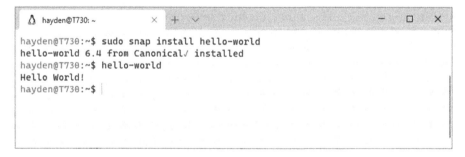

Figure 10-2. *Successfully installing and running the "hello-world" Snap package*

Installing Microk8s

Congratulations, you now have everything you need to install microk8s. Let us install it then:

```
sudo snap install microk8s --classic
sudo usermod -a -G microk8s $USER
newgrp microk8s
sudo chown -f -R $USER ~/.kube
microk8s status
```

Enabling Microk8s Add-Ons

Now that microk8s is installed, you may access the Kubernetes control plane with `kubectl` as normal and deploy and manage services and pods with the usual tools you would use to administer an in-production cluster. You can also quickly enable and disable various add-ons via `microk8s enable` and `microk8s disable` commands (Figure 10-3).

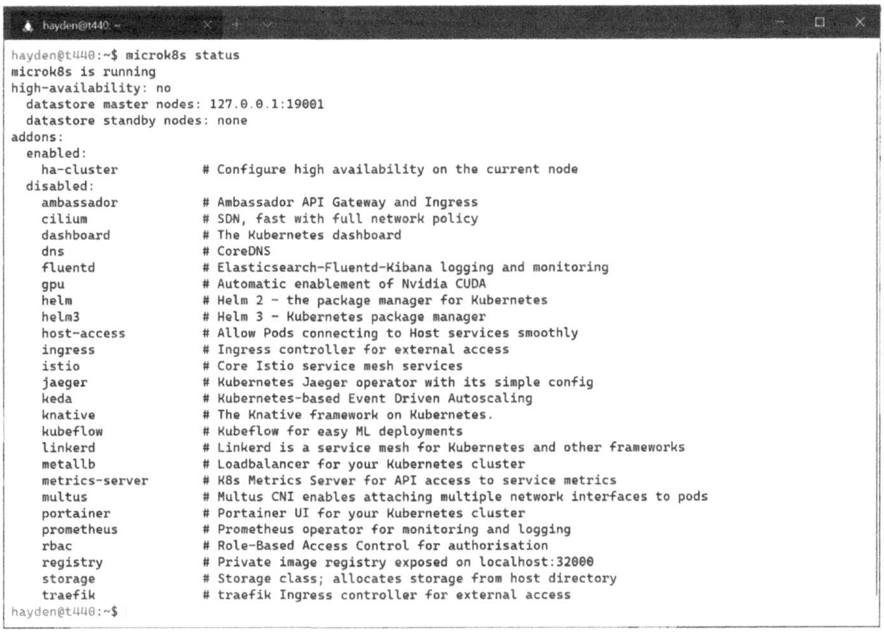

```
hayden@t440:~$ microk8s status
microk8s is running
high-availability: no
  datastore master nodes: 127.0.0.1:19001
  datastore standby nodes: none
addons:
  enabled:
    ha-cluster           # Configure high availability on the current node
  disabled:
    ambassador           # Ambassador API Gateway and Ingress
    cilium               # SDN, fast with full network policy
    dashboard            # The Kubernetes dashboard
    dns                  # CoreDNS
    fluentd              # Elasticsearch-Fluentd-Kibana logging and monitoring
    gpu                  # Automatic enablement of Nvidia CUDA
    helm                 # Helm 2 - the package manager for Kubernetes
    helm3                # Helm 3 - Kubernetes package manager
    host-access          # Allow Pods connecting to Host services smoothly
    ingress              # Ingress controller for external access
    istio                # Core Istio service mesh services
    jaeger               # Kubernetes Jaeger operator with its simple config
    keda                 # Kubernetes-based Event Driven Autoscaling
    knative              # The Knative framework on Kubernetes.
    kubeflow             # Kubeflow for easy ML deployments
    linkerd              # Linkerd is a service mesh for Kubernetes and other frameworks
    metallb              # Loadbalancer for your Kubernetes cluster
    metrics-server       # K8s Metrics Server for API access to service metrics
    multus               # Multus CNI enables attaching multiple network interfaces to pods
    portainer            # Portainer UI for your Kubernetes cluster
    prometheus           # Prometheus operator for monitoring and logging
    rbac                 # Role-Based Access Control for authorisation
    registry             # Private image registry exposed on localhost:32000
    storage              # Storage class; allocates storage from host directory
    traefik              # traefik Ingress controller for external access
hayden@t440:~$
```

Figure 10-3. *Successful installation of microk8s*

For example, most workloads deployed to a Kubernetes cluster usually access other services on the same cluster via DNS names. These are names internal to the cluster that are resolved to their respective IP addresses via normal DNS lookups. Due to the minimalist nature of microk8s, the DNS service provided by CoreDNS is not enabled out of the box, but is easily enabled (Figure 10-4):

```
microk8s enable dns
```

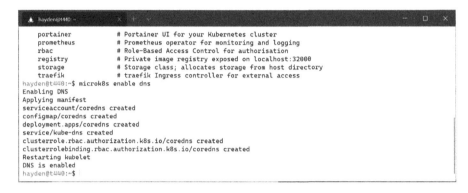

Figure 10-4. *Enabling CoreDNS service on microk8s*

You may remove the CoreDNS feature again when it is not needed any longer with

```
microk8s disable dns
```

Helm can be enabled for installing Helm charts with (Figure 10-5):

```
microk8s enable helm3
```

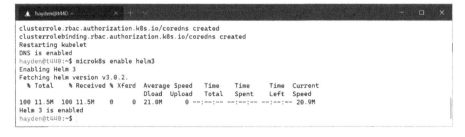

Figure 10-5. *Enabling Helm 3 for microk8s*

Deploy a Cluster with Helm

A common way to deploy workloads to a Kubernetes cluster is via the use of Helm. This is accessed in microk8s with the microk8s.helm or microk8s.helm3 commands. The first is for Helm 2 and the second for Helm 3. Which you choose is up to you and likely depends on the version you use for your production environment. If you do not have a preference, then start with Helm 3. Whichever you choose, you must enable it in your microk8s system with the enable command:

```
microk8s enable helm3
```

To be able to reach our services, we need to enable microk8s' ingress controller (Figure 10-6) with:

```
microk8s enable ingress
```

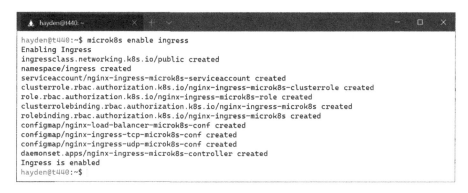

Figure 10-6. *Enabling microk8s' ingress controller*

Now we can install the Ghost blog (Figure 10-7) with:

```
microk8s.helm3 repo add groundhog2k https://groundhog2k.github.io/helm-charts/
microk8s.helm3 repo update
microk8s.helm3 install ghost groundhog2k/ghost
```

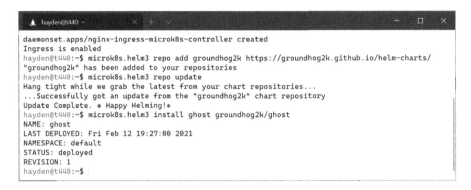

```
daemonset.apps/nginx-ingress-microk8s-controller created
Ingress is enabled
hayden@t440:~$ microk8s.helm3 repo add groundhog2k https://groundhog2k.github.io/helm-charts/
"groundhog2k" has been added to your repositories
hayden@t440:~$ microk8s.helm3 repo update
Hang tight while we grab the latest from your chart repositories...
...Successfully got an update from the "groundhog2k" chart repository
Update Complete. ⎈ Happy Helming!⎈
hayden@t440:~$ microk8s.helm3 install ghost groundhog2k/ghost
NAME: ghost
LAST DEPLOYED: Fri Feb 12 19:27:00 2021
NAMESPACE: default
STATUS: deployed
REVISION: 1
hayden@t440:~$
```

Figure 10-7.   *Installing Ghost blog with Microk8s and helm3*

You can now use `microk8s.helm3` for development as you would use Helm in your production environment. See `microk8s.helm3 help` for usage information and `https://helm.sh/` for documentation on Helm if you get stuck.

Using Docker Desktop

Installing Docker Desktop on WSL

Once you have installed Docker Desktop onto Windows from `www.docker.com/get-started`, we can configure it to enable support for WSL. Find the Docker icon in your system tray (next to your taskbar's clock), and double-click it (Figure 10-8).

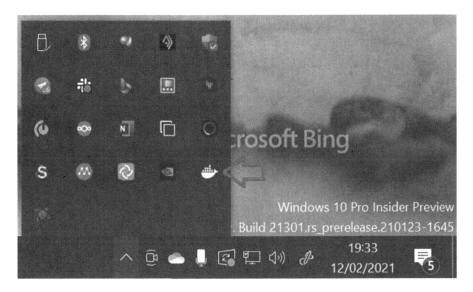

Figure 10-8. *Showing the Docker Desktop icon in the system tray*

From the new window, click the settings icon at the top right – it looks like a gear.

The first option to make sure is enabled is to use the WSL 2–based engine
(Figure 10-9). This replaces the Docker Desktop virtual machine with a lightweight
environment utilizing the WSL 2 infrastructure.

Figure 10-9. *Enabling the option to use the WSL 2–based engine for Docker Desktop*

Now, navigate to Resources followed by WSL Integration. Here, we can enable and disable Docker Desktop integration with our WSL distros to enable use of the same Docker Engine from Windows and each of our enabled Distros (Figure 10-10).

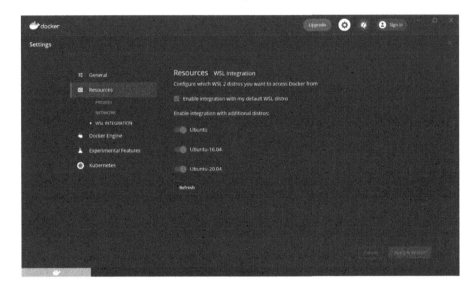

Figure 10-10. *Configuring Docker Desktop's WSL Integration for our distros*

Building Docker Container

After configuring WSL integration in the Docker Desktop settings window, we can use Docker commands inside our WSL distro the same way we would on Windows in PowerShell or cmd.exe. To prove this, we will use Docker's getting-started example application to show that you can build container images from WSL using Docker Desktop.

First, use git to clone `https://github.com/docker/getting-started`:

```
git clone https://github.com/docker/getting-started
```

Move into the getting-started directory, and execute the Docker build command. The build will, when finishing successfully, show an image ID which we will use to run a container (Figure 10-11):

```
cd getting-started
docker build .
```

```
Step 19/22 : RUN mkdocs build
 ---> Using cache
 ---> 81bcf6ea3cfd
Step 20/22 : FROM nginx:alpine
 ---> 629df02b47c8
Step 21/22 : COPY --from=app-zip-creator /app.zip /usr/share/nginx/html/assets/app.zip
 ---> d5c36ecc0d7b
Step 22/22 : COPY --from=build /app/site /usr/share/nginx/html
 ---> 8fc6e32f5c0e
Successfully built 8fc6e32f5c0e
hayden@t440:~/getting-started$ docker run --rm -it -p 80:80 8fc6e32f5c0e
/docker-entrypoint.sh: /docker-entrypoint.d/ is not empty, will attempt to perform configuration
/docker-entrypoint.sh: Looking for shell scripts in /docker-entrypoint.d/
/docker-entrypoint.sh: Launching /docker-entrypoint.d/10-listen-on-ipv6-by-default.sh
10-listen-on-ipv6-by-default.sh: info: Getting the checksum of /etc/nginx/conf.d/default.conf
10-listen-on-ipv6-by-default.sh: info: Enabled listen on IPv6 in /etc/nginx/conf.d/default.conf
/docker-entrypoint.sh: Launching /docker-entrypoint.d/20-envsubst-on-templates.sh
/docker-entrypoint.sh: Configuration complete; ready for start up
```

Figure 10-11. *Successful build and launch of the getting-started Docker example container*

We can now navigate to `http://127.0.0.1/` in a web browser in Windows to view the example web page (Figure 10-12).

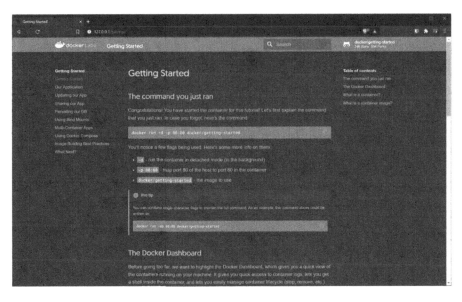

Figure 10-12. *The getting-started web page served from the container we just built and started using Docker Desktop's WSL integration*

Connecting to Editors/IDEs

Visual Studio

The de facto standard IDE for enterprises is Microsoft's Visual Studio, which can be integrated with WSL to build and debug .NET Core and .NET 5.0 applications for deployment to Linux systems.

Installing in Visual Studio Version 16.8 and Earlier

In Visual Studio 16.8 and earlier, enable the feature with the following steps:

1. Open Visual Studio, and select "Continue without code."

2. Find and open the Extensions menu, and select "Manage Extensions."

3. Type into the search box the word `Dot-Net-Core-Debugging-With-Wsl2`.

4. Click the Download button on the item labeled ".NET Core Debugging with WSL 2 – Preview" (Figure 10-13).

5. Once the download is complete, close Visual Studio, and let the installer finish (be ready for a UAC prompt).

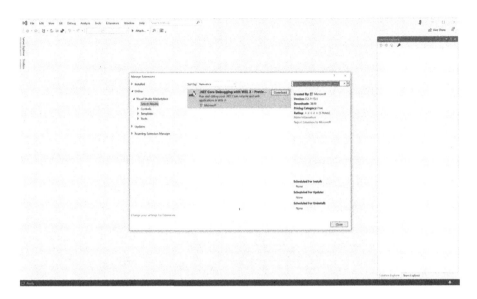

Figure 10-13. *Downloading and installing .NET Core Debugging with WSL 2 Visual Studio extension*

Installing in Visual Studio Version 16.9 and Later

The feature is included as part of Visual Studio 16.9 and later, so to enable, we will use the "Visual Studio Installer" application – this is the same application that you use to initially install Visual Studio on a workstation, update it to newer versions, and add and remove features.

You can enable the ".NET Core Debugging with WSL 2" feature either as part of the ".NET Core cross-platform development" item in the workload tab or by selecting it from the "Individual components" tab (Figure 10-14).

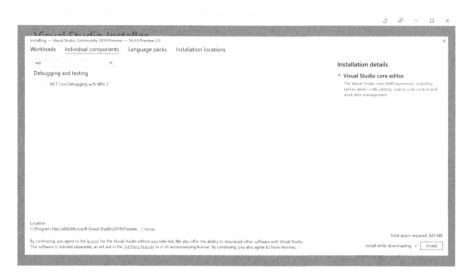

Figure 10-14. *Selecting the .NET Core Debugging with WSL 2 item in Visual Studio Installer*

Debugging Your App in WSL

To be able to debug your app in WSL 2, it must target .NET Core or .NET 5.0. You can create a new project that is compatible by selecting Linux from the platforms drop-down in the "New project" window (Figure 10-15).

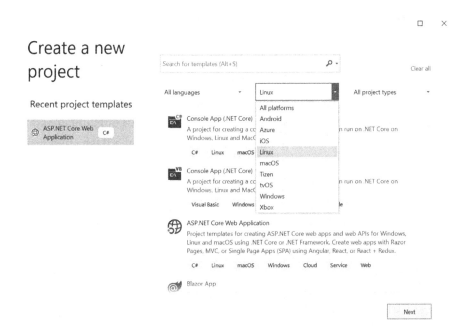

Figure 10-15. *Creating a new project that targets Linux*

Once you have a compatible project, the drop-down to select which platform to use for debugging should list "WSL 2" as an option (Figure 10-16). When you select this item, it will configure your WSL environment to run .NET Core or .NET 5.0 applications and then allow you to launch your debugging session.

Figure 10-16. *Selecting "WSL 2" as the environment to debug within*

Visual Studio Code

Many developers are moving to using Visual Studio Code as their editor of choice. Code allows for seamless integration with WSL by using its "WSL Remote" extension. With this extension to Code, the editor is split into two parts where the User Interface runs on Windows, but the tools that are used for development and debugging are started in WSL. You can even open a terminal inside Code that shows you a Bash shell from the WSL environment.

To get started, we need to install the "WSL Remote" extension inside Code:

1. To Start Code, select it from the Start/Flag menu in Windows; or open the run dialog (windows key + R), type code, and hit enter; or use Windows search by pressing the Windows key on your keyboard, then type code, and finally press enter.

2. Press Ctrl+P, and type ext install remote-wsl, and then press Enter. This will open the extensions screen with the WSL Remote extension.

3. Click the "Install" button in the right-hand pane of Code underneath the extension title "Remote – WSL" (Figure 10-17).

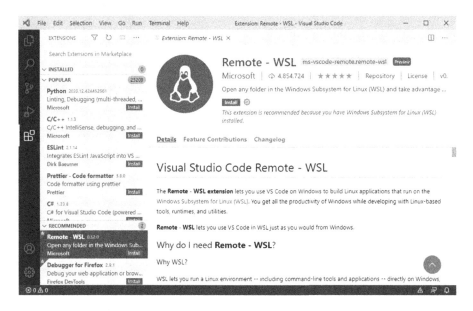

Figure 10-17. *Installation screen of WSL Remote extension for Visual Studio Code*

Now that we have the extension, we may open a file or folder from our WSL distro:

1. Press Ctrl+Shift+P.

2. Type remote-wsl.

3. Choose the "New Window..." option to open a new window with the default WSL distro, or "New Window using distro..." to choose which distro you want to use (Figure 10-18).

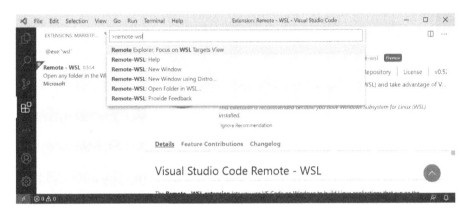

Figure 10-18. *Opening a new Code window connected to WSL*

4. Select "Open Folder" to find and open a folder from your WSL distro (Figure 10-19).

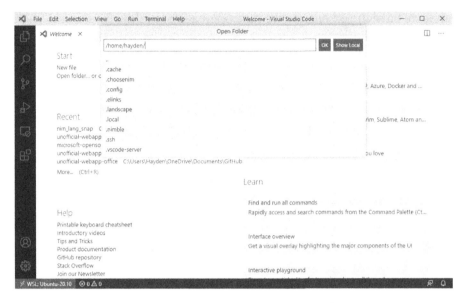

Figure 10-19. *Opening a folder from the now-connected WSL instance*

You will note that when you connect to a WSL instance, the terminal automatically opens in the bottom right of the Visual Studio Code window. This terminal is a direct view to BASH running inside WSL, so anything that would be possible on the command line without Code is possible here (Figure 10-20).

Figure 10-20. *Showing that the terminal inside Code is the real WSL terminal*

With the client-server mechanism that Code uses, you can even debug your code running in WSL from Code running in Windows. Here, we are hitting a breakpoint in a .NET web application that is running in WSL with Code running in Windows (Figure 10-21).

Figure 10-21. *Debugger hitting a breakpoint in Windows while debugging a .NET web app running in WSL*

JetBrains IDEs

JetBrains IDEs support opening a project from within a WSL 2 instance by showing the \\wsl$ special paths in the File ➤ Open dialog (Figure 10-22). When opening or creating a project from a \\wsl$ path, the JetBrains IDE will automatically switch to using Git from within the WSL instance.

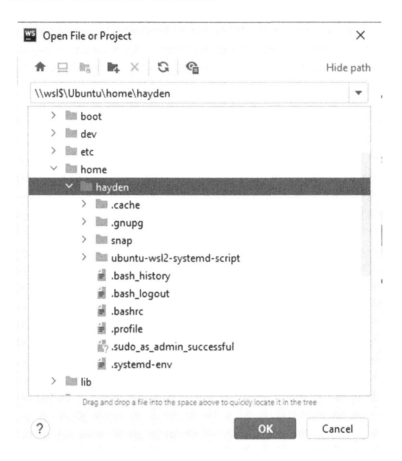

Figure 10-22. *The JetBrains IDE's "Open File or Project" window showing available WSL paths*

Like with Visual Studio and Visual Studio Code's remote debugging in WSL, JetBrains IDEs are growing support for executing more build and debug steps within the WSL instance. One of the better supported experiences is within WebStorm when building a NodeJS project. When creating a project, you can specify that WebStorm uses the node and npm executables from your WSL instance.

When creating a new project, you can specify tooling inside WSL:

1. Select the "Node interpreter" drop-down, and choose add (Figure 10-23).

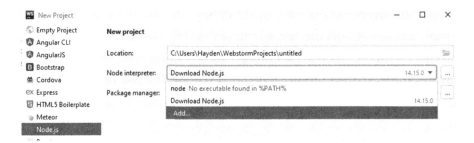

Figure 10-23. *Adding a new "Node interpreter" to WebStorm*

2. Inside the new dialog, enter the path to your node executable, which is likely /usr/bin/node but might be different on your system (Figure 10-24).

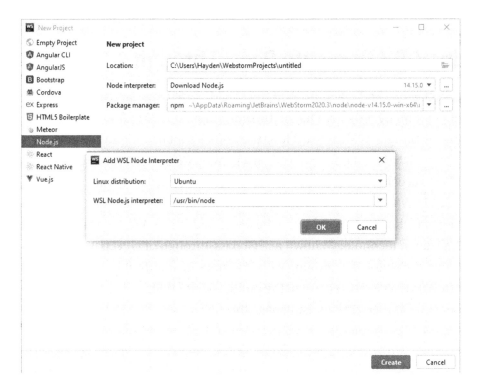

Figure 10-24. *Setting the path to the "node" executable in the Ubuntu WSL distribution*

3. Now, add any code, and then run or debug your application using the normal JetBrains methods. In the following, you see that a trivial example is indeed executing inside WSL as indicated by the word "linux" in the output "Hello linux World!" (Figure 10-25).

Figure 10-25. *Running a trivial example to show it is executing in WSL*

Utilizing GPU Compute Pass-Through

Artificial intelligence and machine learning (AI/ML) are becoming almost a staple requirement for many projects. One of the most popular AI/ML frameworks is TensorFlow by Google. With TensorFlow, use comes a lot of compute-intensive calculations, which do not perform well on a generic CPU, and TensorFlow recommends using a GPU to accelerate the calculation speed by many orders of magnitude.

However, in WSL 2, the GPU is being used in Windows to run your display, and it cannot be detached from Windows to be dedicated to the WSL 2 virtual machine via a virtualization technology known as PCI pass-through or GPU pass-through. AI/ML workflows are enabled beginning with Windows Insider Build number 20150 and available in Windows 21H1 release to the public, where WSL 2 exposes an API to access your workstation's GPU without using pass-through to detach it from your Windows system.

NVIDIA CUDA

- To enable NVIDIA CUDA, you must have an NVIDIA GPU and have downloaded and installed the developer drivers from NVIDIA at `https://developer.nvidia.com/cuda/wsl`.

The best experience with TensorFlow for NVIDIA CUDA is to use Docker inside your WSL instance. If you have Docker Desktop installed on Windows, please ensure that WSL integration is disabled for the WSL instance because we will install a native Docker on that system. Docker Desktop support for GPU Compute is planned.

1. Install Docker in your WSL instance. Here, we are assuming either Debian or Ubuntu:

```
sudo apt -y install docker.io
sudo adduser $USER docker
```

2. Enable the NVIDIA APT repositories:

```
distribution=$(. /etc/os-release; echo $ID$VERSION_ID)
```

```
curl -s -L https://nvidia.github.io/nvidia-docker/gpgkey |
sudo apt-key add
```

```
curl -s -L https://nvidia.github.io/nvidia-
docker/$distribution/nvidia-docker.list | sudo tee /etc/
apt/sources.list.d/nvidia-docker.list
```

```
curl -s -L https://nvidia.github.io/libnvidia-container/
experimental/$distribution/libnvidia-container-
experimental.list | sudo tee /etc/apt/sources.list.d/
libnvidia-container-experimental.list
```

3. Refresh your APT caches, and install the NVIDIA runtime to support our containers' access to our workstation's GPU:

```
sudo apt update
sudo apt install -y nvidia-docker2
```

4. It is necessary, now, to shut down the WSL instance. Assuming it is called Ubuntu-20.04, run

```
wsl.exe --terminate Ubuntu-20.04
```

5. Now, run a benchmark to test that CUDA is working correctly. It
    should report your GPU Device name; here, it is "GeForce GTX
    960" (Figure 10-26).

```
docker run --gpus all nvcr.io/nvidia/k8s/cuda-sample:nbody
nbody -gpu -benchmark
```

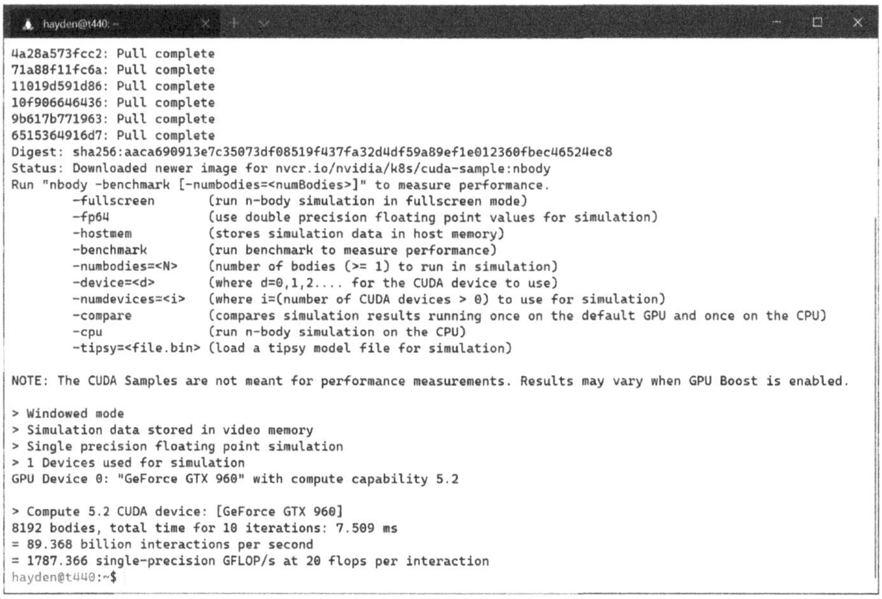

Figure 10-26. *Running an NVIDIA CUDA benchmark in a Docker container*

6. We can now start to play around with TensorFlow. Start a new
    container running Jupyter Notebooks (Figure 10-27):

```
docker run -u $(id -u):$(id -g) -it --gpus all -p 8888:8888
tensorflow/tensorflow:latest-gpu-py3-jupyter
```

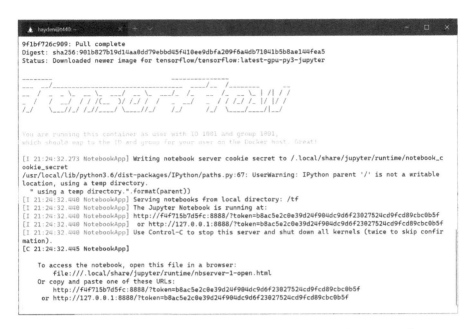

Figure 10-27. *Successfully starting Jupyter Notebooks with TensorFlow*

7. Find the URL on the last line of the output from starting the
    container, and copy it into your browser's address bar, replace
    127.0.0.1 with the word localhost, and press enter to navigate
    there (Figure 10-28).

Figure 10-28. *The welcome page of Jupyter Notebooks showing the tensorflow-
tutorials subfolder*

You are now all set to start using TensorFlow with NVIDIA CUDA inside WSL 2.

DirectML for Non-NVIDIA GPUs

- To enable DirectML on an AMD GPU or an AMD CPU that has graphics built into the CPU, you must download and install the developer drivers from AMD at `www.amd.com/en/support/kb/release-notes/rn-rad-win-wsl-support`.

- To enable DirectML on an Intel GPU or an Intel CPU that has graphics built into the CPU, you must download and install the developer drivers from Intel at `https://downloadcenter.intel.com/download/29526`.

We will install TensorFlow with DirectML support using "Miniconda."

1. Download and install Miniconda:

   ```
   wget https://repo.anaconda.com/miniconda/Miniconda3-
   latest-Linux-x86_64.sh

   bash Miniconda3-latest-Linux-x86_64.sh
   ```

2. Create a new Python environment, and activate it inside your current shell session:

   ```
   conda create --name directml python=3.6

   conda activate directml
   ```

3. Install the TensorFlow package using "PIP," the Python package installer:

   ```
   pip install tensorflow-directml
   ```

4. Verify that you can run accelerated workloads with a simple example. Paste the following code into an interactive Python session, which can be started by running `python`:

   ```
   import tensorflow.compat.v1 as tf

   tf.enable_eager_execution(tf.ConfigProto(log_device_placement=True))

   print(tf.add([1.0, 2.0], [3.0, 4.0]))
   ```

For more examples, see Microsoft's GitHub repository at `https://github.com/microsoft/DirectML`.

CHAPTER 11

Troubleshooting WSL

Installation

When it comes to installing WSL, it is generally smooth sailing, but there are a few scenarios where things can go wrong. In this section, we will go through a few of these scenarios and things to check.

Ensure the Windows Optional Features Are Enabled

The first thing to check when you have problems enabling WSL is that the required bits of Windows are enabled. You must ensure that the Windows components are named "Virtual Machine Platform" and "Windows Subsystem for Linux." The easiest way to do this, without navigating through menus, is to open a PowerShell window as Administrator and execute two commands. These two commands will enable the required Windows Optional Features. Alternatively, you may use the "Turn Windows features on or off" dialog (Figure 11-1).

© Hayden Barnes 2021
H. Barnes, *Pro Windows Subsystem for Linux (WSL)*, https://doi.org/10.1007/978-1-4842-6873-5_11

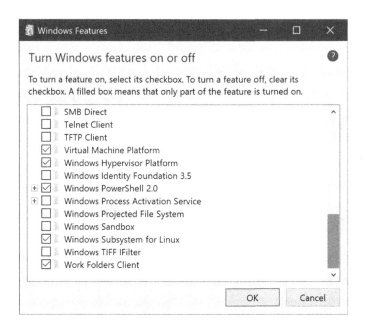

Figure 11-1. *Enabling Windows features GUI*

To turn the Windows features on using PowerShell (Figure 11-2), press the Windows key on your keyboard, and type "powershell":

1. Click the item in the right-hand pane labeled "Run as Administrator."

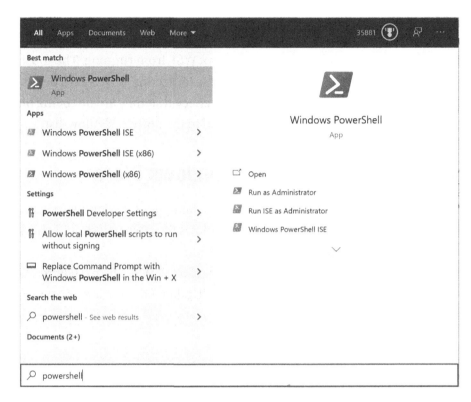

Figure 11-2. *Locating PowerShell using the Windows key and running as Administrator*

2. In the new PowerShell window, run as follows (Figure 11-3):

```
Enable-WindowsOptionalFeature -Online -FeatureName
VirtualMachinePlatform
```

```
Enable-WindowsOptionalFeature -Online -FeatureName
Microsoft-Windows-Subsystem-Linux
```

Figure 11-3. *Enabling WSL 1 and 2 using PowerShell*

Check Your Security Application

Some third-party antivirus applications can prevent WSL from running. The most common way they impact WSL is by blocking access to "lxcore" or "lxsys." These are required for WSL to operate correctly. You should check that they are not being blocked by your antivirus application or that they are added to the antivirus' Allow-list.

Get the Latest Distro from the Windows Store

It is always a good idea to ensure you have the latest launcher for your distro installed. The launcher is what is downloaded from the Windows Store, so you should check that it is up to date with the standard Windows Store methods.

Navigate to the Microsoft Store entry for your preferred WSL Distro (Figure 11-4), and click "Install," if it is not currently installed, or "Update," if there are any updates available.

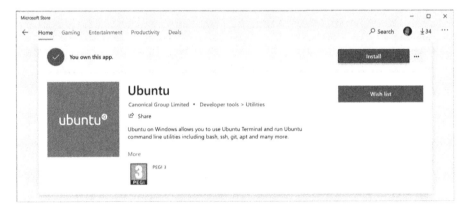

Figure 11-4. *Ubuntu WSL distro entry on the Microsoft Store*

Alternatively, navigate to the Store's "Downloads and Updates" page to see if your distro has an update available (Figure 11-5).

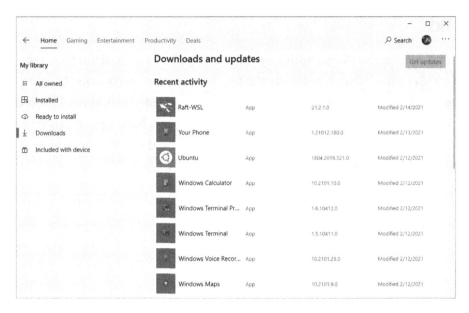

Figure 11-5. *Checking for updated WSL distro images in Downloads and updates section of the Microsoft Store*

Virtualization

Another common issue is encountered when running Windows inside of a virtual machine such as those created by VirtualBox. Unless your virtualization platform allows you to expose "nested virtualization," WSL 2 will not run. You may find that you can still use WSL 1 when you are running inside a virtual machine because WSL 1 does not rely on hardware-based virtualization technologies, sometimes known as VT-x (Intel's name) or SVM (AMD's name).

Linux Component Dependencies

Like any complex operating system, the Linux ecosystem is heavily intertwined with dependencies. Many applications will require features to be available and running to work. Some of these include "systemd," "DBUS," and kernel modules.

systemd

The standard mechanism for handling system services in a Linux distro is usually provided by "Systemd." This is normally the first process that starts when booting up. Due to the way that WSL 1 and WSL 2 are implemented, Systemd is either blocked from running, in WSL 1, or requires a work-around using Process Namespaces, in WSL 2. When you issue a command that interacts with the Systemd process, such as `systemctl` to manage services, it will emit the following (Figure 11-6).

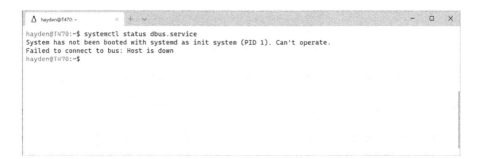

Figure 11-6. *A Linux application failing to run because of a systemd dependency*

This indicates that Systemd is inoperable and that you need to find an alternative way of running your application.

Some applications will refuse to start unless they are run through Systemd. One prime example is the Snapd daemon that manages Linux Snap Packages (see `https://snapcraft.io/` for information about Snaps.) This means that Snaps are not usable in WSL without work-arounds.

dbus

Common in GUI applications, the DBUS service is used to pass messages between applications in a consistent way. Normally the DBUS service is started and stopped with your session by the Systemd process. In WSL, however, Systemd is nonoperational by default as we explored earlier. When an application tries to use the DBUS service, it will likely emit messages to the console indicating the error, or it might refuse to start (Figure 11-7).

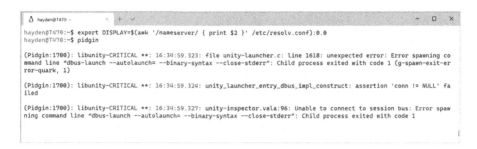

Figure 11-7. *A Linux GUI application attempting to contact DBUS*

You can fix this with the following command every time you enter the WSL environment:

```
dbus-launch --exit-with-x11
```

It might be useful to add the line into your WSL user's `.bashrc` file so that it is run every time you start a shell. However, the first time you try this, you will receive an error message (Figure 11-8).

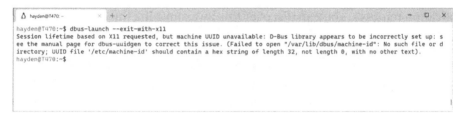

Figure 11-8. *DBUS refusing to run without a unique DBUS UUID*

To fix this, run the following (Figure 11-9). It is only required once:

```
sudo dbus-uuidgen –ensure
```

Figure 11-9. *Having generated a DBUS UUID and manually started DBUS, our Linux GUI application now starts successfully*

Kernel Modules

Some applications might require specific kernel modules to be enabled. These require that you use WSL 2 for its native Linux kernel so that you can use real Linux kernel modules. However, the kernel supplied by Microsoft might not include the module that your application requires. You can discover this by examining the output of running your application for warnings or errors indicating the kernel module is missing, or the output of dmesg, which is a utility to show the internal kernel log messages.

Linux Applications

When a Linux application fails, there are a few tools that you may find useful:

- GDB – The GNU debugger
- strace – Trace system calls and signals

The most useful of these for WSL is "strace," which allows us to see into the system calls that an application uses.

Using "strace" on WSL 1

Since WSL 1 is a translation layer that has been written from scratch without using any Linux source code, some system calls may be unimplemented. We can use "strace" to see all the system calls that an application makes to try to pinpoint a missing feature in WSL 1.

For an example, consider that we want to investigate the `ls` command's system calls. We prefix the command with `strace` and execute (Figure 11-10):

```
strace ls
```

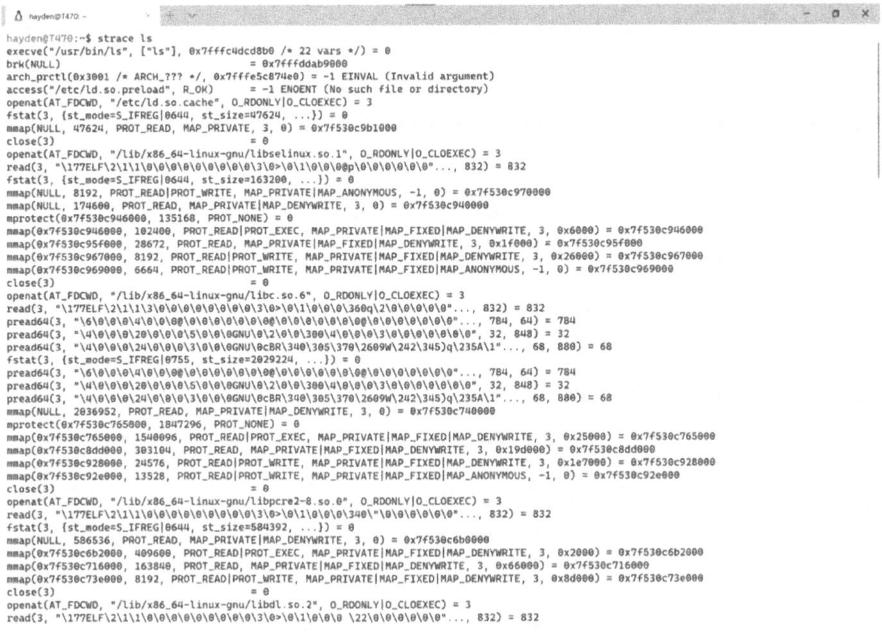

```
hayden@T470:~$ strace ls
execve("/usr/bin/ls", ["ls"], 0x7fffc4dcd8b0 /* 22 vars */) = 0
brk(NULL)                               = 0x7fffddab9000
arch_prctl(0x3001 /* ARCH_??? */, 0x7fffe5c874e0) = -1 EINVAL (Invalid argument)
access("/etc/ld.so.preload", R_OK)      = -1 ENOENT (No such file or directory)
openat(AT_FDCWD, "/etc/ld.so.cache", O_RDONLY|O_CLOEXEC) = 3
fstat(3, {st_mode=S_IFREG|0644, st_size=47624, ...}) = 0
mmap(NULL, 47624, PROT_READ, MAP_PRIVATE, 3, 0) = 0x7f530c9b1000
close(3)                                = 0
openat(AT_FDCWD, "/lib/x86_64-linux-gnu/libselinux.so.1", O_RDONLY|O_CLOEXEC) = 3
read(3, "\177ELF\2\1\1\0\0\0\0\0\0\0\0\0\3\0>\0\1\0\0\0@p\0\0\0\0\0\0"..., 832) = 832
fstat(3, {st_mode=S_IFREG|0644, st_size=163200, ...}) = 0
mmap(NULL, 8192, PROT_READ|PROT_WRITE, MAP_PRIVATE|MAP_ANONYMOUS, -1, 0) = 0x7f530c970000
mmap(NULL, 174600, PROT_READ, MAP_PRIVATE|MAP_DENYWRITE, 3, 0) = 0x7f530c940000
mprotect(0x7f530c946000, 135168, PROT_NONE) = 0
mmap(0x7f530c946000, 102400, PROT_READ|PROT_EXEC, MAP_PRIVATE|MAP_FIXED|MAP_DENYWRITE, 3, 0x6000) = 0x7f530c946000
mmap(0x7f530c95f000, 28672, PROT_READ, MAP_PRIVATE|MAP_FIXED|MAP_DENYWRITE, 3, 0x1f000) = 0x7f530c95f000
mmap(0x7f530c967000, 8192, PROT_READ|PROT_WRITE, MAP_PRIVATE|MAP_FIXED|MAP_DENYWRITE, 3, 0x26000) = 0x7f530c967000
mmap(0x7f530c969000, 6664, PROT_READ|PROT_WRITE, MAP_PRIVATE|MAP_FIXED|MAP_ANONYMOUS, -1, 0) = 0x7f530c969000
close(3)                                = 0
openat(AT_FDCWD, "/lib/x86_64-linux-gnu/libc.so.6", O_RDONLY|O_CLOEXEC) = 3
read(3, "\177ELF\2\1\1\3\0\0\0\0\0\0\0\0\3\0>\0\1\0\0\0\360q\2\0\0\0\0\0"..., 832) = 832
pread64(3, "\6\0\0\0\4\0\0\0@\0\0\0\0\0\0\0@\0\0\0\0\0\0\0@\0\0\0\0\0\0\0"..., 784, 64) = 784
pread64(3, "\4\0\0\0\20\0\0\0\5\0\0\0GNU\0\2\0\0\300\4\0\0\0\3\0\0\0\0\0\0\0", 32, 848) = 32
pread64(3, "\4\0\0\0\24\0\0\0\3\0\0\0GNU\0cBR\340\305\370\2609W\242\345)q\235A\1"..., 68, 880) = 68
fstat(3, {st_mode=S_IFREG|0755, st_size=2029224, ...}) = 0
pread64(3, "\6\0\0\0\4\0\0\0@\0\0\0\0\0\0\0@\0\0\0\0\0\0\0@\0\0\0\0\0\0\0"..., 784, 64) = 784
pread64(3, "\4\0\0\0\20\0\0\0\5\0\0\0GNU\0\2\0\0\300\4\0\0\0\3\0\0\0\0\0\0\0", 32, 848) = 32
pread64(3, "\4\0\0\0\24\0\0\0\3\0\0\0GNU\0cBR\340\305\370\2609W\242\345)q\235A\1"..., 68, 880) = 68
mmap(NULL, 2036952, PROT_READ, MAP_PRIVATE|MAP_DENYWRITE, 3, 0) = 0x7f530c740000
mprotect(0x7f530c765000, 1847296, PROT_NONE) = 0
mmap(0x7f530c765000, 1540096, PROT_READ|PROT_EXEC, MAP_PRIVATE|MAP_FIXED|MAP_DENYWRITE, 3, 0x25000) = 0x7f530c765000
mmap(0x7f530c8dd000, 303104, PROT_READ, MAP_PRIVATE|MAP_FIXED|MAP_DENYWRITE, 3, 0x19d000) = 0x7f530c8dd000
mmap(0x7f530c928000, 24576, PROT_READ|PROT_WRITE, MAP_PRIVATE|MAP_FIXED|MAP_DENYWRITE, 3, 0x1e7000) = 0x7f530c928000
mmap(0x7f530c92e000, 13528, PROT_READ|PROT_WRITE, MAP_PRIVATE|MAP_FIXED|MAP_ANONYMOUS, -1, 0) = 0x7f530c92e000
close(3)                                = 0
openat(AT_FDCWD, "/lib/x86_64-linux-gnu/libpcre2-8.so.0", O_RDONLY|O_CLOEXEC) = 3
read(3, "\177ELF\2\1\1\0\0\0\0\0\0\0\0\0\3\0>\0\1\0\0\0\340\"\0\0\0\0\0\0"..., 832) = 832
fstat(3, {st_mode=S_IFREG|0644, st_size=584392, ...}) = 0
mmap(NULL, 586536, PROT_READ, MAP_PRIVATE|MAP_DENYWRITE, 3, 0) = 0x7f530c6b0000
mmap(0x7f530c6b2000, 409600, PROT_READ|PROT_EXEC, MAP_PRIVATE|MAP_FIXED|MAP_DENYWRITE, 3, 0x2000) = 0x7f530c6b2000
mmap(0x7f530c716000, 163840, PROT_READ, MAP_PRIVATE|MAP_FIXED|MAP_DENYWRITE, 3, 0x66000) = 0x7f530c716000
mmap(0x7f530c73e000, 8192, PROT_READ|PROT_WRITE, MAP_PRIVATE|MAP_FIXED|MAP_DENYWRITE, 3, 0x8d000) = 0x7f530c73e000
close(3)                                = 0
openat(AT_FDCWD, "/lib/x86_64-linux-gnu/libdl.so.2", O_RDONLY|O_CLOEXEC) = 3
read(3, "\177ELF\2\1\1\0\0\0\0\0\0\0\0\0\3\0>\0\1\0\0\0 \22\0\0\0\0\0\0"..., 832) = 832
```

Figure 11-10. *Output of an strace on the ls command*

This will output a lot of log messages as the command runs. It can be useful to restrict the system calls that are monitored by adding the -e flag. The following command will restrict the output to only the `openat` and `close` system calls (Figure 11-11):

```
strace -e openat,close ls
```

You can find a list of Linux system calls in the "manpage" documentation at `https://man7.org/linux/man-pages/man2/syscalls.2.html`, or with the following command, if you have the manpages-dev package installed:

```
man 2 syscalls
```

If you use the man command, navigate the manpage with the page up and page down buttons or the arrow keys, and quit by typing q.

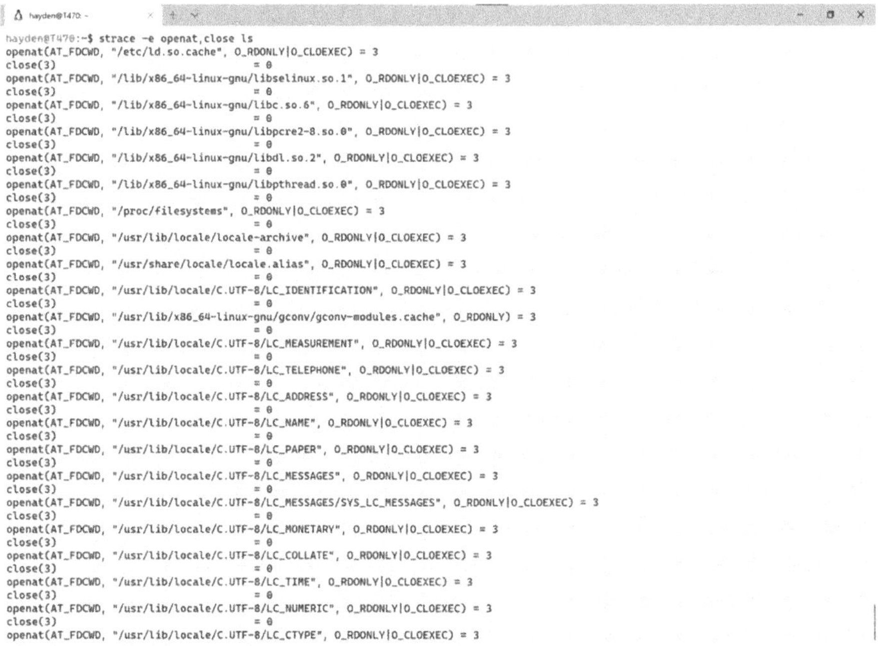

Figure 11-11. *Using strace options to limit output to file operations*

CHAPTER 12

Deploying WSL at Scale

Considerations for Deploying

Deploying WSL at scale requires you to be aware of some important things for the best experience.

It is important to make sure that when a user restarts their system, the %APPDATA%\ local directory of their user account is preserved. If the directory is erased, the user will need to reinstall their WSL distro(s) every time that they log in to Windows. This is because the WSL file systems are stored within this directory. As an alternative, you could install the distros on behalf of the user via automation with the wsl.exe --import command, which allows you to specify where to save the WSL file system. This would let you choose a location that is persistent.

Once a WSL distro has been installed, it is important to remember that the user of the Windows PC will have root access to the WSL distro. The Linux root user is like the Windows Administrator account in that it is fully privileged within the Linux distro. While the user will have root access to their WSL distros, and can do anything inside that distro, your Windows security policies will still apply to Windows resources. So, even with root access in the WSL distros the user has installed, they will only have as much access to Windows resources as their Windows account allows.

You will likely find that managing multiple PCs and users with WSL installations is challenging. It is advised to use Ansible or Landscape or another management system to ensure that you have full visibility into the distros you have deployed.

With Windows use comes the inevitable challenge of keeping the systems clear of malware and viruses. If you are using a third-party security system, you may find that they block the WSL drivers from being loaded. Make sure you test the deployment before rolling out to your users to help prevent any unexpected surprises.

© Hayden Barnes 2021
H. Barnes, *Pro Windows Subsystem for Linux (WSL)*, https://doi.org/10.1007/978-1-4842-6873-5_12

Using Intune to Deploy Ubuntu on WSL

In the enterprise world, Mobile Device Management is a common practice to ensure that all business computers and mobile devices have a standard set of applications and settings. To fill the MDM role, Microsoft has its Intune product, which you can use to preload your users' Windows systems with WSL distros direct from the Windows Store. By using Intune to deliver WSL distros, your users will have WSL ready to go as soon as they log in to a corporate device.

Using Landscape to Manage Ubuntu on WSL

Canonical's Landscape server is the officially blessed way to manage large Ubuntu on WSL installations, such as an enterprise network. It allows you to monitor and actively maintain your fleet of Ubuntu systems by running scripts or installing packages on a subset or all systems.

Enroll Ubuntu WSL into a Landscape Server

We will assume you have a Landscape server installed by following the instructions at `https://docs.ubuntu.com/landscape/en/`.

This chapter builds on the SystemD-enabled environment we explored earlier, because `landscape-client` expects to be managed by the `systemd` process.

The first step, once you have Launchpad server running, is to log in to the Launchpad admin screen (Figure 12-1) and navigate to the instructions to find your registration and ping URLs. Click the link on the leftmost panel of the admin pages labeled `following these instructions`. It is important to note that the ping URL is always HTTP (non-secure), while the registration URL is likely HTTPS (secure).

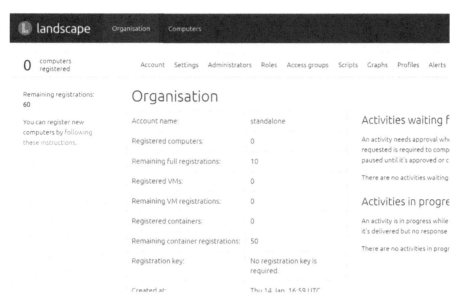

Figure 12-1. *The Launchpad admin screen showing the link to instructions for registering new computers*

The instructions are reproduced in summary as follows:

1. Update the repositories:

   ```
   sudo apt-get update
   ```

2. Install the client:

   ```
   sudo apt-get install landscape-client
   ```

```
△  hayden@T440: ~              ×  +  ⌄                                    —  □  ×
hayden@T440:~$ sudo apt-get update
Hit:1 http://archive.ubuntu.com/ubuntu focal InRelease
Hit:2 http://archive.ubuntu.com/ubuntu focal-updates InRelease
Hit:3 http://archive.ubuntu.com/ubuntu focal-backports InRelease
Hit:4 http://security.ubuntu.com/ubuntu focal-security InRelease
Reading package lists... Done
hayden@T440:~$ sudo apt-get install landscape-client
Reading package lists... Done
Building dependency tree
Reading state information... Done
The following additional packages will be installed:
  python3-pycurl
Suggested packages:
  libcurl4-gnutls-dev python-pycurl-doc python3-pycurl-dbg
The following NEW packages will be installed:
  landscape-client python3-pycurl
0 upgraded, 2 newly installed, 0 to remove and 99 not upgraded.
Need to get 155 kB of archives.
After this operation, 791 kB of additional disk space will be used.
Do you want to continue? [Y/n] y
Get:1 http://archive.ubuntu.com/ubuntu focal/main amd64 python3-pycurl amd64 7.43.0.2-1ubuntu5 [46.9 kB]
Get:2 http://archive.ubuntu.com/ubuntu focal-updates/main amd64 landscape-client amd64 19.12-0ubuntu4.1 [108 kB]
Fetched 155 kB in 0s (983 kB/s)
Preconfiguring packages ...
Selecting previously unselected package python3-pycurl.
(Reading database ... 42826 files and directories currently installed.)
Preparing to unpack .../python3-pycurl_7.43.0.2-1ubuntu5_amd64.deb ...
Unpacking python3-pycurl (7.43.0.2-1ubuntu5) ...
Selecting previously unselected package landscape-client.
Preparing to unpack .../landscape-client_19.12-0ubuntu4.1_amd64.deb ...
Unpacking landscape-client (19.12-0ubuntu4.1) ...
Setting up python3-pycurl (7.43.0.2-1ubuntu5) ...
Setting up landscape-client (19.12-0ubuntu4.1) ...
Processing triggers for man-db (2.9.1-1) ...
hayden@T440:~$
```

Figure 12-2. *Installing landscape-client through apt-get*

3. If you followed the Quickstart installation instructions for your
    Landscape server, you will also need to copy the server encryption
    key to each host, because it is not signed by a recognized or your
    company's own SSL Certification Authority.

    a. Log in to the Landscape server's console, and copy the file from `/etc/ssl/`
        `certs/landscape_server_ca.crt` to a known shared location.

    b. On each system you want to add to the Landscape server, copy the file we
        saved earlier in 3.a to `/etc/landscape/server.pem` on the client.

    c. When you run the command in 4., append the following parameter to use
        the saved public key:

        `--ssl-public-key /etc/landscape/server.pem`

4. Register the computer – your `landscape-url` will likely differ, you
    will want to change `My Computer Title` to a suitable description
    of your WSL instance, and you may need to change the account
    name to the name of your Launchpad organization. If in doubt
    about the organization name or `landscape-url`, then consult the
    instructions in your Launchpad admin pages.

```
sudo landscape-config --computer-title "My Computer Title"
--account-name "standalone" --url https://landscape-url/
message-system --ping-url http://landscape-url/ping
```

To be able to run commands as root, you need to add the username when prompted for users that landscape is allowed to use to run script. In the screenshot, it is configured as the special keyword ALL which means that landscape may use any user.

Figure 12-3. *Successfully registering with Landscape*

5. If the registration is successful, you must accept the computer by navigating to the Launchpad "Pending Computers" page. The registration might fail if the hostname is not resolvable by DNS, in which case you can either use an IP address or add the hostname to your WSL instance's `/etc/hosts` file.

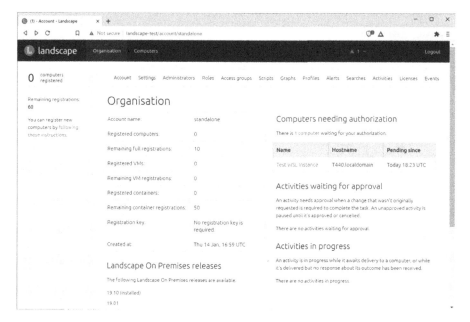

Figure 12-4. *Pending registration for the new computer*

Executing a Script on the WSL Instance with Landscape

Now that we have the connection established, we can start to run scripts or update packages. First, we will run a script to show the disk usage of the WSL instance. Navigate to the computer, and select "scripts" along the top of the rightmost panel.

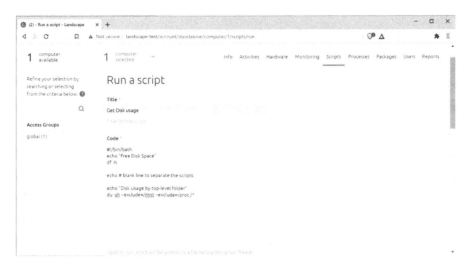

Figure 12-5. *Configuring the Get Disk usage script*

Insert the following script into the Code box:

```
#!/bin/bash
echo "Free Disk Space"
df -h

echo # blank line to separate the scripts

echo "Disk Usage by top-level folder"
du -sh --exclude=/mnt --exclude=/proc /*
```

Scroll to the "Run as user" box, and input "root" or another user of your choice – this user must be allowed by the landscape-client configuration, which is prompted when you first set up the client. Finally, click the "Run" button at the bottom of the page, and wait till the script finishes, at which point the page will update to indicate success or failure.

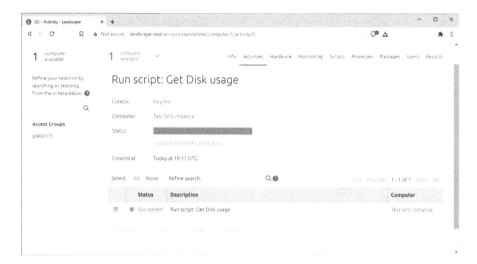

Figure 12-6. *Successful execution of our Get Disk usage script*

You can then click the command status to see the output of the script.

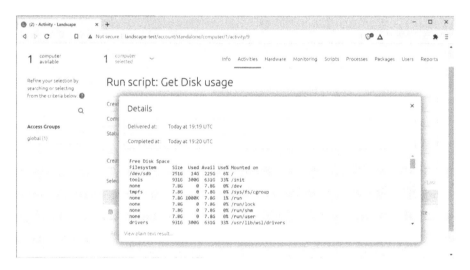

Figure 12-7. *The results of running our Get Disk usage script*

Managing Packages of the WSL Instance with Landscape

We can also manage installed packages by navigating to the Packages tab. To install a package, enter its name, for example, `ffmpeg`, into the Search for packages box, and then click the magnifying glass, or press Enter.

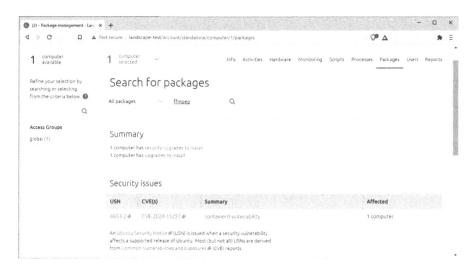

Figure 12-8. *Searching for a package*

In the search results page, use the ⊞ symbol next to any packages you wish to install. In this example, we have selected the ffmpeg package only.

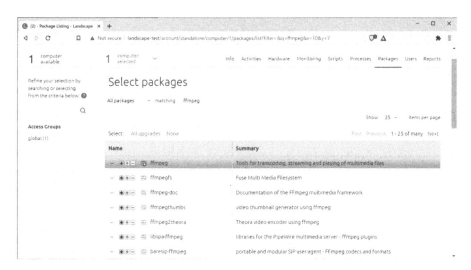

Figure 12-9. *Selecting a package to install*

Click the "Apply changes" button at the bottom, and wait for the task to finish.

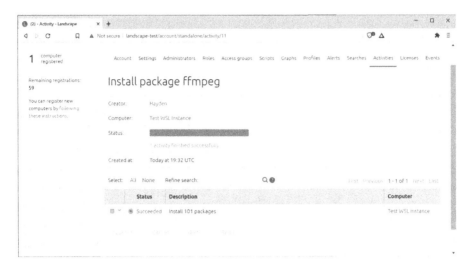

Figure 12-10. *Successful package installation*

Finally, we can also perform complete upgrades or security-only upgrades. For security-only upgrades, if there are any available, you will see a screen similar to the following on the Packages tab.

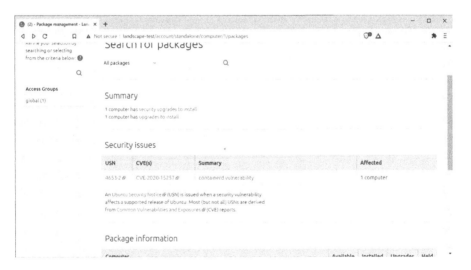

Figure 12-11. *Available upgrades on the Packages tab*

You will also see the following information on the Organization tab and the Alerts drop-down.

Figure 12-12. *Organization alerts showing available upgrades*

Clicking through the alerts or selecting the computer(s) and choosing the Packages tab will take you to the same screen where you may select which upgrades to apply. Here, packages can either be removed by clicking the ▬ symbol or upgraded by clicking the ▲ symbol (Figure 12-13). In either case, you apply the changes with the "Apply changes" button at the bottom.

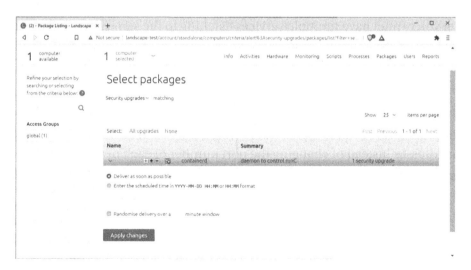

Figure 12-13. *Selecting a package to upgrade*

Using Ansible to Manage Ubuntu on WSL

Ansible is one of the leading configuration management automation platforms. Being open source, it is readily available for download from `https://github.com/ansible/ansible` and is also available in the Ubuntu APT repository. Developed by Red Hat, there are also paid plans for support through your journey available at `https://ansible.com`.

You need a Linux or macOS system to host the server-side part of Ansible, as Windows is currently unsupported for the server. For the systems you want to manage from Ansible, you also need to run an SSH server such as OpenSSH. On an Ubuntu WSL distro, you can install OpenSSH through APT:

```
sudo apt install openssh-server
```

However, as WSL does not start services automatically, you will need to set up the systemd environment as we discussed earlier. Alternatively, if you do not want to run a SystemD setup, you must invoke the `sshd` command via some other means such as by a Windows Task Scheduler job. The Windows Task Scheduler job should run on login to Windows and use the `wsl.exe` command to start the distro(s) and `sshd` within.

To manage multiple WSL distros with Ansible on the same Windows PC, you need to configure each WSL distro's `sshd` to use a unique network "port," unless both the management server and the managed WSL 2 instances are on the same PC, the reason being that you cannot have multiple services listening to the same port; and to manage from a remote server, rather than the same PC, you need to target the Windows PC's hostname or IP address to access the port that is proxied to Windows from each WSL instance. By default, `sshd` binds to port 22.

If the server and managed WSL clients are *all* on the same PC in separate WSL 2 distros, *and* the distros are using WSL 2, then you may target the relevant distros by their internal addresses instead of changing the port number of each of the `sshd` services. However, the server and clients *must* use WSL 2 to be reachable by an internal address separate from the PC's physical network.

When creating the host inventory for Ansible, you must add the relevant port number if the WSL distro is configured to use anything other than port 22. On the management server, create a file at `/etc/ansible/hosts` to hold your hostnames, or IP addresses, and optionally their port numbers if not 22:

```
192.0.2.50
windows-pc.example.org
windows-pc.example.org:8022 ; alternative port number 8022.
```

You should set up an SSH key pair on the server, with `ssh-keygen`, and configure each client to use that for authentication. Ubuntu is set up to support public-key identification out of the box. You need to copy the SSH public key into each client's `$HOME/.ssh/authorized_keys` file for the user you will be connecting from the server as. This can be streamlined by using the `ssh-copy-id` command on a system with both public and private keys installed, the easiest place being the system you ran `ssh-keygen` upon. You might need to reconfigure the clients' `sshd` to allow password authentication for `ssh-copy-id` to copy the SSH key correctly.

Index

© Hayden Barnes 2021
H. Barnes, *Pro Windows Subsystem for Linux (WSL)*, https://doi.org/10.1007/978-1-4842-6873-5

G

H

I

J

K

U

Ubuntu, 87–88
    Ansible, 278–279
    groovy build, 32
    images, 30
    Intune product, 268
    landscape server, 268
        apt-get, 270
        Launchpad admin screen, 268
        package installation, 274–277
        pending registration, 272
        Quickstart installation, 270
        registration, 270–271
    Linux, 27
    package management
        installation, 276
        organization alerts, 277
        packages tab, 276
        search option, 274
        selection, 275
        upgrade process, 277
    releases, 31

V

Virtual Application Integrated Locally
        (VAIL), 16
Virtualization extensions, 23
Visual Studio
    debugging app, 244–245
    16.9 version/later, 243
    .NET Core debugging, 244
    source code
        debugging process, 249
        distro, 247
        folder process, 248
        installation screen, 246

terminal inside code, 248
    window connection, 247
version 16.8/earlier, 242–243

W, X, Y, Z

Windows interoperability
    environmental variables, 223–225
    file systems (*see* Mount file systems)
    piping (*see* Piping)
    WSLENV, 223
    Wslpath tool, 209
    Wslutilities tool
        empty file creation, 213
        gedit installation, 210
        icons search, 211
        shortcut creation, 211
        splash screen, 212
        system information, 212
        tools, 210
        .txt file, 214
        web browser, 213
        wslvar, 212
        wslview, 213
Windows services
    apache2 batch file/script file, 163–164
    Apache web server, 159
    batch file testing, 161–163
    pane management, 165
    shell script, 160
    sudoers file, 162
    task scheduler, 165, 166
        actions tab, 172–174
        active tasks, 175–176
        naming field, 167
        program specification, 171
        properties dialog, 171–172
        start program, 170

Printed in the United States
by Baker & Taylor Publisher Services